The WAY of CATECHESIS

The WAY of CATECHESIS

Exploring Our History, Renewing Our Ministry

GERARD F. BAUMBACH

AVE MARIA PRESS AVE Notre Dame, Indiana

Nihil Obstat: Reverend Monsignor Michael Heintz
                    Censor Librorum

Imprimatur: +Most Reverend Kevin C. Rhoades
                    Bishop of Fort Wayne–South Bend
                    January 23, 2017

Library of Congress Cataloging-in-Publication Data
Names: Baumbach, Gerard F., author.
Title: The way of catechesis : exploring our history, renewing our ministry / Gerard F. Baumbach.
Description: Notre Dame : Ave Maria Press, 2017. | Includes bibliographical references and index.
Identifiers: LCCN 2016054196 (print) | LCCN 2017010613 (ebook) | ISBN 9781594717147 (pbk.) | ISBN 9781594717154 (ebook)
Subjects: LCSH: Catechetics--Catholic Church | Catechetics--History. | Christian education--History.
Classification: LCC BX1968 .B37 2017 (print) | LCC BX1968 (ebook) | DDC 268/.82--dc23
LC record available at https://lccn.loc.gov/2016054196

For my grandchildren,
Gabriel, Michelle, Charlotte,
William, Tegan, Katherine,
and baby on the way,
with lasting love

CONTENTS

PREFACE

The idea for this book originated with Ave Maria Press, a ministry of the United States Province of Holy Cross and located on the campus of the University of Notre Dame, where for many years I taught a course that incorporated highlights of catechetical history along with contemporary catechetical issues. My students made history come alive in creative and memorable ways as they navigated the Church's experience of catechesis over the ages.

My goal in this work is to foster a catechesis rooted in its own history while continuing to grow in fresh and invigorating ways, especially at a time of "New Evangelization." A natural paradigm is the exploration of catechesis in the life of the contemporary Church in light of some of our historical foundations. Awareness of these foundations affords us the opportunity to employ life lessons derived by our forebears as we catechize and evangelize today.

As we look back over the last two millennia, we see that we stand on the broad catechetical shoulders of countless people for whom "handing on the faith" framed their life commitment. As members of the Catholic Church, we are a community of living faith, still inquiring, emerging, and developing. Disciples never graduate from the catechetical way; we continue to accompany others in forging, through the grace of God, mutually enriching relationships on the Way of Jesus Christ.

You are invited to view as your own this history of eras and centuries—earthly yet building toward eternity—that form part of the holy ground on which we stand, especially in relation to the present catechetical moment. I hope that this approach enriches your understanding of the catechetical surface on which we respectfully take our places, a past that is at once sacred and sorrowful, compelling and questioning, enlightening and unsettling, encouraging and challenging.

As we make our way through centuries and decades long past, we may find our journey refreshed by our own catechetical memory and energized by what we experience today along the way of faith. Our lively "crossover" experience between evangelization and catechesis feeds our spirit and fashions our faith-filled movement together to Jesus, the Way. Whatever confronts us, we do not lose hope, for "our eyes [are] fixed on Jesus, the leader and perfecter of faith" (Heb 12:2).

Love in Christ carries us, all of us. "I give you a new commandment: love one another. As I have loved you, so you also should love one another" (Jn 13:34). Listening carefully to and interacting with others can build relationships of trust while gently offering witness to the faith we share and hand on as members of the Church. Far from being a lockstep task, this spirited ministry—a merciful discipleship of accompaniment—seizes and embraces us. Confidence in the guidance of the Spirit of God within the community of faith—even when we do not fully comprehend the ways of God—goes a long way in nurturing trusting relationships. The New Evangelization, emblazoned with catechetical opportunity, offers newly lighted and transformative pathways to the heart of the Gospel, Jesus Christ. Catechesis through the Church fuels energetic communal witness to this faith-driven continuum by way of an inherited past, a developing present, and an emerging future. We are community in motion, one in Christ, alive together.

Consider this book an invitation to enter into and echo what secures and challenges our common identity as we catechize and live the Way of Christ today. None of us walks this way alone. Read this book not from the outside, but from within the heart of the Church—loving, wounded, healed, forgiving, rejoicing. Our developing story is vital to the life of the Church. More than a record of past events and personalities, our shared story swells with passion and possibilities. The turn of a page does not summon us to bid farewell to past events, personalities, or understandings;

rather, movement through ages past bolsters catechetical ministry and renews faith today.

You are encouraged to claim the Church's story of catechesis as your own; for this reason, I have woven contemporary catechetical insights throughout the historical presentations. Since this ministry has directed most of my adult life, I periodically include autobiographical examples to make connections to the contemporary scene. I encourage you to claim or discover your own examples for reflection and have provided many reflection questions to help you get started.

This book offers a look at selected highlights of catechesis over the ages. The topic is vast, and I recognize that many histories of catechesis could be written, for history takes us in many directions. Therefore, I propose here an interpretation of a limited number of highlights from across the centuries. Although a variety of topics is presented, many more could have been chosen. Informative older and contemporary sources are identified, and perhaps something you see here will lead you to further study. Many of the endnotes provide first steps for such a purpose. I have sought to ensure the accuracy of the historical information presented. A list of selected documents and other sources since the Second Vatican Council appears in the appendix.

Our own experiences of the Church, ministry, catechesis, and life guide our perspectives on catechetical topics that sometimes rest atop complex layers of history. This work is a segment, a capsule if you will, of selections that engage us and support exploring our history and renewing our ministry. Although I have sought to provide an informative interpretation, there remains much more to discover and digest.

The many pastoral challenges of our age demand an assortment of approaches as we seek to implement the Church's catechetical agenda. My approach and topical interests reflect several decades of catechetical practice and study. Other interpreters might choose to pursue topics different from my own, offering assessments and preferences informed by their own scholarship, experience, and historical and cultural perspectives. I encourage others to probe even further this broad historical spectrum, thereby contributing fresh insights for the Church of the twenty-first century.

I hope that *The Way of Catechesis* enlivens interpretation of our history, strengthens foundations for those who will come after us, and fortifies our efforts in service to the Church's ministry of catechesis.

I wish to thank the staff of Ave Maria Press, especially Robert Hamma, who was vice president and editorial director there when this project got underway. Bob saw the book through from beginning to end, clarified many questions, and provided a guiding hand in transforming words and phrases into a shimmering display. His patience in responding to my many questions was limitless. I drew inspiration from Notre Dame's McGrath Institute for Church Life and Department of Theology, and in a particular way the institute's Echo Program, a continuing sign of catechetical hope for the future. The staffs of the Hesburgh Library at the University of Notre Dame and the Cushwa-Leighton Library at Saint Mary's College were generous in accommodating my research needs. Matthew Halbach provided critical commentary on an early draft, and I remain grateful for his insights, availability, and friendship. Gracious support from a distance came from Mary Elizabeth Sperry, associate director for USCCB permissions and NAB utilization at USCCB Publishing. Many others offered affirmation of this project along the way, and I am most appreciative of their support and good wishes. I found and continue to benefit from prayerful support from the parish of St. Pius X Catholic Church in Granger, Indiana.

Finally, I express with lifelong gratitude and an insufficiency of words my lasting thanks to my wife, Elaine, who has patiently supported my writing for nearly five decades. I also owe a particular debt of appreciation to my sons, daughters-in-law, and grandchildren. They joined with Elaine in generously giving me the space and time needed to prepare this work. Their kindness goes beyond words, as does my thanks to each of them.

I dedicate this book to my grandchildren, loving signs of hope for the future.

ABBREVIATIONS

AA   *Apostolicam Actuositatem* (*Decree on the Apostolate of Lay People*), in *Vatican Council II: The Conciliar and Postconciliar Documents*, ed. Austin Flannery (Collegeville, MN: Liturgical Press, 1975).

AG   *Ad Gentes Divinitus* (*Decree on the Church's Missionary Activity*), in *Vatican Council II: The Conciliar and Postconciliar Documents*, ed. Austin Flannery (Collegeville, MN: Liturgical Press, 1975).

AN   Pius X, Encyclical Letter *Acerbo Nimis* (*On the Teaching of Christian Doctrine*), in *Catechetical Documents of Pope Pius X*, trans. and ed. Joseph B. Collins (Paterson, NJ: St. Anthony Guild Press, 1946).

CCC   *Catechism of the Catholic Church*, 2nd ed. (Vatican City: Libreria Editrice Vaticana; Washington, DC: United States Catholic Conference, 1994, 1997).

CD   *Christus Dominus* (*Decree on the Pastoral Office of Bishops in the Church*), in *Vatican Council II: The Conciliar and Postconciliar Documents*, ed. Austin Flannery (Collegeville, MN: Liturgical Press, 1975).

CS   Pontifical Council for Justice and Peace, *Compendium of the Social Doctrine of the Church* (Washington, DC: USCCB Publishing, 2004).

CT   John Paul II, Apostolic Exhortation *Catechesi Tradendae* (*On Catechesis in Our Time*) (Washington, DC: United States Catholic Conference, 1979).

DCE   Benedict XVI, Encyclical Letter *Deus Caritas Est* (*On Christian Love*) (Washington, DC: United States Conference of Catholic Bishops, 2006).

DH   *Dignitatis Humanae (Declaration on Religious Liberty)*, in *Vatican Council II: The Conciliar and Postconciliar Documents*, ed. Austin Flannery (Collegeville, MN: Liturgical Press, 1975).

DM   John Paul II, Encyclical Letter *Dives in Misericordia (Rich in Mercy)* (Vatican City: Libreria Editrice Vaticana, 1980), https://w2.vatican.va/content/john-paul-ii/en/encyclicals/documents/hf_jp-ii_enc_30111980_dives-in-misericordia.html.

DV   *Dei Verbum* (*Dogmatic Constitution on Divine Revelation*), in *Vatican Council II: The Conciliar and Postconciliar Documents*, ed. Austin Flannery (Collegeville, MN: Liturgical Press, 1975).

EE   John Paul II, Encyclical Letter *Ecclesia de Eucharistia* (*On the Eucharist in Its Relationship to the Church*) (Boston: Pauline Books & Media, 2003).

EG   Francis, Apostolic Exhortation *Evangelii Gaudium* (*On the Proclamation of the Gospel in Today's World*) (Washington, DC: United States Conference of Catholic Bishops, 2013).

EN   Paul VI, Apostolic Exhortation *Evangelii Nuntiandi* (*On Evangelization in the Modern World*) (Washington, DC: United States Catholic Conference, 1975).

EV   John Paul II, Encyclical Letter *Evangelium Vitae* (*On the Value and Inviolability of Human Life* [*The Gospel of Life*]) (Washington, DC: United States Catholic Conference, 1995).

GCD   Sacred Congregation for the Clergy, *General Catechetical Directory* (Washington, DC: United States Catholic Conference, 1971).

GDC   Congregation for the Clergy, *General Directory for Catechesis* (Washington, DC: United States Catholic Conference, 1997).

GE   *Gravissimum Educationis* (*Declaration on Christian Education*), in *Vatican Council II: The Conciliar and Postconciliar Documents*, ed. Austin Flannery (Collegeville, MN: Liturgical Press, 1975).

GS   *Gaudium et Spes* (*Pastoral Constitution on the Church in the Modern World*), in *Vatican Council II: The Conciliar and Postconciliar Documents*, ed. Austin Flannery (Collegeville, MN: Liturgical Press, 1975).

IM   *Inter Mirifica* (*Decree on the Means of Social Communication*), in *Vatican Council II: The Conciliar and Postconciliar Documents*, ed. Austin Flannery (Collegeville, MN: Liturgical Press, 1975).

LG   *Lumen Gentium* (*Dogmatic Constitution on the Church*), in *Vatican Council II: The Conciliar and Postconciliar Documents*, ed. Austin Flannery (Collegeville, MN: Liturgical Press, 1975).

MV   Francis, Bull of Indiction of the Extraordinary Jubilee of Mercy *Misericordiae Vultus* (*The Face of Mercy*) (Vatican City: Libreria Editrice Vaticana, 2015), https://w2.vatican.va/content/francesco/en/apost_letters/documents/papa-francesco_bolla_20150411_misericordiae-vultus.html.

NA   *Nostra Aetate* (*Declaration on the Relation of the Church to Non-Christian Religions*), in *Vatican Council II: The Conciliar and Postconciliar Documents*, ed. Austin Flannery (Collegeville, MN: Liturgical Press, 1975).

NABRE   Confraternity of Christian Doctrine, *The New American Bible Revised Edition* (Washington, DC: 2010, 1991, 1986, 1970, in edition published by World Catholic Press, A Division of Catholic Book Publishing Corp., Totowa, NJ, 2010).

NDC   United States Conference of Catholic Bishops, *National Directory for Catechesis* (Washington, DC: USCCB, 2005).

OE   *Orientalium Ecclesiarum* (*Decree on the Catholic Eastern Churches*), in *Vatican Council II: The Conciliar and Postconciliar Documents*, ed. Austin Flannery (Collegeville, MN: Liturgical Press, 1975).

OT   *Optatam Totius* (*Decree on the Training of Priests*), in *Vatican Council II: The Conciliar and Postconciliar Documents*, ed. Austin Flannery (Collegeville, MN: Liturgical Press, 1975).

PC   *Perfectae Caritatis* (*Decree on the Up-to-Date Renewal of Religious Life*), in *Vatican Council II: The Conciliar and Postconciliar Documents*, ed. Austin Flannery (Collegeville, MN: Liturgical Press, 1975).

PO   *Presbyterorum Ordinis* (*Decree on the Ministry and Life of Priests*), in *Vatican Council II: The Conciliar and Postconciliar Documents*, ed. Austin Flannery (Collegeville, MN: Liturgical Press, 1975).

QS   Pius X, Decree *Quam Singulari* (*On the Age of Children Who Are to Be Admitted to First Holy Communion*), in *Catechetical Documents of Pope Pius X,* trans. and ed. Joseph B. Collins (Paterson, NJ: St. Anthony Guild Press, 1946).

RCIA   *Rite of Christian Initiation of Adults* (Chicago: Liturgy Training Publications, 1988).

RH   John Paul II, Encyclical Letter *Redemptor Hominis* (*The Redeemer of Man*) (Vatican City: Libreria Editrice Vaticana, 1979), http://w2.vatican.va/content/john-paul-ii/en/encyclicals/documents/hf_jp-ii_enc_04031979_redemptor-hominis.html.

RMa   John Paul II, Encyclical Letter *Redemptoris Mater* (*On the Blessed Virgin Mary in the Life of the Pilgrim Church* [*Mother of the Redeemer*]) (Boston: Pauline Books & Media, 1987).

RMi   John Paul II, Encyclical Letter *Redemptoris Missio* (*On the Permanent Validity of the Church's Missionary Mandate* [*Mission of the Redeemer*]) (Boston: Pauline Books & Media), 1990.

RN   Leo XIII, Encyclical Letter *Rerum Novarum* (*The Condition of Labor*), (Glen Rock, NJ: Paulist Press, 1939, 1963).

SCa   Benedict XVI, Apostolic Exhortation *Sacramentum Caritatis* (*Sacrament of Charity*) (Boston: Pauline Books & Media, 2007).

SCo   *Sacrosanctum Concilium* (*The Constitution on the Sacred Liturgy*), in *Vatican Council II: The Conciliar and Postconciliar Documents*, ed. Austin Flannery (Collegeville, MN: Liturgical Press, 1975).

SLF   National Conference of Catholic Bishops, *Sharing the Light of Faith: National Catechetical Directory for Catholics of the United States* (Washington, DC: United States Catholic Conference, 1979).

TMA   John Paul II, Apostolic Letter *Tertio Millennio Adveniente* (*On Preparation for the Jubilee of the Year 2000*) (Vatican City: Libreria Editrice Vaticana, 1994).

UR   *Unitatis Redintegratio* (*Decree on Ecumenism*), in *Vatican Council II: The Conciliar and Postconciliar Documents*, ed. Austin Flannery (Collegeville, MN: Liturgical Press, 1975).

1

OUR JOURNEY ON THE WAY OF CATECHESIS

Make known to me your ways, LORD;
  teach me your paths.
Guide me by your fidelity and teach me,
  for you are God my savior,
  for you I wait all the day long.

—Psalm 25:4–5

What demanded your attention the last time you traveled a familiar pathway? Perhaps you were on a road, field, alley, or avenue. Was it then that something moved you to emulate or learn more about another, perhaps an ancestor whose life continues to challenge you to unravel the meaning of your own?

What are the ways of the Lord that direct your seeking to live the Way, a journey marked by the faithful witness of generations gone by and those still to come (cf. Acts 9:2)? What guideposts seize your attention as you pursue "the way of wisdom" (Prv 4:11)? What is it that you are truly seeking?

Imagine yourself in familiar surroundings, searching for an old family artifact, perhaps a family record book. You long to make it available to others, for it contains entries handwritten by your ancestors. Surely, you think, others will share in your joy at locating this distant family account of past generations. Love demands no less, you surmise.

A tightly covered basket whose odor hints at its age catches your eye. You remove the lid, and a loosely bound book seems to stare up at you. Its worn cover, yellowed pages, and sewn binding show their years. Your search is over, you think. But as you lift the book out of the basket, paper flakes scatter about you. Some pages of the old volume, dried, tattered, and worn, scatter beyond your immediate reach. You hold the book close now, your grasp more firm, as memories flood your senses and people and events seem to come to life.

Rich and joyful echoes of past lives and events suddenly emanate from this old family book that demands more of you than mere recollection. Your heart is on call now, on fire now, as an assortment of memories, perspectives, and traditions overtakes you, inviting you to discern anew your participation in what is, of course, your own living heritage, your "way." Love demands no less. *Belonging* and *believing* take on newly discovered meaning as momentary reflection carries you.

Somehow you have arrived, secure in the history that holds you and makes you who you are. It becomes difficult to wrap words around this aging yet still present love. Images may surface of family members and others who helped to form you, persons who have accompanied you through the "living, dying, and rising" moments of your life. A community of others surrounds you, albeit from a distance, as you preserve the past in a present moment now destined to waft through a future horizon. For what you have found is not just an old artifact ripe with temporary or fading sentiment. It is that which, over time, you will hand on to another . . . and another . . . and another—all along the way.

Catechesis: "Stepping Lively"

What does this scene have to do with catechesis? Pope Francis tells us, "The believer is essentially 'one who remembers'" (EG, 13). Remembering (both in the standard sense of recalling and in the sense of bringing in new members or recharging existing members) is a significant activity within the Church's ministry of catechesis. Catechesis, over time, helps to shape and identify us as Christians, disciples of Jesus Christ, as we progress and remember along the way.

Catechesis engages and combines many elements that nurture formation in faith: listening and finding; discovering and uncovering; celebrating and remembering; believing and professing; teaching and learning; and adhering, replenishing, and enacting. The *General Directory for Catechesis* asserts that "catechesis is nothing other than the process of transmitting the Gospel, as the Christian community has received it, understands it, celebrates it, lives it and communicates it in many ways" (GDC, 105).

Essential, of course, to the activity and ministry of catechesis is Jesus Christ, given and offered for all. "The definitive aim of catechesis is to put people not only in touch but in communion, in intimacy, with Jesus Christ: only He can lead us to the love of the Father in the Spirit and make us share in the life of the Holy Trinity" (CT, 5; cf. GDC, 80, and NDC, 19B). Such communion and intimacy are foundational to our developing spirituality, which is enriched by a holistic sense of why and how we live by faith.

Catechesis is a term of Greek origin. Simply put, to *catechize* is to "resound" or to "echo."[1] Catechesis offers us both an invitation to and a participation in echoing the depth, core, and fullness of what the Church proclaims and teaches. We do so "in the Spirit" eagerly and energetically, for the Word of God frees us and enlivens us. This is no ordinary or static resounding, different only in degree from a search through (or for) a highly valued old family artifact, as important as that may be. Rather, it is a deliberate and sustained echo that enters our hearing (and, I would argue, all our senses) and lasts for a lifetime.

Anyone who has hollered "Hello!" in an underground cavern has surely heard in reply "Hello! Hello! . . . Hello!" as the word found its way back to the speaker. In the case of catechesis, the word reaches beyond familiar limits, finding welcome in its movement to another (or others), returning to be uttered again, now with even greater resonance, power, and confidence—for the source of our echo is Jesus Christ, the Word made flesh. It is he whom we echo, he whom we follow, he for whom we live as disciples and stewards of the Word. The living and life-giving Word of

God pierces time and history, resounding from generation to generation, community to community, person to person.

Catechesis offers us the opportunity to participate (as we ourselves are renewed) in a historic ministry of offering to others the Church's living faith through gifts ever ancient and ever new, alive through the "five inner senses: will, reason, memory, imagination, [and] thought."[2] We echo that which rings true, that which we have been given and are compelled to share. And—surprise!—so often the echo is reheard deep within ourselves, within that inner sanctum of soul and identity, as our words of living faith and belief fall gently and confidently from our lips to touch the heart of another.

"Go, therefore, and make disciples of all nations" (Mt 28:19). The Church carries out the mission given by Christ through evangelization efforts that move us beyond perceived limitations and worrisome liabilities. "Evangelizing is in fact the grace and vocation proper to the Church, her deepest identity. She exists in order to evangelize" (EN, 14). Today we serve through a New Evangelization, rich in ways of encouraging and inviting already baptized people who may have moved away from the community of the Church to explore returning to the faith of their baptismal heritage. The New Evangelization reaches people of many types and situations, including those who sense the movement of the Spirit in their lives for the first time. It also impacts the faithful, for the need for a renewal of faith recurs during a lifetime.

In the ever-lively opportunity presented by the New Evangelization, we experience anew the confluence of evangelization and catechesis. The Gospel cannot be contained, neatly sealed and stored away in an enclosure that is more coffin than memory keeper. It is destined to resound, to burst into and through minds and hearts orally, joyfully, communally. This Gospel movement is particularly encouraging at a time when inculturation is so visibly appreciated and apparent in the life of the Church. "Inculturation involves listening to the culture of the people for an echo of the word of God. It involves the discernment of the presence of authentic Gospel values or openness to authentic Gospel values in the culture" (NDC, 21C).[3] The shared beauty of faith and culture is demonstrably identifiable in these new-millennium days.

Catechesis is a type of "handing on" that is not easily constrained to a measurable moment in time, one among many—which implies that perhaps it is devoid of serious purpose or intent. Nor is it a rapidly constructed and momentary "handing off," as in a sporting event or business transaction. Rather, gifted emissaries of faith "step lively" and over time share a timeless treasure made more vibrant through living relationships of mercy, justice, compassion, and understanding.

We offer, through the grace of God, a catechesis of love. The Holy Spirit abides within the community of faith from age to age, from the apostles who walked with Jesus to disciples who find their way in him today. Generation after generation—stripped of all but Christ himself and living in and through the community of the Church—become one in a symphonic melody that resounds from the Church's ongoing expression and experience of the One who is way, truth, and life.

Entering Catechetical History

What are some starting points for exploring the historical and contemporary world of catechesis?

How might we characterize our catechetical passage through life, marked by joyful hope for an eternity of life in God's own presence? Happily seized by Christ and confidently motivated by mission, the catechist offers herself or himself within the community of faith not as mouthpiece but as "life-piece," expressing discipleship beyond words and telling beyond familiar stories. This lifelong journey, vibrant through the remembered witness of faithful generations, is marked by anticipation and expectation.

Living and journeying the Way calls us to probe, explore, and understand our heritage as proclaimed and professed over the ages as we seek to embrace it today in the light of faith. We do this as part of a community of sisters and brothers in the Lord. Indeed, our support of and for one another is essential and must be presumed along the Way.

The image of the Way is fitting for anticipating and describing our movement through the Church's catechetical journey, here applied to Catholic life and teaching (cf. Acts 9:2). It is scripturally rich, with layers of meaning. We may first see it as a pointer, suggesting a particular direction. As time passes and as we come to grips with the meaning and expression of our Catholic identity, it may even become an emblem for us, a summary descriptor of all we are and do as Christians in giving our lives over to the One who is "the way and the truth and the life" (Jn 14:6).

Just as Jesus began his public ministry within the geographic and cultural setting of Galilee, so do we serve in this ministry of the Church from within our own local, regional, cultural, and geographic environs. We do so remembering that Jesus

> made himself a *catechist* of the Kingdom of God for all categories of persons, great and small, rich and poor, healthy and sick, near and far, Jews and pagans, men and women, righteous and sinners, rulers and subjects, individuals and groups. He is available to all. He is interested in the needs of every person, body and soul. He heals and forgives, corrects and encourages, with words and deeds. (GDC, 163)

Notice the use of the present tense. Ponder the emphasis of Jesus on others, regardless of their elevated or downtrodden state in life. This statement of Jesus' presence and availability is as true today as it was two millennia ago. What he offers is so essential that nothing can prevent its fulfillment. Indeed, he offers himself to the Father for all generations, redeeming us, healing us, encouraging us, giving his life for us, and rising for us. Jesus loves people. The truth of his promise to be with us in the Spirit carries forward through our daily witness and determined discipleship.

Our entry into the still-developing and complex history of catechesis emerges from expectations born of the blended and culturally rich experience of our current milieu. Just as others have done before us, each of us joins the journey of faith along the way of living faith. The difference is our time of entry. It seems natural to suggest that we join this bright pathway through the present moment of our lives. But what is this moment? How might it be assessed through the lens of catechesis?

One commonly understood meaning of *moment* invokes a brief duration of time. Another, more expansive meaning is a period of time. Many moments of life may attract us to the Gospel and to all who accompany us on the walk of faith. We may even be tempted to idealize a single moment of life that teases our imagination as natural memory gradually recedes, increasingly moving beyond timely awareness as days turn to weeks, weeks to months, and months to years. We age.

Some of us may hear "Live in the moment!" proclaimed as an indictment—as if we have failed ourselves or others if every passing second of our lives does not yield inspiring and measurable success. Think of a less-than-stellar workday, a conflict-laden meeting of parish organizations, or a catechetical workshop that does not go as intended.

Frustration can set in for those of us who seem to live, either professionally or personally, from moment to moment. Fed by promises of immediate life fulfillment that may surface from deep within ourselves, from well-meaning colleagues and friends, or from across the Internet and other media,[4] we may find ourselves laying claim only to anxiety, discomfort, and even greater challenges for achieving tomorrow's success.

Perhaps these are all reasons why the New Evangelization must begin within and with ourselves. In reality, limited momentary experiences, as well intended as they may be, are insufficient for the remembering believer. Such moments fade and slip away before our eyes. They limit our way.

Through unmuted voices joined to the still resounding witness of those who have preceded us in faith, catechesis boldly seeks to confirm a new and ceaseless moment of no short duration, for "now is a very acceptable time; behold, now is the day of salvation" (2 Cor 6:2). This is a lasting moment of anticipation, expectation, and participation through which our ongoing conversion, initiated by the Holy Spirit along the baptismal way, takes root. It is time that offers us welcome, challenge, and change, for it is the time of Christ among us.[5] It is a time of the experience of Christ all day long, all life long, even when we may be unaware of or even doubt his presence. It is the Christ moment.

In entering this eminently lasting, overarching, and life-changing moment, we find new meaning for the present as we secure roots linked to past lives and renew hope for generations to come. As with generations before us, regular participation in the celebration of the Eucharist confirms that we are called to the day of salvation and to something beyond the successive brief or passing moments of our lives.

Through the abiding grace of God, we can choose to live in harmony within the all-encompassing milieu of the "Christ moment"—a new stage for all God's children. This Christ moment perdures through the witness of faith professed by our ancestors and is entrusted with confidence to us and to our descendants who, with fresh understanding, will bear the message of Christ in millennia to come.

The handing on of faith in past eras—for example, orally from person to person, by preaching, by moral decision-making formed in light of the Gospel, or through Christian witness in socially threatening or nonthreatening times—may at first call to mind similarities to conditions today. However, there are differences, based in part on how we perceive the social order.

For example, we may find that such sociological labels as urban, suburban, and rural that carried us into the twenty-first century are now inadequate.[6] They may even appear to blend together along electronic pathways whose storefronts display an endless variety of high-tech world-wide communications systems. People in one part of the world welcome the dawn as others enjoy fading hues of daylight, all while communicating with one another at lightning-fast speeds that, with a simple click, merge sunrise and sunset, ranches and cities, farms and residential developments, and apartment buildings and the rich greens of barely populated mountain foothills. Time zones become irrelevant and unnecessary for many. Opportunities for interaction abound!

However, instantaneous communication, offered through devices that rest at a forty-five-degree angle on one's knees, may make for all too swiftly deleted memories. "In the moment" may be seen as nothing more than a few seconds on their way to the shadows of time, soon to be replaced by other happenings. For some Catholics, *60 Minutes* may be more of a statement about time at church than the name of a popular television show.

Complaints about "not getting anything out of" Mass ("Boring!") might actually suggest our need to recommit ourselves to being "in the moment" in all its depth and breadth. Who encourages us to extend our pause from lightning-fast living during the eucharistic celebration? How might mystagogical reflection and engagement invite us to savor this sacred moment, not just for an hour but for a lifetime? How might "at church" become "as Church"?

Jesus surely accompanies us in the daily events of our lives. We are one with him along the way in the great and memorable experiences of faith and of life. Clearly, his everlasting presence and promise of life with God forever is neither passing nor momentary. It is he who surrounds, supports, and elevates us, through the gift of his Spirit, as we encounter demands brought forth by the sweep of a second hand. In entering our own communal catechetical history, the present moment stretches in many directions, always with Christ at the center.

> So then you are no longer strangers and sojourners, but you are fellow citizens with the holy ones and members of the household of God, built upon the foundation of the apostles and prophets, with Christ Jesus himself as the capstone. Through him the whole structure is held together and grows into a temple sacred in the Lord; in him you also are being built together into a dwelling place of God in the Spirit. (Eph 2:19–22)

The Plan of the Book

The history of catechesis can be approached in a number of valuable and diverse ways. While there may be differences among authors' perspectives, there is also likely to be some overlap in identifying important dimensions of the history, the study of which has been richly served by many scholars whose work continues to inform the field.[7]

The remaining chapters of the book present pertinent topics of historical and contemporary interest along the way of catechesis, from millennia gone by to the present. The presentation is intentionally limited. My experience and understanding of catechesis within the Catholic Church and, in particular, the Latin Church, inform the overall perspective and topical selections, with a diversity of references identified in the endnotes.

We move from some Old Testament foundations, an essential beginning for rooting and tracing our history, to the One who is the Way, Jesus
Christ. Our journey continues with highlights of the New Testament and
the emerging Church, followed by a look at the development of the catechumenate and catechesis. We then span the fifth to the fifteenth centuries,
review catechesis in light of the fracture in the Church at the time of the
Reformation, and look at succeeding centuries, down to the movement
into the new millennium.

The flow of our journey is captured by the chart that follows. Locate
the "Start" arrow in the chart to trace some aspects of the historical development presented here.

Catechesis: A Historical Overview

One Approach

 **START**

Chapters 2–5: Foundations and Early Church

Old Testament; Jesus Christ, Teacher and Catechist; New Testament; proclamation and
teaching; scripture, tradition; Creed; deepening faith; emerging catechumenal and
communal process of initiation

Chapter 6: Spanning the Fifth to Fifteenth Centuries

The Middle Ages; catechesis through changing times; diminished catechumenal reality; "lived faith" in
home, life, community; reliance on Creed, Lord's Prayer; examples of the era

Chapter 7: Fracture and Reform

Sustaining catechesis during a time wounded by division; catechisms and shaping a
pattern in print; some representative persons and communities; growing awareness
of the "person"

Chapter 8: Bridging a Millennium

Nineteenth to twenty-first centuries; content, method, kerygma, experience; Vatican Council II; renewal
(many areas); community and ministry, catechumenal lens; New Evangelization; cultural diversity;
Catholic social tradition; mercy; Jesus Christ, the Way

Each chapter includes a broad look at the catechetical climate of the era under study. The scope of catechesis underwent adjustment over the course of several centuries, especially after the emergence of the printing press in the West in the mid-fifteenth century. To today's catechists, this may seem to have been a sudden move, but the changes actually happened over a period of time. Subsequently, there was a reawakening of the understanding of foundational linkages among scripture, liturgy, sacrament, and catechesis, along with the integration of important insights from education and related social sciences.[8] Today we are witness to the Church's expansive catechetical agenda, rich in doctrinal understanding; pastoral integration; increasing awareness of the necessity of catechesis for all; and renewed understanding of Catholic social teaching, especially for peace and justice. We do not seek applause for yesterday's achievements but remember that "the salvation which God offers us is the work of his mercy" (EG, 112).

Forging Connections: Catechetical History and Contemporary Catechesis

The image of a weaver helps us to review and expand our understanding of the Church's catechetical journey. A weaver combines strands of material (e.g., yarn) to create a whole cloth. Similarly, catechesis is in part born of the merger of various strands into a single whole, one that is representative of a still-developing history.

Regardless of era or event, Christ remains the center of faith and life and the focus of our way in living the faith we profess as the Church. Christ establishes the context for who we are and for what we proclaim on the way of faith. He is our spiritual core and the *living* content of our experience of faith. Catechetically, we see this content proclaimed and embraced through scripture and tradition and as interpreted by the Magisterium, "the servant of the word of God" (NDC, 18).

The Second Vatican Council reaffirmed the guiding role of bishops, our chief catechists (see NDC, 54A), in caring for the baptized and in calling all people to Christ (see CD, 11ff.). As a result of the Second Vatican Council,[9] new opportunities arose for the laity to join with the ordained in serving the people of God. Persons serving in consecrated life secured many positions as part of a catechetical schematic that also attracted married and single laypeople.

Jesus offers us the way of life and the way to live in the Spirit as the Church, through which we come to participate in the life of the Risen One. For example, *Lumen Gentium* declares that the laity "in their own way share the priestly, prophetic and kingly office of Christ" (LG, 31).[10] This is enlivening and stimulating. According to the *Catechism of the Catholic Church*, "The whole People of God participates in these three offices of Christ ['priest, prophet, and king'] and bears the responsibilities for mission and service that flow from them" (CCC, 783).

The movement of the Spirit guides and inspires us as we welcome the integration of many aspects of Catholic life and practice within the fertile soil in which the Gospel continues to take root. Gifts of collaborative trust, including leadership formation and the witness of catechetical leaders, continue to reinforce such a perspective, especially—though not exclusively—in diocesan and parish life. All participate in the essential ministry of catechesis during an era of New Evangelization.

The New Evangelization, bolstered by effective and ongoing catechesis, offers a gateway for exploring and enacting a diversity of approaches for proclaiming and teaching the faith. One helpful aspect is the review of the state of catechesis in the life of the Church, especially since the Second Vatican Council. This is more than a summary of practices and perspectives; rather, we engage the past in helping to inform and shape catechesis for now and for the future. A wealth of ecclesial documents since the council continues to influence this necessarily vigorous effort, one framed in part by the six tasks of catechesis and for which clarity of teaching remains a priority. The broad sweep of pastoral needs demands heightened attention to the implementation of the Church's evangelizing mandate; well-formed and well-informed catechists are essential, especially as people respond to the Spirit's call to consider anew their relationship with Christ and, for some, explore a return to the Church.

Our main topic here is the evolution of the way of catechesis over the ages. Countless persons strove to hand down the gift of faith from within the heart of the Church. They belonged, as do we. They believed, as do we. They discerned matters of faith and of life, as do we. They experienced firsthand what it is to live, die, and rise during life's joys and challenges, keeping faith alive! As do we. I propose that this witness in faith through the years forms an important strand of the historically woven tapestry of what are known today as evangelization, catechesis, and New Evangelization.

This long and evolving history includes highs and lows of the catechumenate; "the domestic Church" (LG, 11; cf. CCC, 1655ff.) stoking the fire of faith alive; extensive reliance on printed resources for catechesis; renewed awareness of the importance of catechesis for all in the midst of a rebirth of emphasis on the role of initiation in coming to faith; and shifts in catechetical practice and service, including service in catechetical leadership through lay ecclesial ministry.[11]

As we read "through" history and not merely about history, and as we derive meanings and possibilities for catechesis today, our history can serve as a type of catechetical mirror for the contemporary community of faith, the Church. Catechetical history—*our* history by faith and inheritance—is welcomed within these pages as a dear friend to be received and interpreted as we serve within our own cultural and catechetical milieu along the way of faith.

Four Characteristics along the Way

In view of the appeal to the witness of the faithful, four characteristics are proposed here for aiding our reflection along the way of faith: (1) belonging; (2) believing; (3) discerning and reflecting; and (4) living, dying, and rising.

These characteristics, briefly described below, appear intermittently in the chapters in a variety of ways, as befits the topic under review. They often form an implicit perspective for a chapter and may be identified by name only infrequently. And they need not be sequentially applied. No attempt is made here to make all eras of catechetical history look alike; each era has its own distinguishing features. But the characteristics are there, especially when you see them—even in the background—through *your* experience and reflection.

The four characteristics are derived in part from my experience, study, and implementation of the *Rite of Christian Initiation of Adults*[12] and are intended to serve as a tool for reflecting on highlights of the catechetical enterprise in the history, life, and practice of the Church.

Though intentions may vary, all who are baptized represent *belonging* to and within the Church every day. Belonging implies the obvious: being who we are and what we do in relation to Christ, the Church, and others. "Everyone who belongs to the truth listens to my voice," Jesus says to Pilate (Jn 18:37).

Why do we belong? We long to belong: a neat phrase, but there is more to it than meets the eye. What is it for which we long? For whom do we long? Longing to belong is not simply a state of mind but a state of relationship. Such longing is not an appeal for living within safe havens to which access is granted only by ourselves to ourselves when necessary. Rather, this healthy sense of belonging finds its breath and resonates within supportive relationships of trust through which risks, joys, and challenges populate daily life and where, to apply an overused phrase, "real life" happens beyond familiar comfort zones that are more shield than doorway to God's children. We hear Jesus' voice and yearn for his presence. We belong to him.

Pope Francis tells us of Jesus' enduring love: "Mission is at once a passion for Jesus and a passion for his people. . . . He takes us from the midst of his people and he sends us to his people; without this sense of belonging we cannot understand our deepest identity" (EG, 268). For the Church, evangelizing necessity and catechetical reality draw from shared wisdom and ongoing experience in fostering living faith.

Believing is linked dynamically to belonging. Believing offers us the graced opportunity to cherish the treasure of what we are charged to hand on with vigor, clarity, and passion—though not alone ("just me and my God") but through witness in faith commonly professed; not in drudgery but in the strength of loving resolve. Scripture and tradition ground us within contexts born of faith and of life. As we "encourage a living, explicit and fruitful profession of faith" (GDC, 66), we seize fresh opportunities for living our baptismal call and the call to evangelize and catechize. The life-giving Word of God sustains us as we risk seeking new horizons. We are neither a creedless nor a lifeless community. Strengthened by faith within the sacramental life of the Church, we belong as we believe and believe as we belong. We model a collaborative spirit through care for one another, especially those new to Catholic faith and life.

Teachings and doctrinal understanding are welcomed affirmations of faith, essential to heritage and identity, faith and life. They frame and give shape to our understanding of who we are and invite active engagement in the ways, words, and witness that help to form us in faith all our lives long. Believing does not occur in a catechetical closet; rather, believing serves the catechetical mission with linkages to belonging and opportunities for discernment that, among other benefits, heighten understanding. "May the God of hope fill you with all joy and peace in believing, so that you may abound in hope by the power of the holy Spirit" (Rom 15:13).

In Genesis, we see images of Joseph as both "discerning and wise" (Gn 41:39) and also, upon seeing his brother Benjamin, "on the verge of tears" (Gn 43:30). The call to belong and to believe summons us to *discernment* and its partner, *reflection*. Through prayerful discernment, our vulnerabilities (historical and otherwise) are exposed within and before the community of faith. We live within and through this humbling need. We ponder and reflect on who we are becoming, what we believe, and whom we believe in as we enter into mysteries rich in truth and promise. This may happen for us in the midst of the daily "living, dying, and rising" (to self and others) experiences that we offer and share through the witness of the heart.

Living, dying, and rising converge where "way" becomes actualized in the people and events that cleanse and paint afresh the portrait of our lives. This is no painting to be viewed from a distance but rather one best viewed from within the fibers of the brush itself. For the "distance" of the centuries is now absorbed in one grand display of the community of faith from which we inherit our past and through which the future unfolds. Indeed, Christ the Artist and our Redeemer continues to teach us about living, dying, and rising as he invites us into his own. "For to me life is Christ, and death is gain" (Phil 1:21).

I invite you to explore these characteristics briefly in your own life and hope that this engagement will enhance your consideration of the chapters that follow.

For example, how does belonging affect the way you interact with others? What does it mean for maintaining regular communication with parents, family, friends, or caregivers? Does belonging necessarily mean having others nearby? Or might you be one of the multitude of people whose family is scattered across the nation or around the world? What sustains "belonging" for you if that is your reality? How does your parish, as a locus of belonging, occupy a place of fellowship and discipleship for you? Are you welcome? Do you welcome others, even if you are shy about such things?

As you ponder the movement of faith in your life, consider what it is that you believe and whom it is you believe in. Who is Jesus for you right now? What does he call you to do and to become? What confession of faith keeps you going day after day? What power resonates from within as you profess faith during Mass with the community to which you belong (not just the local parish but the diocese and universal Church)? What power resonates from within as you make belief come alive in faith and action?

Life can be a whirlwind. Is it a challenge for you to stop periodically and take time to reflect on your life? On where you are headed and why you are moving in a particular direction? On why you believe and belong as you do? Consider choices you may be facing or decisions that you have been asked to assist in making on behalf of others. What factors come to mind? How does prayer help to set the context for what you are discerning?

Our discernment can calm us as we deal with life's challenges and unpredictable outcomes. What joys, what hopes, what griefs, and what anxieties (see GS, 1) welcome or confront you, perhaps almost ceaselessly? How do "dying and rising" occasions of life describe your way as you live by faith each day?

For the baptized, born of water and Spirit, a cradle of hope offers perspective and promise, often through the common witness in faith of the Christian community, especially through the celebration of the sacraments. But this is not hope understood as a golden wish. Rather, catechists "hold fast to the hope that lies before us" (Heb 6:18) in times that simultaneously suggest both uncertainty and simplistic self-assurance. Indeed, faith sustains us as we strive to be "bearers of paschal joy and hope, in the name of the Church."[13]

Getting Started

To assist in our reception of historical perspectives that go well beyond the boundaries of this book, we need the support of other voices. Discussion with others about historical trends and practices can enhance our own understanding and influence our own practices.

Each chapter begins with a scriptural selection for your reflection. Reflection questions appear at the end of each of the remaining chapters and sometimes elsewhere in a chapter. They are intended to assist in facilitating these conversations, often with regard to the four characteristics of belonging; believing; discerning and reflecting; and living, dying and rising that were identified earlier.

Catechetical and related documentation lend other support. We are blessed with many sources that support our efforts to look forward as we remain mindful of our past. Examples of such sources are the *General Directory for Catechesis* and the *National Directory for Catechesis*. They offer us opportunities for reflection as we run, walk, and stumble along, and sometimes even drift away from, the Way who is Christ and the way we seek to travel together. They extend ready and contemporary assistance for understanding and reflecting on the catechetical journey.

Enjoy this look at our past. Going forward, embrace it as your own the way you would someone you love. Raise new questions as you answer old ones. Raise critical issues. Be merciful toward someone whom you may seek to avoid. Seek more information. Keep alert: the echo is near, even in whispers. Listen to other voices as you hear again the One who is "the way and the truth and the life" (Jn 14:6).

Approach others in a spirit of love and charity as you probe the joys and the challenges of catechesis over the ages. Do not read only for yourself, but think of at least one other person as you rediscover the way of faith that is yours but not yours alone—and surely not yours to lay to rest in a tightly covered basket. Consider that person's gifts. See in that person a living reminder of a history that is still evolving. And pause to look in the mirror—you might be surprised by what you see beyond and beneath the image of yourself. Listen for the echo.

"At present we see indistinctly, as in a mirror, but then face to face. At present I know partially; then I shall know fully, as I am fully known. So faith, hope, and love remain, these three; but the greatest of these is love" (1 Cor 13:12–13).

2
ROOTING THE JOURNEY
Some Old Testament Foundations

Hear, O Israel! The LORD is our GOD, the LORD alone! Therefore, you shall love the LORD, your God, with your whole heart, and with your whole being, and with your whole strength. Take to heart these words which I command you today.

—Deuteronomy 6:4–6

I love roaming among the stacks of a library. A glimpse of an unexpected title may delay my search for a volume shelved farther on down the aisle. A new title, standing alongside the one sought, beckons me to stay longer as I spot a nearby carrel. After all, there is something new to read and to discover—right now. Feasting on insights unknown to me yesterday, I yearn for more.

History, like a library, takes us beyond ourselves. A historical search can escort the inquirer through many paths without jettisoning connections to his or her own beginnings. Wondering about what things were like in millennia gone by may stimulate our curiosity; the "what, how, and why" of ancient civilizations piques our interest and feeds our imagination. For example, the marvels of Newgrange and other burial mounds in Ireland and the geographically distant pyramids of Egypt provide concrete witness to extraordinary undertakings from ages past, now resting secure in earth's memory.

Longstanding religions such as Judaism, Christianity, and Islam possess extensive histories with their own distinctive memories. As he looked toward the turn of the millennium and dialogue between the Church and other religions, St. John Paul II stated, "In this dialogue the Jews and the Muslims ought to have a pre-eminent place" (TMA, 53).[1]

Buddhism and Hinduism also present their own historic foundations. Siddhartha Gautama, the Buddha, lived around the same time as the Babylonian exile (sixth century BC). Whether religious and spiritual development found a home in Buddhism's eight-fold path or Hinduism's pursuit of Brahman, the quest for inner harmony and fulfillment (both clearly inadequate terms) led searchers in many directions.

Today, religious traditions and accompanying loyalties cross vast continents and numerous countries.[2] In this first quarter of the new millennium, we note the benefits to be gained through mutuality of respect, learning about other religious traditions, and ongoing interreligious interaction.[3] And within Christianity, ecumenical dialogue is of increasing importance. In a world dominated by technological advances, electronic "meeting places" are more accessible than ever before for ecumenical and interreligious interaction.

The historically significant and firmly rooted relationship between Judaism and Christianity helps to sharpen our focus for the present work, which relies in this chapter on God's self-revelation through such dimensions as Law, prophets, and wisdom literature. Early expressions of Christian life, worship, and witness bear testimony to linkages with Jewish tradition and practice. Our bond with Judaism and the Jewish people, from whom we learn much about living by faith, is of particular importance. We are reminded of "the spiritual ties which link the people of the New Covenant to the stock of Abraham. The Church of Christ acknowledges that in God's plan of salvation the beginning of her faith and election is to be found in the patriarchs, Moses and the prophets" (NA, 4).

These roots produce a rich religious heritage. We know the story. Elizabeth's offspring would eventually profess Mary's child as greater than himself: "I am baptizing you with water, for repentance, but the one who is coming after me is mightier than I. I am not worthy to carry his sandals. He will baptize you with the holy Spirit and fire" (Mt 3:11). "Jesus was born of the Chosen People, in fulfilment of the promise made to Abraham and constantly recalled by the Prophets" (TMA, 6).

We trust through our Judeo-Christian heritage that God comes to us in the midst of humanity's ongoing quest for life (not just "living" but life in all its depth and risk and challenge) and for truth (not just clear verbal expression but a knowing inclusive of body, mind, and spirit). Such an assertion may upon reflection overwhelm our ability to comprehend God's self-revelation and intimate presence in history. Indeed, the Incarnation is a turning point not only for time but for humanity.[4]

As our thoughts find their way to our hearts (or the reverse), we come to see that the immanence and transcendence of God combine to wrap us, secure us, in God's own saving and merciful care. This is a love so sweeping and so limitless that we may at first fail to realize that in actuality we share together in God's own blessing. Think about that for a moment—we share together in God's own blessing. "In order to gather together scattered humanity God calls Abram from his country, his kindred, and his father's house, and makes him Abraham, that is, 'the father of a multitude of nations.' 'In you all the nations of the earth shall be blessed'" (CCC, 59).[5]

Faith and Life

The way of faith moves us along the way of covenant, including God's covenant with Abraham and the Sinai covenant, tendered by God to Moses after the saving event of the exodus.[6] Though God yearns for the Israelites' ongoing faithfulness, they struggle to maintain faith in the God of the covenant as they continue their pursuit of the promised land.

Consider such personages as Abraham, Sarah, Isaac, Rebekah, Jacob, Leah, Rachel, Joseph, Moses, Miriam, Ruth, Saul, David, Solomon, and Esther. These and many more give color to a portrait of faith painted on a canvas formed by the lived experience of a chosen and resolute people. Each teaches us something about faith and about life. Such images as a burning bush, stone, soil, and manna nourishment help to tell the story of a people who, at one point, would find solace in a calf of gold before hearing and responding again to the call of a loving and patient God.

From the time of the great patriarchs until and beyond "Passover, the Exodus, the gift of the Law, and the ratification of the covenant" (CCC, 2574), we see a people finding their way, a way like a river with many tributaries winding through times of hunger, resistance, sin, confusion, and change along with times of repentance, hope, trust, and faithfulness.

It was important for the Israelites to band together. They were, after all, one people, God's own. They had endured enslavement from generation to generation. Within God's care, they were knit together, despite troubles that would come their way, including troubles of their own making. They needed to belong—not just to themselves or to immediate family members but to the self-revealing God of life and covenant. This was their only lasting security. That sense of God's call and of belonging remains alive and robust today.

Yet belonging is tied to and thrives within believing. These escapees were not freed from pursuing chariots just to reach safe and dry land. Rather, they were called to something that would secure their life together: belief in the living God and faithfulness to God's exhortations, through prophets and others, to stand firm in their belief. On such a foundation, belonging would thrive.

These fleeing people, led by Moses, are to discern next steps within God's care, for the way of wilderness can be harsh and unpredictable. They hunger. Moses bears the wilderness distress of the Israelites, hearing their complaint to him and Aaron (a familiar sentiment in our own day) (see Ex 16:3). Move ahead a chapter in Exodus: a different location, more complaining: they thirst (see Ex 17:1–3). Among the people trust in Moses is evaporating. We can almost hear his frustration when Moses says to the Lord, "What shall I do with this people?" (Ex 17:4). Frustration will drive Moses to go so far as to ask God to kill him (see Nm 11:15).

The Lord knows his people's need and is with them and takes care of them, despite their bickering and uncertainty (cf. Ex 16:4ff. and 17:5–7). God's love for his people is beyond measure. And Moses would be the one to hear the Word of the Lord and carry it to his people:

> Now, if you obey me completely and keep my covenant, you will be my treasured possession among all peoples, though all the earth is mine. You will be to me a kingdom of priests, a holy nation. That is what you must tell the Israelites. So Moses went and summoned the elders of the people. When he set before them all that the LORD had ordered him to tell them, all the people answered together, "Everything the LORD has said, we will do." Then Moses brought back to the LORD the response of the people. (Ex 19:5–8)

Over the ages, the Israelites would meet with grand success, utter failure, renewed hope, more disappointment, and enhanced hope. Indeed, faithfulness to covenant and the commandments would demand a "whole-life" response.

What might have challenged the Israelites in their discernment? Why could they sometimes not "see" what was in their midst? Why did they sometimes not "see the forest for the trees"? What might they have learned from their "dying" experiences? From experiences of God's care? What does their ongoing story and experience offer us?

One particularly important life-giving and spirit-sustaining scriptural excerpt comes from Deuteronomy, the last book of the Pentateuch. It offers a focused look into the breadth and demands of faith and life within the Israelite community. The book's main speaker is Moses, faithful and prophetic servant of God; this prayerful scripture, known as the Shema ("Hear, O Israel! . . ."),[7] appears one chapter after the Deuteronomic rendering of the Decalogue.

> Hear, O Israel! The LORD is our GOD, the LORD alone! Therefore, you shall love the LORD, your God, with your whole heart, and with your whole being, and with your whole strength. Take to heart these words which I command you today. Keep repeating them to your children. Recite them when you are at home and when you are away,

> when you lie down and when you get up. Bind them on your arm as
> a sign and let them be as a pendant on your forehead. Write them
> on the doorposts of your houses and on your gates. (Dt 6:4–9; cf.
> Mt 22:37–38, Mk 12:29–30, Lk 10:27)

We see here the beauty, power, and convergence of Law and life.
This foundational exhortation commands the attention of both head
and heart. Our senses step up with keen awareness of the demands and
commands of the Lord. Notice the blend of verbs that in catechetical
discourse may not always be seen as complementary: hear, love, take (to
heart), command, repeat, recite, bind, and write. Yet they are complementary. Indeed, in some mysterious way life *is* a convergence experience, one that draws us out of a comfort zone born of "my world" and
that may do no more than confirm our own opinion. Sadly, we may even
find it preferable to accept all sides of an issue instead of taking a stand
on important matters of faith and life.

Listening with the Heart

Perhaps we sometimes find ourselves sidetracked along the way of faith,
disappointed in ourselves or others—or God. However, the "sidetrack"
may actually present a new opportunity, for we are called to raise up goodness and goodwill wherever it is found—including within ourselves—even
when fear and anxiety may tempt us to choose a bypass lane on one of
life's many highways.

Consider Moses and all who followed him out of Egypt toward freedom across the sea. Consider, too, commitments of faithful generations
over the past millennia. Imagine people embracing the Ten Commandments (cf. Ex 20) long ago, in the recent past, and this day, this hour. And
imagine calling faith-filled believers to love and live in the rich preserve
of heart, soul, and strength, not merely for or within the self but for and
within the life that God offers to each of us and all of us as saving Lord,
beckoning us to himself.

"Hear, O Israel! The LORD is our GOD, the LORD alone!" (Dt 6:4).
Our hearing moves us to listen carefully not only with ears but also with

hands and heart. How might we respond in the affirmative to the resolute voice of the Lord urging us to hear, to listen attentively? Might our own next thought get in the way of the voice and message of another? Such questions are relevant regardless of age or setting.

As I think of these things, I am drawn to the prophets Elijah and Elisha. The tender story of Elisha, about to succeed Elijah, gives us a message to hear and digest today. Elisha says to Elijah, "As the LORD lives, and as you yourself live, I will not leave you" (2 Kgs 2:2, 4, 6).

The reluctant prophet Jeremiah, whose life spanned from the mid-seventh into the sixth centuries before Christ, insisted to the Lord God that he was not one to bear the Word of the Lord to others. He knew his own limitations. However, he underestimated God's ongoing presence (see Jer 1:4–10). From Jeremiah's lips falls the Word of God. Immersed in the culture of the time, he knows the people to and of whom he speaks. He proclaims a new covenant:

> See, days are coming—oracle of the LORD—when I will make a new covenant with the house of Israel and the house of Judah. It will not be like the covenant I made with their ancestors the day I took them by the hand to lead them out of the land of Egypt. They broke my covenant, though I was their master—oracle of the LORD. But this is the covenant I will make with the house of Israel after those days—oracle of the LORD. I will place my law within them, and write it upon their hearts; I will be their God, and they shall be my people. . . . For I will forgive their iniquity and no longer remember their sin. (Jer 31:31–34)

When I think of Jeremiah, the terms *weary* and *frustrated* come to mind (cf. Jer 20:7–9). Perhaps I am putting myself in his shoes (a bit prideful, perhaps), commiserating from across millennia about the way in which I might respond to God's call in the midst of political uncertainty and religious unfaithfulness. Yet does that not describe in some ways aspects of our own age? Despite the hardships he endures, Jeremiah cannot fail to proclaim the Word of the Lord, for the Word "is as if fire is burning in my heart" (Jer 20:9). The Word also consumes us. Perhaps there is a little bit of Jeremiah in each of us.

Centuries after the Sinai covenant, about 600 BC, "the hand of the LORD came upon" Ezekiel (Ez 1:3). Exiled to Babylon, Ezekiel would seek to stir the hearts of his hearers from within the experience of separation from his homeland.

Ezekiel's voice would render the Word of the Lord with the power of God's own commitment to his people: "I will give you a new heart, and a new spirit I will put within you. I will remove the heart of stone from your flesh and give you a heart of flesh. I will put my spirit within you so that you walk in my statutes, observe my ordinances, and keep them" (Ez 36:26–27).

The term *spirit* carries popular meanings; for example, it may designate a type of outward enthusiastic display, such as during a sporting event. For catechesis, however, we dig deeper, to that Breath that comes from God and that gives voice to our hearts and power to our witness. The Holy Spirit is with us, freely given through Baptism. The gift of God's grace sustains us as we inhale and exhale, even subconsciously, second by second. The practice of habitually breathing in the Spirit the words "Lord Jesus Christ, Son of the living God, have mercy on me, a sinner" can strengthen our resolve—without our even knowing it—as we seek to live by faith and keep faith alive in relationships formed in Christ. How fortunate we are to be "endowed with the special strength of the Holy Spirit" in Confirmation (LG, 11; see CCC, 1285, 689–690, 1241).

Similarly, the significance of the image of the heart, employed in numerous though limited ways in our age to express love and affection, is not to be understated. The image of the heart implies a holistic understanding not only of who we are but also of who we are coming to be. The heart is not to be defined only by its ability to pump blood. The life-sustaining fluid that courses its way to and from this central organ opens up to us meanings of hearts hardened, broken, healed, troubled, repentant, joyful, and made whole.

The scriptures offer an abundance of such uses, and catechesis is a beneficiary, as we seek to educate the whole person, whether child or adult. For example, we do not catechize the child as a "partial person" in the expectation that he or she will be "full" in adulthood. Rather, we recognize and affirm the gifts of the child *as* child, aware that growth emerges as the child grows in the life of faith offered through Baptism and lived through the witness and welcome of generations young and old.

"Attend, My People, to My Teaching"

Biblical scholar Lawrence Boadt, C.S.P. (1942–2010), reminds catechists of the importance and breadth of the Old Testament for catechetical understanding. Parental responsibility in Old Testament times sounds similar to what parents claim as their duty today. Writes Boadt: "Parents were to train their children in the various skills needed for daily life." Later he adds, "The first teacher was the parent."[8] He goes on to say, "Much was learned the old-fashioned way, by example and family practice. Ancient Judaism, like the modern, emphasized whole family participation in religious rites at home, such as the Sabbath, or feast days during the year, at which children were to learn their faith."[9]

Indeed, it would appear to be unnatural for teaching and practice to be considered apart from each other. Judaism continues to teach by example the value of both.

Writing on Jewish education, the distinguished scholars James Reed and Ronnie Prevost indicate that "teaching was conducted by repetition and memorization. Boys learned to read in order to read the Torah in the synagogue."[10] These authors also note that "women had always taught their children, particularly their daughters, in and through their domestic duties. Jewish laws were lessons in obedience and piety. In later Judaism, the mother often had a more formal role in the literary education of her children, and her domestic role was interpreted in terms of freeing her husband to study the law."[11]

Prayerful reading and reflection on the psalms, which were composed during different time periods, yields a portrait of a people struggling with themselves, their allies, their enemies, and their God. Such a "poetic treasure" characterizes life itself, rich in thanks and pain, joy and sorrow, regret and resilience. In a word, these scriptures, so vital in the past and to Jewish people today, serve to inform, shape, and form us along the way of faith and life. Let us sing praise to God!

One particularly enriching and encouraging scripture for catechesis from this font of wisdom literature is Psalm 78:1–4:

> Attend, my people, to my teaching;
>   listen to the words of my mouth.
> I will open my mouth in a parable,
>   unfold the puzzling events of the past.
> What we have heard and know;
>   things our ancestors have recounted to us.
> We do not keep them from our children;
>   we recount them to the next generation,
> The praiseworthy deeds of the LORD and his strength,
>   the wonders that he performed. (Ps 78:1–4)

Notice emphases on elements that capture much of what catechesis today relies on: teaching, listening, words, parable, recounting, generational sharing, and deeds and wonders of the Lord. Again we see convergence. Opportunities for belonging and believing coincide in an interplay founded on faith and faithful witness. Psalm 78 goes on to assert—but not without a comparison to a previous generation deemed "rebellious and defiant" (Ps 78:8; cf. Dt 31:27, 32:5)—the obligation to hand on the teaching to generation after generation, for the generations belong to one another in shared belief and practice.

Psalm 19 provides an unfiltered opportunity to embrace "the law of the LORD" (Ps 19:8) in a positive way, seeking and seeing the Law and its accompanying precepts as helps rather than hindrances for our lives. Psalm 19 blends rich images that climax in praise of the "LORD, my rock and my redeemer" (Ps 19:15). One hundred psalms later, the majestic and prayerful Psalm 119 confirms through its own instructional style[12] God's lasting presence with the well-intentioned and faithful seeker, who "reminds" God that "all my ways are before you" (Ps 119:168).

In an age that tends to equate "law" with "legalism," we can benefit from a fresh reading of Psalm 19 and later Psalm 119, the longest of all the psalms. Verse by verse, these psalms show us the way through the joys and challenges of faithful living in union with praise for the God who lovingly pierces our lives with plentiful guidance and abundant care. Indeed, God's revelation sustains us.

Proverbs, another book of wisdom literature, also formed part of religious development and does so for people of faith today as well. "To seek wisdom above all things is a fundamental option and a way of life."[13] Catechists surely can relate to such a path (e.g., see Prv 4).[14]

Proverbs offers wise counsel and a reservoir of support as we grow in openness to God's presence and to relationships with one another. "Other books urge readers to perform wise acts, but Proverbs urges them to seek wisdom itself and portrays wisdom as a woman seeking human beings as disciples and companions."[15] Probing its sayings sometimes leads me to remember my late mother and the holistic mindset that shaped her life and characterized her activity: graced living in relation to others.

Considering the Old Testament *as a catechesis* enables us to mine the rich depth of the book of Proverbs (and other books) for obvious meanings and more. For example, chapter 4 exhorts the hearer/reader to live faithfully and justly by "the way of wisdom" and to avoid the way of wickedness. It says in part:

On the way of wisdom I direct you,
  I lead you on straight paths.
When you walk, your step will not be impeded,
  and should you run, you will not stumble.
Hold fast to instruction, never let it go;
  keep it, for it is your life. (Prv 4:11–13)

The integration of instruction and life not only confirms an ancient exhortation but also reinforces contemporary approaches that blend such elements together. Catechesis today does not "live" by itself. The New Evangelization and catechesis bond well, as do worship and witness, and all four together. The message of the scriptures is "whole." Of course, such an assertion does not suggest that particular portions of the scriptures cannot be studied in depth or mined for diverse understandings. The point here is that such study happens within the grand schematic of the living Word of God, a Word alive and active in the pre-Christian era and alive today. "Does not Wisdom call, and Understanding raise her voice?" (Prv 8:1).

Prophetic awareness, so richly portrayed by our elders in faith, offers another look into our catechetical heritage, as we have already seen through Jeremiah and Ezekiel. We thirst for the Word of God. Isaiah the prophet offers us opportunities to probe, for example, trust, justice, and witness associated with living by faith.[16] Catechists today relate well to Isaiah 6:8: "Then I heard the voice of the Lord saying, 'Whom shall I send? Who will go for us?' 'Here I am,' I said; 'send me!'" Perhaps you see yourself in this exchange. And Isaiah chapter 55, for example, is rich in catechetical application:

•   "All you who are thirsty, come to the water!" (v. 1).

•   "Pay attention and come to me; listen, that you may have life. I will make with you an everlasting covenant, the steadfast loyalty promised to David" (v. 3).

•   "Yet just as from the heavens the rain and snow come down and do not return there till they have watered the earth, making it fertile and fruitful, giving seed to the one who sows and bread to the one who eats, so shall my word be that goes forth from my mouth; it shall not return to me empty, but shall do what pleases me, achieving the end for which I sent it" (vv. 10–11).

The Word of God lives! The prophets provided an exhortatory voice with an urgency born of real-time challenges and real-life concerns. Falling from their lips were words of encouragement, judgment, and hope along with vigorous calls for justice.

For many years I relied on Isaiah 43 to invite persons engaged in catechetical ministry to remember that each of the people with whom they interact is called by name by God. Sometimes we would also listen to a recording of the recollections of a Jewish Holocaust survivor whose named identity was changed from her name to an assigned number tattooed on her body while she was held captive during World War II.[17] A quiet unease would come over the room as the catechists listened to this survivor's strong yet painful testimony. I continue to be reminded of the comforting words of Isaiah the prophet's assertion of God's protective care for his people: "Do not fear, for I have redeemed you; I have called you by name: you are mine" (Is 43:1). No number or marking can ever steal the soul of a named person; such attempted theft cries out for justice.

We must never forget the millions of Jews who perished less than a century ago in the horror of the Holocaust.[18] We must rely on words and actions that "respect the continuing existence of God's covenant with the Jewish people and their faithful response, despite centuries of suffering, to God's call" (NDC, 51D).[19] Remembrance is no distant recollection bordered by fading memories of centuries made less present by the passage of time. The enduring heritage of faith of "the Jewish people, the first to hear the word of God" (NDC, 51D) gives witness to God's loving and sustaining care. "Our two traditions are so related that they cannot ignore each other."[20] We need to apply this fundamental perspective in catechetical ministry.

Indeed, there are many benefits to be derived from ongoing and extended dialogue and from building up this essential relationship. For example, the Vatican's Commission for Religious Relations with the Jews indicates, in part (in treating "Relations between the Old and New Testaments"):

> In underlining the eschatological dimension of Christianity we shall reach a greater awareness that the people of God of the Old and the New Testaments are tending toward a like end in the future: the coming or return of the Messiah—even if they start from two different points of view. . . .
>
> Attentive to the same God who has spoken, hanging on the same word, we have to witness to one same memory and one common hope in him who is the master of history. We must also accept our responsibility to prepare the world for the coming of the Messiah by working together for social justice, respect for the rights of persons and nations and for social and international reconciliation.[21]

Our exploration of some roots of our journey and the emergence of catechesis within Christianity combines humble awareness of ages gone by with ongoing understanding of Judaism today. "All the paths of the LORD are mercy and truth toward those who honor his covenant and decrees" (Ps 25:10). God's gifts, mercy, and love abound. The Lord of all creation and all humanity awaits us, is with us, and seeks us out.

As we move to chapter 3, we engage with eyes of faith the historical context from within which the Christ moment penetrates humanity. "And the Word became flesh and made his dwelling among us" (Jn 1:14). Our rejoicing is boundless as we affirm in faith the reality of the Incarnation. The Son of God "became truly man while remaining truly God" (CCC, 464). Jesus Christ, the second person of the Blessed Trinity, reaches us and reaches out to us, especially now through the gift of the Spirit and the sacramental life of the Church. We take comfort, though not selfishly (catechists are not "faith hoarders"), as witnesses to faith alive. Jesus is with us; the Spirit abides.

Jesus teaches as part of his Sermon on the Mount, "Do not think that I have come to abolish the law or the prophets. I have come not to abolish but to fulfill" (Mt 5:17). As Christians and catechists in this place and time, may our memory making, memory keeping, and memory healing continue to strengthen our faith and guide us along the way of catechesis. And may we rejoice as our prayer, expressed in thought, word, and action, resounds anew with thanksgiving to the God who calls and who comes. We remember: "For the gifts and the call of God are irrevocable" (Rom 11:29).[22]

Reflection Questions

1. To whom do you turn every day for security and a renewed sense of belonging? How?
2. What does the Jewish experience of faith and life offer you?
3. What sense of community identity do you derive from what you have read?
4. Imagine yourself struggling to sustain faith after years of searching and toil. Perhaps this has already been your experience. What would

sustain you? What would you do when you experienced shortness of "faith-breath"?

5. What is your experience of belonging "within" believing? How do the two come together for you?

6. Why, sometimes, don't we "see the forest for the trees"?

7. Why do we sometimes expect life to be rich in "living" without embracing the "dying" that is part of life and that brings us back to what we are seeking?

8. How might you help to "raise up" someone you may know for whom life seems to be a daily and perhaps even monumental struggle? What hope might you offer?

3

IDENTIFYING THE WAY
Jesus Christ, Teacher and Catechist

Do you realize what I have done for you? You call me "teacher" and "master," and rightly so, for indeed I am. If I, therefore, the master and teacher, have washed your feet, you ought to wash one another's feet. I have given you a model to follow, so that as I have done for you, you should also do.

—John 13:12–15

How might we explore Jesus as teacher and catechist as we continue on our way through catechetical history?

Over time, we come to know, through the grace of God and through sacred and life-sustaining words, the One who became one of us. Sacred scripture, itself a comprehensive catechesis, speaks to us in the eucharistic language of love, mercy, and redemption. It bleeds godly care in the midst of human sentiment. It nourishes us with words that soothe and satisfy, yet leaves us yearning for more.

Jesus is with us and calms us as we face our worries, cares, and concerns; he is the saving Word himself. "Christ is the light of humanity" (LG, 1), and his light spreads far and wide, beyond the three dimensions we perceive. "Blessed be the Lord, the God of Israel, for he has visited and brought redemption to his people" (Lk 1:68).

Christ entrusts his disciples with a mission, now inherited and transferred from generation to generation: "Go, therefore, and make disciples of all nations, baptizing them in the name of the Father, and of the Son, and of the holy Spirit, teaching them to observe all that I have commanded you. And behold, I am with you always, until the end of the age" (Mt 28:19–20).

Christ remains with us in and through the community of the Church he founded, a living body—the Body of Christ. In community, we seek Christ. "In the Christian community the disciples of Jesus Christ are nourished at a twofold table: 'that of the word of God and that of the Body of Christ'" (GDC, 70).[1] In community, we find Christ. And in community—in the life of the Church—we live, die, and rise in Christ through the power and abiding presence of the Holy Spirit, especially through the sacraments, "efficacious signs of grace, instituted by Christ and entrusted to the Church, by which divine life is dispensed to us" (CCC, 1131; cf. CCC, 1407).

Nurtured by the gift of God's revelation in sacred scripture and sacred tradition, we come to see who we are spiritually as we reach out to others.[2] Sacred scripture, "truly the Word and work of God,"[3] offers us both the promise and the presence of God as we enter through familiar yet ever-new doorways for exploring life with God and with one another. Sacred tradition has to do with the wealth of the Church's "doctrine, life and worship" (DV, 8) handed on in life, faith, and belief over the centuries.

We affirm the reality that "both the living Tradition and the written Scriptures have their common source in the revelation of God in Jesus Christ."[4] Our faith is a living faith, enabling us to embrace ever more vigorously the living Word of God in our lives. Sacred scripture and sacred tradition form an essential foundation for all the Church as we profess Christ as Messiah and Lord and seek to live his Way and teach the Good News that he is and that he shares, the Gospel that still forms us in faith.

God the Father never stops loving us. "In love he destined us for adoption to himself through Jesus Christ" (Eph 1:5). By the blood of Christ we are redeemed (cf. LG, 4; CCC, 766). The saving Word lives in and through the Church instituted by Christ and sanctified by the Holy Spirit (cf. LG, 4; CCC, 874, 767–768). We strive to comprehend the Word by living and to live the Word by comprehending. Through his self-revelation in Christ,[5] God our Father provides ways and means for us to do so. The Good News must be preached and taught. Where there is one believer, there are two, then three, then more. They need not be in close geographic proximity to be united—to one another and, through the grace of the Holy Spirit (which binds believers together in the first place), to the One who offers himself sacrificially as redemptive gift for all humanity.

Although it is often stated that *we* are the Church, we may sometimes speak more from routine than from powerful affirmation drawn from practice. The Church, filled with the Spirit of Christ, grows within continents and across vast seas. We neither wander aimlessly by ourselves across rugged lands nor swim alone in such waters. We carry the community of faith in our hearts as we wend our way through rivers that pierce mountains, lakes and streams that water plains and valleys, and urban centers that stand firm on solid soil as they reach for the sky.

Joining the Journey of Jesus

Imagine traveling by foot or donkey between two locations of your choice, many miles apart. Selma to Montgomery and South Bend to Fort Wayne are two trips that come to mind for me.

Now imagine another journey of long distance: that of Joseph and Mary from Nazareth to Bethlehem. What might they have experienced not only along the way to the city of Jesus' birth but also during their ensuing flight into Egypt and subsequent return to Nazareth? What might their conversations regarding Jesus' future have been like? Where might they have stopped along the way on each of these journeys? What might have strengthened their sense of belonging to one another and to their community of faith?

The faithful family of Jesus traveled again, this time to the Temple in Jerusalem so that Joseph and Mary could "present him to the Lord" (Lk 2:22). Simeon and Anna both attest to the wonder of their experience of the child in their midst. Their hope is affirmed, their discernment secure. Imagine Simeon gently receiving the child, holding him with great care, as one would any infant, and marveling at what is happening before him, gratefully offering to God a blessing with the now-familiar words "my eyes have seen your salvation" (Lk 2:30). Anna, a prophetess and a fixture in the Temple, came forward and "gave thanks to God and spoke about the child to all who were awaiting the redemption of Jerusalem" (Lk 2:38).

After Jesus' family "had fulfilled all the prescriptions of the law of the Lord," they returned to Nazareth, where "the child grew and became strong, filled with wisdom; and the favor of God was upon him" (Lk 2:39–40).

Jesus became one of us in and through the cultural, political, and religious world of his day. His faithful family lived according to the pre-scriptions of the Jewish tradition to which they belonged, formed and shaped by adherence to the Shema and influenced by the religious prac-tices of the day. Catechetical scholar James Campbell notes that "education in the time of Jesus was primarily religious. God was at the center of all life and culture. For the Jews, all truth came from God. . . . Every day in the life of a faithful Jew was a day of prayer."[6]

Both the Temple in Jerusalem, a place of sacrifice and prayer, and the local synagogue held special meaning for the Jewish people. In tracing the development of the synagogue from the time of the exile in Babylon (sixth century BC), Campbell states that it "became a place of assembly where all the concerns of Jewish life could be discussed. People came to pray, worship, and learn."[7] One can imagine the intergenerational blending in and around such a place. Learning for Jesus would have been typical of the time and multi-dimensional, incorporating religious, scriptural, and historical foundations, along with practical skills.[8] What we call today "family catechesis" was part of the greater responsibility of parents to prepare their children for life.

It would have been natural for people of the time to rely on oral tradition to hand on great truths of faith. This was more than a teaching device; it was an essential means for handing on foundational beliefs and practices. Storytelling was also an important tool. Storytelling does more than keep details of the story or account alive; storytelling enables the teller to enter into the narrative with vigor and personal witness, often drawn from his or her own reflection on and experience of life's challenges (ups and downs, "dyings and risings") and hand it on to others not just with words but with spirited understanding and, when it is a scriptural account, spirited recollection. Similarly, memorization,[9] sometimes judged as rote or meaningless, fosters more than repetition of words. Rather, this tool enables an immediacy of recall for accessing the truth being taught or prayed.

Jesus was immersed in the culture of his time. The *General Directory for Catechesis*, in addressing the Incarnation, notes, "The Word of God became man, a concrete man, in space and time and rooted in a specific culture: 'Christ by his incarnation committed himself to the particular social and cultural circumstances of the men among whom he lived.' This is the original 'inculturation' of the word of God and is the model of all evangelization by the Church, 'called to bring the power of the Gospel into the very heart of culture and cultures'" (GDC, 109).[10] From within the domain of cultural settings we learn to belong, to believe, and to discern future life steps along the way, not sure perhaps of where they might lead us, but confident in our hope that critical moments of our lives can be faced within networks of love, care, and mutual support.

Just as the life-sustaining core of the body is the heart, so is the core of the Church's catechesis Jesus Christ. No wonder we say that catechesis has at its heart "the Person of Jesus of Nazareth" (CT, 5) and has as its source "the word of God revealed by Jesus Christ" (NDC, 18). We look to Christ as priest, prophet, and king, knowing that "we share in Christ's triple mission" (RH, 18)[11] as we explore and study catechesis.

Jesus' Way of Teaching

Here we consider briefly Jesus as teacher and catechist in the context of our review of some highlights of catechetical history, which can aid our becoming more effective teachers and catechists. The scriptures provide extensive evidence of the way in which Jesus taught not only his disciples but also those who did not embrace his message.

One can see in Jesus' childhood his ability to capture the attention of his elders. Consider the twelve-year-old Jesus separated from his family in Jerusalem following the feast of Passover. He has been gone now for a few days, unable to be found by his religiously observant family. Families today might describe such a worrisome separation as a time of anxiety, even emotional "dying." "After three days" Mary and Joseph finally locate him "in the temple, sitting in the midst of the teachers, listening to them and asking them questions, and all who heard him were astounded at his understanding and his answers" (Lk 2:46–47). Even as a child, Jesus uses listening as he teaches by his responses.

In the meantime, Mary and Joseph are "astonished," and Mary questions his absence. His parents are perplexed by Jesus' response ("Why were you looking for me? Did you not know that I must be in my Father's house?"[Lk 2:49]). After all, Jesus belonged to Mary and Joseph. Any parent who has recovered a lost child, or any adult child who has had to go looking for a parent suffering from dementia, knows the sense of relief and "resurrection" that overtakes them upon finding the one who is lost. Yet Jesus' response, even to them, displays his embrace of a greater mission, one beyond the natural boundaries of immediate family. Luke goes on to say that Jesus returned with Mary and Joseph to Nazareth, "and Jesus advanced [in] wisdom and age and favor before God and man" (Lk 2:52). Later, after Jesus begins his public ministry, the Temple becomes a usual place for him to teach (see Mt 26:55; cf. NDC, 8).

Nearly two decades later, Jesus is baptized by John, even though John objects (see Mt 3:14). Jesus is to share fully in his people's experience, in all ways but sin. Many of us know the account from repeated telling and reflection. Jesus tells John, "'Allow it now, for thus it is fitting for us to fulfill all righteousness.' Then he allowed him. After Jesus was baptized, he came up from the water and behold, the heavens were opened [for him], and he saw the Spirit of God descending like a dove [and] coming upon him. And a voice came from the heavens, saying, 'This is my beloved Son, with whom I am well pleased'" (Mt 3:15–17).

Matthew tells us that "Jesus was led by the Spirit into the desert to be tempted by the devil" (Mt 4:1). Jesus experiences that most human of challenges, temptation, after lengthy fasting and accompanying hunger. But Jesus does not yield to Satan: "You shall not put the Lord, your God, to the test" (Mt 4:7; see also Lk 4:12). Indeed, nothing can contain Jesus and his ministry: "Get away, Satan! It is written: 'The Lord, your God, shall you worship and him alone shall you serve'" (Mt 4:10).

We read in the Gospel of Mark, "After John had been arrested, Jesus came to Galilee proclaiming the gospel of God: 'This is the time of fulfillment. The kingdom of God is at hand. Repent, and believe in the gospel'" (Mk 1:14–15).[12] The kingdom of God, present in the Lord Jesus and given witness by his words, his signs, and his works (see GDC, 140; NDC, 28), is here. "In him the kingdom itself became present and was fulfilled" (RMi, 18). Signs of the kingdom, especially in the ultimate sign of eucharistic celebration, surround us.

Jesus taught in a way that expands our understanding of who a teacher is and what a teacher does. His appeal was to mind and heart, spirit and soul. He and his teaching (actually, he *is* the teaching) not only permeate the gospels but also are foundational to the entire New Testament. And he taught not only his followers but also those who opposed him (see NDC, 8). Whether he was teaching in the synagogues of Galilee (Lk 4:15) or standing, sitting, or walking out in the world, Jesus' sense of what his hearers needed to hear and do was uncanny.

The proclamation of the kingdom of God was central for his exhortations to others: life matters; eternal life is in the balance. It is in the synagogue in Nazareth, his hometown, that Jesus proclaims from the prophet Isaiah to those assembled:

> The Spirit of the Lord is upon me,
>   because he has anointed me
>   to bring glad tidings to the poor.
> He has sent me to proclaim liberty to captives
>   and recovery of sight to the blind,
>   to let the oppressed go free,
> and to proclaim a year acceptable to the Lord. (Lk 4:18–19)[13]

Luke continues: "Rolling up the scroll, he handed it back to the attendant and sat down, and the eyes of all in the synagogue looked intently at him. He said to them, 'Today this scripture passage is fulfilled in your hearing'" (Lk 4:20–21).

However, Jesus will experience rejection in this place of childhood memories (he knows and says that "no prophet is accepted in his own native place" [Lk 4:24]). Anger and disapproval reach fever pitch. And rejection is something he will face again. Yet Jesus will call and serve, lead and save. He will die and rise for all people.[14]

Communication and Relationship in Christ

Jesus teaches his disciples and us not only about the demands of faith and depth of rejection but also about the need to look beyond the immediate culture, place, and population. Indeed, the Spirit of the Lord moves beyond familiar peoples and boundaries and sustains us as we seek to stretch beyond comfort zones that may seem to make of the Gospel a template for easy living by limiting its reach. Well-known catechist Judith Dunlap writes, "God constantly gathers a people in loving covenant, inviting them to grow closer to him and to each other in community. God, never sacrificing the truth, revealed himself in and through the culture of each generation, offering liberation from the evil and bondage encountered within that culture."[15]

Jesus faced many questioners, right up until his death.[16] When asked by a scribe, "Which is the first of all the commandments?" Jesus replies with some familiar words ("Hear, O Israel! . . .") that hold a significant place within his Jewish tradition. He says to the scribe, "The first is this: 'Hear, O Israel! The Lord our God is Lord alone! You shall love the Lord your God with all your heart, with all your soul, with all your mind, and with all your strength.' The second is this: 'You shall love your neighbor as yourself.' There is no other commandment greater than these." More interaction ensues, after which Jesus, seeing that the scribe answers "with understanding," assures him, "You are not far from the kingdom of God" (see Mk 12:28–34).[17]

Jesus invites his listeners into relationship, an overused term often reduced to no more than a synonym for polite acknowledgment of another. But Jesus invites his listeners into a relationship beyond words: a participation in the love he shares with the Father and the Spirit. God exists in eternal relationship: three persons in one God. "God is eternal blessedness, undying life, unfading light. God is love: Father, Son and Holy

Spirit" (CCC, 257). Within the Body of Christ, the Church, we profess belief that "the mystery of the Most Holy Trinity is the central mystery of the Christian faith and of Christian life" (CCC, 261).

Our relationship of love in Christ may stretch human understanding beyond words but not beyond human participation. One essential truth of our relationship in Christ—and through him with one another—is that God shares his own life with us. His self-revelation invites us to explore the "pedagogy of God," his saving action over time that is not reducible to a daily lesson plan; rather, it is love so vast and so intimate that we may struggle at first to understand it.

Our first declaration as we pray the Creed with the whole Church—"I believe in one God . . ."—begins our "whole-self" affirmation of belief in the one true God, Creator of all things, the God of the covenant, of saving self-sacrifice, of abiding merciful love, of wisdom of the ages, of advocacy for life itself. "God has revealed himself fully by sending his own Son, in whom he has established his covenant for ever" (CCC, 73).

Such a statement about the author of life asserts and confirms God's presence among us. It encourages us to probe faith grounded in the pedagogy of God, for the gift of faith is both a treasure humbly received and a gift to be handed on. "The divine plan of Revelation is realized simultaneously 'by deeds and words which are intrinsically bound up with each other' and shed light on each other. It involves a specific divine pedagogy: God communicates himself to man gradually" (CCC, 53).[18]

We are the beneficiaries of God's own pedagogy, for God's saving action over time, fulfilled in Christ, teaches us and forms us today. God transforms us into his people, setting us free from sin and enabling us to love in witness to an enduring and salvific covenant of eschatological import (see NDC, 28). God models love, for God is love. Dunlap writes that "God's self-revelation serves as the original model for catechesis."[19]

The *National Directory for Catechesis* puts it this way: "God's self-communication is realized gradually through his actions and his words. It is most fully achieved in the Word made flesh, Jesus Christ. The history of this self-revelation itself documents the method by which God transmits the content of Revelation as contained in Sacred Scripture and

Tradition. This is the pedagogy of God. It is the source and model of the pedagogy of the faith" (NDC, 28; cf. DV, 15).

One anchor for us in this regard, set decades before the national directory just cited, emerged from the Second Vatican Council. *Dei Verbum* teaches that "Sacred Tradition and sacred Scripture make up a single sacred deposit of the Word of God, which is entrusted to the Church" (DV, 10). The next sentence references faithful witness to the Word of God, seen in relation to Acts 2:42. A little later we read, "The task of giving an authentic interpretation of the Word of God, whether in its written form or in the form of Tradition, has been entrusted to the living teaching office of the Church alone. Its authority in this matter is exercised in the name of Jesus Christ" (DV, 10). In a chapter focused on catechesis and evangelization, the *National Directory for Catechesis* states, "The Magisterium ensures the Church's fidelity to the teaching of the apostles in matters of faith and morals.... The Magisterium is the servant of the Word of God" (NDC, 18).

By faith[20] and by our passage through saving baptismal waters, we are drawn to and enter into relationship with God—Father, Son, and Holy Spirit—and in that loving communion enter into sacred mystery. We are claimed by Christ, "the eternal high priest of the New Covenant" (CCC, 1410), who gives all for all in redemptive sacrifice: "He took the bread, said the blessing, broke it, and gave it to them, saying, 'This is my body, which will be given for you; do this in memory of me.' And likewise the cup after they had eaten, saying, 'This cup is the new covenant in my blood, which will be shed for you'" (Lk 22:19–20). We are blessed to live and enact faith through his Paschal Mystery, now celebrated with thanks and praise at the table of the Lord.

By faith, we seek to promote the Gospel, avoid sin, and live in the promised Holy Spirit as we develop new relationships and sustain existing ones. Relationships may lead to or flow from communion in Christ, to whom we belong (see CT, 9). We know that relationships benefit from communication between individuals and within communities.

Communication is fundamental for any catechist or teacher. We need to remember this, especially because the term *communication* runs the risk of losing its depth of meaning for the community of faith. Jesus exemplifies communication for mission as he forms his disciples for mission (see GDC,

137). They belong to him. Jesus is "the Teacher who saves, sanctifies and guides, who lives, who speaks, rouses, moves, redresses, judges, forgives, and goes with us day by day on the path of history, the Teacher who comes and will come in glory" (CT, 9; cf. GDC, 137). God's own pedagogy continues to inform, shape, guide, and teach us, especially through the pedagogy of Jesus Christ (see GDC, 140). Jesus' own pedagogy relied in part on "the use of all the resources of interpersonal communication, such as word, silence, metaphor, image, example, and many diverse signs as was the case with the biblical prophets" (GDC, 140).

Jesus shows us how to communicate his distinctive saving message. He prepares us by his own pedagogical presence, for he is "the convincing model for all communication of the faith" (GDC, 137). We teach Christ in conformity with his own words: "My teaching is not my own but is from the one who sent me" (Jn 7:16). In the words of Nicodemus, Jesus is "a teacher who has come from God" (Jn 3:2; cf. NDC, 8).

Jesus *is* the content of faith that, two millennia later, occupies the heart of the New Evangelization and its accompanying catechesis. The *National Directory for Catechesis* asserts that "Christ is the unique Teacher because his teaching is not merely a collection of abstract truths but the Truth itself, 'the communication of the living mystery of God.' In fact, Christ is the 'one teacher,' whose message is identical with himself. His words do not merely express the word of God; he *is* the Word of God" (NDC, 8).[21] For catechesis, this resounding ecclesial and merciful witness is part of the pedagogy of faith.

What might this emphasis on pedagogy of faith have to do with belonging, especially belonging to God? The *General Directory for Cat-echesis* reminds us, "Jesus Christ is the living and perfect relationship of God with man and of man with God" (GDC, 145). The word *belonging* does not do such deep relationship justice but does at least help us to sense through our own experience all that God offers to us through Christ and in the Spirit. In such an encounter we find out who we really are and what we are called to be, for faith—including though not limited to its catechet-ical dimension—has to do with ultimate expressions of life: relationships, principles, truths, decisions, risks, and life with God forever. People live for faith and people die for faith (the Church counts many catechists among its martyrs). God's presence to us is so compelling that our response in obedience is itself an act of love. Expressions of faith among believing witnesses are enlivened by gesture, symbol, word, and action.

In Galilee when crowds in Capernaum seek Jesus out, he says to them, "To the other towns also I must proclaim the good news of the kingdom of God, because for this purpose I have been sent" (Lk 4:43). Jesus moves on mission. He is "the Father's Emissary" (CCC, 858).

Jesus, Teach Us

In Jesus the kingdom of God is present, though unrecognized by many, including in our time. Perhaps the greatest pain occurs when we fail to see. Unrelenting schedules and a whirlwind of events and activities can cloud our vision and limit our listening. Not a day seems to go by without reports of new developments in personal resources designed to make life easier. Used wisely, they probably do. But is an easier life what we truly seek?

How ironic that in the midst of such human-friendly develop-ments—noble successors to television and personal computers in the last century—we seek wisdom from Jesus' use of parables, one of the most common, low-tech teaching tools from his own faith tradition. One might have surmised that new technology would satisfy, in a flash, our need for what the parables offer. But life's greatest needs are timeless, and the parables, made lively by Jesus, give meaning to our time and purpose to our lives. Their lessons remain fresh, ripe for new discovery. "Through his parables he invites people to the feast of the kingdom, but he also asks for a radical choice: to gain the kingdom, one must give everything. Words are not enough; deeds are required" (CCC, 546).

Jesus challenges us to assess what we value and to whom we belong—and what we might be willing to become and to do—through these compelling and diverse stories. No matter how often we reflect on them, we can find new layers of meaning in the parables. I propose that we "listen" attentively with all our senses as we seek "to teach Christ" (CCC, 428; cf. Phil 3:8–11), the One inseparable from incarnation, redemption, and the kingdom of God.

Parables were fundamental to the way Jesus taught. He told these stories about faith time and time again. Parables enlighten us and can form us anew with each prayerful reading or hearing. Scholars mine the parables and offer helpful commentary, identifying nuances and distinctions from within the preserve of scriptural study and theological development.

A respected catechetical voice from the twentieth century, Bishop G. Emmett Carter notes that "the structure of the parables is relatively simple. Each has a moral and each has two parts. The first part is the narrative; the second is the key to understanding what the narrative means."[22] The parables continue to engage and challenge us because they invite us to go deeper into the well of faith and of truth as they touch—and we touch—our own cultural and societal experience. As we proceed, unexpected twists and turns may confront us, but the appeal of the parable's message becomes more enticing and more inviting. An antagonist or doubter may fail to see—or be unwilling to see—what Jesus is getting at. As we likely know from our own experience, even believers may struggle or look away. Yet parables yield "Aha!" moments of scriptural engagement that can alter our spiritual and catechetical orientation and solidify our commitment to Christ and the faith we claim to profess.

For example, in Luke 15 Jesus shares three parables with his listeners. Tax collectors and sinners move closer to listen to him, while others object: "This man welcomes sinners and eats with them" (v. 2). But Jesus proceeds, telling the parables that we know as the parable of the lost sheep, the parable of the lost coin, and the parable of the lost son, identified together by one scholar as "the parables of mercy."[23] Mercy is a prominent theme of *Evangelii Gaudium*, one of the apostolic exhortation of Pope Francis.

For catechetical purposes, whether probed through the example of a weary shepherd carrying a lost sheep, a determined yet likely tired woman finding a lost coin, or a compassionate father welcoming back a son who "was lost and has been found" (Lk 15:32), we come to see that God's inexhaustible and all-merciful love abounds. In the end, all is not lost. Repentance and rejoicing commingle. And a "dead" son lives!

For catechesis, what is Jesus saying to us in this time and place about the love of the Father, about repentance and mercy, about rejoicing in the gift of the kingdom given in Christ?

God's love for us is unending, despite our failings and misgivings. In the familiar parable of the lost son, Jesus tells his listeners about a father with two sons, the youngest of whom asks for his part of his father's estate.

"So the father divided the property between them" (Lk 15:12). Going out on his own, leaving both home and community, the younger son "squandered his inheritance on a life of dissipation" (v. 13).[24] However, "coming to his senses" and "dying from hunger" (v. 17),[25] he seeks to return to his father.

Any parent who has "stood by the window" day after day awaiting the return of an errant son or daughter can imagine the sense of pain and loss that the father experienced during the son's absence. Such parents are saving people, living by a code that commands them, in faith and in trust, to help, heal, and protect their children.

Seeing his youngest son from a distance, the father "was filled with compassion" (Lk 15:20). Notice that the father does not simply watch and wait to hear his returning son speak; rather, "he ran to his son, embraced him and kissed him" (v. 20).[26] The son then utters his last spoken words of the parable: "Father, I have sinned against heaven and against you; I no longer deserve to be called your son" (v. 21).

We can visualize the son resting in the arms of his forgiving father. The father's actions speak of reconciling mercy, as do his uplifting and catechetically rich words to his servants: "he was lost, and has been found" (Lk 15:24). Nothing can overshadow this reality; nothing now stands in the way of their restored relationship. "Only the heart of Christ who knows the depths of his Father's love could reveal to us the abyss of his mercy in so simple and beautiful a way" (CCC, 1439).

The interaction between the father and his older son may also command our interest as we continue to explore the parable's message of merciful love, here with the father as catechist for the older son.[27] From a distance, the older son hears the sound of festivities already underway, and servants tell him of his brother's return. We may see ourselves in the older son: loyal, hardworking, faithful—and now angry (see Lk 15:28). He expresses his displeasure over what his father has done to welcome back his repentant sibling. Maybe we see ourselves there, too, sometimes yearning for the reassurance of the father: "My son, you are here with me always; everything I have is yours" (v. 31). The father speaks of celebration and rejoicing over the return of the younger son, who "was dead and has come to life again" (v. 32). The abiding but sometimes hidden claim of belonging has been given new life.

What is unrecorded is how the older brother reacts after hearing his loving father repeat the joyful words "he was lost and has been found" (Lk 15:32). An "unwritten" ending may seek to come alive through our imaginations as we ponder what is unspoken and unreported in the story. We may even be inclined to construct an ending of our own, neat and tidy, that satisfies for the moment. However, the core message of the parable urges us, as a rushing wind at our backs, to bear in mind the parable's robust power to teach and to make us uncomfortable, and for this we should rejoice.[28] Conversion is ongoing; the Spirit of God guides us along the way as we live the gift of faith through the Church that is our home.

The parables never cease to teach us, though the lessons they carry may be familiar to us, prompting such claims as, "Oh, yes, I already *know* the story of the prodigal son." The parables encourage us to strengthen and apply our well-founded understanding with clear eyes as we nurture living witness born of living faith. Indeed, the parables propel us in this regard. This is an important consideration as we work hard to present and apply them to the sweeping diversity of people and priorities that exists in parish life today.

God continues to reach out to us; his merciful love abounds and is a gift for the repentant sinner. "At times we have to be like the father of the prodigal son, who always keeps his door open so that when the son returns, he can readily pass through it" (EG, 46). That door is for the older son, too, and for each of us. The door is always open. How fortunate we are to benefit from the scriptures, which open doors for us along the way of our faith journey as we serve the ministry of catechesis in the life of the Church. God never lets go. We believe in him; we belong to him.

The kingdom of God, present in Jesus, is not merely a descriptive term but a reality for which Jesus gives his life and which he invites us to share, not for a day but for all eternity. As faithful disciples, we proclaim the kingdom of God from within the heart of the Church, "on earth, the seed and the beginning of that kingdom" (LG, 5; cf. CCC, 541). Moved by the Spirit, we await Christ's return as we model the New Evangelization through faithful and just witness. This is not easy or neatly packaged for us or for those whom we evangelize or catechize. It requires a self-examination that propels us to reach out from the heart of the Church to all classes and cultures beyond the community of the Church.

With a refreshed catechetical spirit, buoyed by the living Word, we proclaim the reign of God active here and now. We find ourselves unable to live without the nourishment that comes from the table of Word and sacrament (see GDC, 70) as we humbly offer real-life catechesis. The witness of our lives can attest to nothing less. An idealistic wish? No. Our joyful work with all the faithful? Yes.

Reflection Questions

1.   Why do you stay on the way of Christ? Who or what nurtures your believing and belonging?
2.   What is Jesus teaching you today?
3.   What relationships offer you witness to God's love in Christ? What do you offer as a member of the Church?
4.   Have "dying and rising" recently occurred in your life? How? What gesture might you use to teach such a point?
5.   In the prodigal son story, how would you describe the father's understanding of belonging? His "daily dying" during his son's absence?
6.   Does your experience invite you into the parable? Which character leads you into the parable? Why?
7.   What might encourage the older son to think about his own need for repentance?
8.   Might you need to offer or seek unconditional forgiveness? How might the sacrament of Reconciliation calm your concern?
9.   How might the offer of mercy given in Christ help to heal your parish from an open wound? What might this imply about a catechesis of rejoicing?
10.   Does your parish bear any struggles that might be lessened by your support and participation? How might you help?

Personalizing the Pedagogy of Faith

Jesus' way of teaching—by words, signs, and works (see GDC, 140, NDC 28A2)—is as essential for third-millennium sojourners in faith as it was for his first disciples. "Inviting his disciples to follow him unreservedly and without regret (cf. Mk 8:34–38; Mt 8:18–22), Christ passed on to them his pedagogy of faith as a full sharing in his actions and in his destiny" (GDC, 140).

Although many people of his time could not bring themselves to embrace the "Way" he offered—a phenomenon replicated in our own time—Jesus still seeks to enter into relationship with each of us and with all of us. This relationship may come through solitary searching or (and perhaps this is the usual case) as a result of the efforts of faithful members of the Church whose witness in faith is natural, unencumbered, and selfless. We release any hesitation that may reside within as we make the pedagogy of faith our own. We do this through the witness and experiences of our own lives and as the faith we seek to share becomes more and more identifiable through who we are becoming in Christ through the Church.

The experience of life is not just "out there" in an amorphous sea of relationships, to be set aside as we seek to deepen our relationship with Christ. Interactions, conversations, emails and other electronic exchanges, time alone, and seemingly meaningless fleeting moments can help to form us in faith and inform what we offer to the Church's ministry of catechesis. The stuff of daily life counts. It helps to shape us along the way of faith with a pedagogy that incorporates profession of the Church's scriptural and doctrinal heritage, celebration of the Paschal Mystery, longstanding commitment to the Christian moral life, prayerful witness alone and with others, and the affirmation of a diversity of cultures rich in faithful Christian living.

We are who we are, and we come to faith as we are, sometimes with hands muddied. Jesus has been there and is here for us, welcoming us as we are—all of us—into the community of faith. Our lives do not remain untouched by this daily and perhaps unconscious awareness of who we are becoming as children of God, as catechetical bearers of the Good News. As we offer our experience of life and of faith to the God and Father of all, we do so with growing awareness of what is changing within ourselves. Heightened moral awareness may come to us gradually, enlivened by our experience of the sacraments. Although catechesis relies on words, it stretches them beyond the obvious, inviting all the senses to take in the Word of the Lord.

As Christ teaches by the witness of his life, so must we. As Christ offers himself to others, so do we. As Christ is merciful to others, so are we called to be. He is with us as Pedagogue par excellence, the Master Catechist and Master Teacher of *savoir-faire* (cf. GDC, 238). He knows how to hear a weakened heart and heal one that is broken. He knows how to read an audience, calm an inquirer, challenge a false teacher, soothe a squeamish listener, confront a boastful intruder, comfort a fearful and lonely traveler. In other words, he knows "real life"—with all its complexities, blessings, and challenges—firsthand. "The whole of Christ's life was a continual teaching" (CT, 9).

Though we may at first see in shadows, with the first light of daybreak faith becomes fixed deep inside. We turn to Christ, already before us. Heart and soul seem ready to burst. Jesus wraps us in love, especially as we seek to live his way. "As the Father loves me, so I also love you. Remain in my love. If you keep my commandments, you will remain in my love, just as I have kept my Father's commandments and remain in his love. . . . This is my commandment: love one another as I love you" (Jn 15:9–10, 12; see Jn 13:34–35).

Fear, gusto, or a combination of the two may surround us—an environment not unfamiliar to first-century Christians. Conversion to Christ encompassed then, as it does now, more than verbal affirmation, as important as that is. Rather, it represents a movement of the whole self beyond the familiar, sometimes fraught with uncertainty and risk, making mutual support essential. There is strength in numbers. Changing one's ways demands a change of heart and a new way of "hearing" the Word of God with other disciples. The convergence of "moral and mental" (e.g., in the Beatitudes, the law of love, and so on) leads to greater awareness of "the kingdom of God . . . at hand" (Mk 1:15), the fullness of which we await in eternity. The kingdom comes in Christ the Savior, whom we teach and whom we profess, despite intervening millennia, in a catechesis centered in and derived from the Master Catechist.

Nicodemus would say to Jesus in the night, "Rabbi, we know that you are a teacher who has come from God, for no one can do these signs that you are doing unless God is with him." As more dialogue ensues, Jesus goes on to say to this "teacher of Israel," who lacks understanding, "For God so loved the world that he gave his only Son, so that everyone who believes in him might not perish but might have eternal life" (Jn 3:2, 10, 16).

As with Jesus' words, his signs and works did more than inform the minds of his hearers—they also appealed to the heart and spirit. They witnessed at the time to who he is, the promised Messiah, and they do so in this age as well. "The works that the Father gave me to accomplish, these works that I perform testify on my behalf that the Father has sent me" (Jn 5:36). We, too, accept his testimony. We believe.

If conversion is a turning to a new way, then Jesus' signs and works offer prompts for that turning. All that Jesus offers us as teacher, catechist, and Lord reinforces with fresh awareness our understanding that "catechesis aims to bring about in the believer an ever more mature faith in Jesus Christ, a deeper knowledge and love of his person and message, and a firm commitment to follow him" (NDC, 19A).

The Book of Signs of the Gospel of John is particularly enriching for probing Jesus' message and gift of himself for all humanity; Jesus' signs "invite belief in him" (CCC, 548) and inform and expand our catechetical understanding.

- These signs, seven in all, begin with Jesus at a wedding feast in Cana in Galilee. He changes water into wine, "and his disciples began to believe in him" (Jn 2:11).

- Jesus' word goes forth from his mouth, and a royal official's son is cured in Capernaum, miles from where Jesus is in Cana: "You may go; your son will live" (Jn 4:50).

- A man, ill for nearly four decades, is lying on a mat, unable to get into the pool of water called Bethesda. On this Sabbath day, the strength of Jesus' word brings healing within as he says to the man on the mat, "Rise, take up your mat, and walk" (Jn 5:8). More than the man's body was healed.

- In the account of the multiplication of the loaves and fishes, Jesus feeds a large crowd of people. Jesus will subsequently say to them, "I am the bread of life; whoever comes to me will never hunger, and whoever believes in me will never thirst" (Jn 6:35). Eucharistic sharing is not far off, for Jesus will give of himself to his disciples and then to all through his Last Supper and redemptive Passion, Death, and Resurrection.

- Frightened disciples are rowing in a boat a few miles from shore near Capernaum. They see Jesus walking on the water. "It is I. Do not be afraid" (Jn 6:20).[29] Christ takes our fears unto himself.

- On a Sabbath day and in response to his disciples' question, Jesus assures them that the blindness of a man living all his life without sight is not due to the man's own sin or that of his parents. He tells them, "While I am in the world, I am the light of the world" (Jn 9:5). Jesus gets his hands dirty. He spits on the ground and applies the clay mixture to the eyes of the man and tells him, "'Go wash in the pool of Siloam' (which means Sent). So he went and washed, and came back able to see" (Jn 9:7). The account goes on to show that the authorities can see physically, but are "blind" to Jesus.

- Lazarus, brother of Martha and Mary, has died and has been buried for four days. The moving conversations between Jesus and each sister are exemplary in the depth of their power, beauty, and awe. For example, Jesus assures Martha, "I am the resurrection and the life; whoever believes in me, even if he dies, will live, and everyone who lives and believes in me will never die" (Jn 11:25–26). In the midst of a time of weeping and suffering of others, he asks Martha, "Do you believe this?" (v. 26) as he nears his own end time of suffering in love for all people. Martha answers, "Yes, Lord. I have come to believe that you are the Messiah, the Son of God, the one who is coming into the world" (v. 27). Later in the account, Jesus' strong voice resounds, "Lazarus, come out!" (v. 43). Lazarus, freed of his burial cloths, lives.

Much turning is going on in these seven signs. Conversion "lives" through the lives of people coming to Jesus and choosing his Way. Such turning may swell with risk, for it can be difficult to depart from the familiar, to attend to a new voice. On the Feast of the Dedication in Jerusalem, Jesus would be approached by some Jews there who want to know: Is he the Messiah? They ask him to be plain-spoken, but his response (which includes the assertion "the Father and I are one") fails to satisfy. Although they ready themselves to stone him and pursue arresting him, "he escaped from their power." Jesus crosses "the Jordan to the place where John first baptized, and there he remained. Many came to him and said, 'John performed no sign, but everything John said about this man was true.' And many there began to believe in him." (See John 10:22–42 for the entire account.)

Jesus' words, signs, and works point to far more than the obvious. Eyes of faith see more. For example, consider the account of the healing of the paralytic. The paralytic is brought to Jesus, who tells him his sins are forgiven. Accused of blasphemy by some scribes, Jesus asserts, "'Which is easier, to say, "Your sins are forgiven," or to say, "Rise and walk"? But that you may know that the Son of Man has authority on earth to forgive sins'—he then said to the paralytic, 'Rise, pick up your stretcher, and go home.'" (See Matthew 9:1–8 for the entire account.)

Do you ever wonder what paralyzes your spirit, your soul, that which lies deep within but lives, perhaps barely visible, on the exterior boundaries of your life? What "stretcher" might you hope to pick up today? Who might be on it?

All too frequently people become confused by Jesus' miracles and fail to see their connection to the kingdom of God and Jesus' identity as Messiah, Lord, and Savior. Yearning for signs perhaps identifies us as a concrete people who "need" to "see" (literally) and then "see" some more, leading to misunderstanding. Jesus' signs confirm who he is: the Son of God, the One whose Incarnation (cf. Jn 1:14) turns and sets the believer along the way of the Paschal Mystery of Christ's Passion, Death, Resurrection, and Ascension. Such a turning is not without setbacks, for discipleship demands fortitude to stay the course when our movement along the Way becomes difficult to traverse. "Dyings" along the way of our temporal existence—illness, lost wages, family dissonance, family members who turn away from Christ and the Church—can rattle our resolve. But for those baptized in Christ, life's misfortunes and even death itself do not linger, unattached from lives of faith, for they bridge our living the way of new life. Jesus conquers sin and asks us to trust that he is with us as we live and teach his Way in faithful discipleship. That is a catechetical pedagogy.

With the Master Teacher on the Mount and on the Road

"Teacher, what good must I do to gain eternal life?" a rich young man asks Jesus. "There is only One who is good," Jesus tells him. "If you wish to enter into life, keep the commandments." Jesus gets more specific when the man asks, "Which ones?" Good news for the wealthy man, who has been faithful to the ones Jesus names—a résumé item that would certainly advance his application to serve as a catechist today. Yet when further pressed, Jesus is not shy about pointing out what the man lacks: "If you wish to be perfect, go, sell what you have and give to [the] poor, and you will have treasure in heaven. Then come, follow me." Sadly, the man moves off, "for he had many possessions." (See Matthew 19:16–30 for the entire account.) For this person, going a new way or, better, farther along the Way, demands too much.

For living the way of catechesis, Christ bridges commandment and beatitude. Blessing gives shape to the gospels, and the Beatitudes help us to uncover and build upon foundations for how we are to live along the way of the kingdom of God in Christ. "The Beatitudes are at the heart of Jesus' preaching" (CCC, 1716).

Matthew tells us that Jesus travels all over Galilee, where he attracts many followers. His disciples approach him, and Jesus "began to teach" (Mt 5:2) all who were gathered there. As you ponder the Beatitudes that follow, do so slowly and meditatively. Underline one or two words that stand out for you. Soak in the spirit of those in need, which may include yourself. Discover God's blessing in their lives and yours as you probe the words of the Master Teacher in this portion of the Sermon on the Mount. For now, place yourself at the foot of the mountain in the midst of the crowds. Perhaps straining to hear, you lean forward and listen closely as Jesus says from the Mount:

> Blessed are the poor in spirit,
>   for theirs is the kingdom of heaven.
> Blessed are they who mourn,
>   for they will be comforted.
> Blessed are the meek,
>   for they will inherit the land.
> Blessed are they who hunger and thirst for righteousness,
>   for they will be satisfied.
> Blessed are the merciful,
>   for they will be shown mercy.
> Blessed are the clean of heart,
>   for they will see God.
> Blessed are the peacemakers,
>   for they will be called children of God.
> Blessed are they who are persecuted for the sake of righteousness,
>   for theirs is the kingdom of heaven.

> Blessed are you when they insult you and persecute you and utter every kind of evil against you [falsely] because of me. Rejoice and be glad, for your reward will be great in heaven. (Mt 5:3–12)

As you look in a mirror at the person of faith, hope, and love before you, be aware of your participation in the pedagogy of Christ and active engagement in his salvific mission. We recall that "the Twelve and the other disciples share in Christ's mission and his power, but also in his lot" (CCC, 765). As do we.

Through the witness of the Church of mission (see Mt 28:19–20, Mk 16:15) to which we belong, we move from awareness to action, walking with Jesus as did the disciples he joined on the way to the village of Emmaus (see Lk 24:13–35)[30]—an extraordinary account of "Jesus as catechist," a fitting ending to this chapter but not the last word of our relationship with Christ, our way.

Two disciples who had hoped Jesus was the Messiah set out along the road from Jerusalem to Emmaus, some miles away. Having been in Jerusalem for the events surrounding the Passover and Jesus' death, they discuss as they walk all that has happened during the last few days. Jesus begins to accompany them, "but their eyes were prevented from recognizing him" (Lk 24:16). The disciples are amazed that the inquiring stranger wonders what they are talking about; after all, how could he be "the only visitor to Jerusalem" (v. 18) who is unaware of what had gone on there? So these well-meaning disciples seek to bring the stranger up to date. But it is they who hear the Word, perhaps as though for the first time: "Beginning with Moses and all the prophets, he interpreted to them what referred to him in all the scriptures" (v. 27). His words leave the travelers hungry and eager for more, and so they invite him to stay with them. Before long, the three are sharing a meal.

Though it is not his home, the stranger plays host, giving the two travelers bread blessed and broken. "With that their eyes were opened and they recognized him, but he vanished from their sight. Then they said to each other, 'Were not our hearts burning [within us] while he spoke to us on the way and opened the scriptures to us?'" (Lk 24:31–32).

Strange, isn't it? In the absence of the stranger the Emmaus disciples are conscious of the presence of the Messiah. Nourished by the Word of God on their way to Emmaus, the travelers share the bread that was broken and given to them by the One for whose presence they had hungered. Despite the growing darkness, they hurry back to Jerusalem and tell the story of "what had taken place on the way and how he was made known to them in the breaking of the bread" (Lk 24:35).

Two millennia later, we travelers still walk, pray, and eat. The Church continues to celebrate and partake of "the eucharistic sacrifice, the source and summit of the Christian life" (LG, 11), and we do so with gratitude beyond words. The faithful "offer the divine victim to God and themselves along with it" (LG, 11).

Be confident that you participate in mission by proposing or refreshing new life from within a New Evangelization that often finds its breath through the Church's ministry of catechesis. As travelers and listeners along the way of faith and with hearts ablaze, you seek Christ through faithful presence as you and your parish teach, celebrate, witness, and serve daily as "co-workers in the truth" (3 Jn 1:8).

From the sacred emptying of the womb of the Blessed Virgin to the sacred emptying of a tomb hewn from rock, we are invited into a sharing of love that words describe only weakly and inadequately.[31] Through his Paschal Mystery, the work of our salvation is won for us by Christ. We enter into the Paschal Mystery through God's love given in Christ, now guided by the Holy Spirit in the life of the Church. It is to some highlights of catechesis in the life of the emerging Church that we now turn.

Reflection Questions

1. What is Jesus teaching you through the Beatitudes? About belonging? About catechesis? About the need for a New Evangelization in your life as you seek to promote the Church's mission to evangelize?

2. What might Jesus be reminding you and your parish of as he offers—in words, signs, and works—God's blessing? How might God's blessing lead you to discern next steps for your life, no matter how far reaching?

3. What demands do the Beatitudes place on you? On the choices you make every day? On the Church to which you belong? On how you catechize?

4. What makes you uneasy about the Gospel? Why do you continue to believe in Jesus?

5. How might the Beatitudes, coupled with the Decalogue, heighten your resolve to live and teach the way of the Gospel of Christ? To take time each day to pray with gratitude and reflect on the Word of God in your life?

6. How might Jesus as teacher and catechist teach you a new lesson about living, dying, and rising, especially as you interact with another person? What within you yearns for strengthening or healing? What are you fearful of today?

7.   Whom do you know who suffers from poverty of spirit or who may be mourning this day? Might this person seem to "live" one moment and "die" the next? What might you and your parish community do to discern ways to raise that person up?

8.   What steps might you take to communicate a joyful spirit to persons of no faith tradition or to those who have moved away from the Church?

9.   How might your own experiences of living, dying, and rising serve as humble witness to another? To what you believe and profess?

10.   Have you ever taken an "Emmaus walk"? What would be *your* question along the way to Emmaus? What sustains your spirit? Why are you joyful "in Christ"?

4

MARKING THE WAY
New Testament and the Emerging Church

Some people God has designated in the church to be, first, apostles; second, prophets; third, teachers; then, mighty deeds; then, gifts of healing, assistance, administration, and varieties of tongues. Are all apostles? Are all prophets? Are all teachers? Do all work mighty deeds? Do all have gifts of healing? Do all speak in tongues? Do all interpret? Strive eagerly for the greatest spiritual gifts.

—1 Corinthians 12:28–31

As we explore some highlights of catechesis in the early centuries of the Church, we are likely to do so through the lens of our contemporary understanding of catechesis. In doing so, we are wise to guard against unintentionally suggesting that individual, contemporary understanding implies that catechetical history comes to fulfillment in "my experience." In other words, looking back into history is not the same as entering into the communal history we claim as our own. Such an individualized stance would negate the communal character of the catechetical enterprise to which we belong and through which we believe.

Recent decades have hosted an explosion of linguistic challenges for today's Catholic, not the least of which comes from the terms *catechesis*, *evangelization* (including the adjective *new*), *catechumenate*, and *myst-agogy*. Any resulting confusion is worth it, for descriptors of elements of the Christian life, often brought to the surface from deep wells of ecclesial history, never run dry.

The mission to share the Good News—to evangelize in witness to the Gospel—forms a natural entry point for surveying the emerging Church's efforts to bring people to Christ. A fundamental dimension of this reality is the kerygma, the distinctive proclamation of the Good News of salvation in Christ. By Jesus' preaching and through the fullness of his life, the Good News of salvation is vividly made present and given to his disciples to spread throughout the world. "For the Lord Jesus inaugurated his Church by preaching the Good News, that is, the coming of the kingdom of God, promised over the ages in the scriptures: 'The time is fulfilled, and the kingdom of God is at hand' (Mk 1:15; cf. Mt 4:17)" (LG, 5).

Jesus "emptied himself" for us (Phil 2:7).[1] "At the foot of the Cross Mary shares through faith in the shocking mystery of this self-emptying" (RMa, 18).[2] Through Christ's Passion, Death, Resurrection, and Ascension—the Paschal Mystery "at the center of the Good News that the apostles, and the Church following them, are to proclaim to the world" (CCC, 571)—time itself is transformed. Salvation is at hand. Knees bend, lives turn. Ordinary time that seems to direct or predict our daily activity yields to *kairos* ("now" time, transforming time), for transformation has to do with fundamental and substantial change.[3] Awakened and anticipated through the fiat of Mary, the divine gift of the Incarnation,[4] and the prophetic work of John the Baptist, this is time without an off switch. Jesus beckons people to this "time of fulfillment"; the kingdom "at hand" and the urgency of repentance lie before them (Mk 1:15). For us today, this transformation is a fruit of conversion gone right and testimony to the God who enables us to "walk in newness of life."[5]

The Church took shape and lived within the experience of this transformation. People drawn into the mystery of faith brought with them a multitude of life experiences, as we and others do today. We come as whole people, sometimes stretched and disheveled but still connected within ourselves and interconnected with one another. The whole life we live in faith is the whole life we give in faith.

The living reality of this faith-filled body emerges as Jesus calls and gathers apostles and other disciples who come to embrace his mission. He charges Peter to be the rock upon whom he will build his Church (cf. Mt 16:18).[6] And the Church is built as a living and ongoing communal witness to the One who continues to call all people to himself. How blessed we are to share today in this building for and in Christ. Familiar terms for such a "building" include *People of God*, *Body of Christ*, and *Temple of the Holy Spirit* (see LG, 17; 1 Pt 2:9–20; Eph 4:12; 2 Cor 6:16; cf. CCC, 781ff.).[7] Far more than ecclesial synonyms, these images provide further witness to the depth, resolve, and sustained faithful activity of generations of believers across centuries and millennia.

The distinctive and ongoing sanctification of the Church on Pentecost (LG, 4; see Acts 2; CCC, 767) changes lives and emboldens a community for the way ahead, a movement of confidence through uncertainty, with voices made strong and hearts afire in faith. Gathered together, "they were all filled with the holy Spirit" (Acts 2:4). According to the *Catechism*, "Of his fullness, Christ, the Lord, pours out the Spirit in abundance. . . . By his coming, which never ceases, the Holy Spirit causes the world to enter into the 'last days,' the time of the Church, the Kingdom already inherited though not yet consummated" (CCC, 731–732).

Peter proclaims on Pentecost that "God raised this Jesus; of this we are all witnesses" (Acts 2:32). He is bold and forthright, calling his Jewish hearers to "repent and be baptized, every one of you, in the name of Jesus Christ for the forgiveness of your sins; and you will receive the gift of the holy Spirit" (Acts 2:38).[8] The Pentecost account, with the pouring forth of the Holy Spirit, gives us insight into initiation in the early Church. To cite the late scholar and sacramental theologian Aidan Kavanagh: "There can be little doubt that the stunning experience of 'Spirit baptism' on the first Pentecost, with its ensuing conversions and the establishment of the premier church in Jerusalem, exercised a profound influence both on the earliest churches' understanding of Jesus' own baptism and on subsequent initiatory practice."[9]

Proclamation and Teaching

The proclamation of the Good News was central to the activity of the early Church. The kerygma occupies such a key place in Christianity and the tradition of the Church that there is no substitute for it. Writing about the primitive Church, John McKenzie, S.J., points out:

> The proclamation of the apostolic Church was directed, not to its members, but to non-members. It was an invitation to enter the Church. . . .
>
> The herald of the Christian proclamation was an apostle who proclaimed what he had seen and heard. He was a witness to the truth of the proclamation. . . . The apostle proclaimed by virtue of a commission; and the commission could be given by Jesus Christ alone.[10]

But how might proclamation and teaching relate to each other? Confusion follows when a catechist assumes that others think as he or she does when applying such terms. The *General Directory for Catechesis* offers a helpful example of terminological distinction, not addressing the exact question at hand but close enough for illustrative purposes. In a chapter that treats catechesis and evangelization, the directory compares primary proclamation with catechesis:

> Primary proclamation is addressed to nonbelievers and those living in religious indifference. Its functions are to proclaim the Gospel and to call to conversion. Catechesis, "distinct from the primary proclamation of the Gospel," promotes and matures initial conversion, educates the convert in the faith and incorporates him into the Christian community. The relationship between these two forms of the ministry of the word is, therefore, a relationship of complementary distinction. . . . Both activities are essential and mutually complementary: go and welcome, proclaim and educate, call and incorporate. (GDC, 61)[11]

However, the next sentence describes a likely familiar experience when it states that "in pastoral practice it is not always easy to define the boundaries of these activities. Frequently, many who present themselves for catechesis truly require genuine conversion" (GDC, 62).[12] This contemporary context seems to place conversion as a linchpin of sorts, bringing together proclamation and catechesis (including teaching) within and beyond the Church. The New Evangelization, for example, offers affirming opportunities for inviting and welcoming people back to Christ and his Church.[13] We may also find ourselves encouraging people to explore for the first time the way of Christ. The grace of God creates these opportunities for renewal.

Challenges of the present era in both Church and society are removed by more than years from those of the first century; as discussed above, we live in an age of overlap. Even so, not only can distinctions born of early Church history help us to understand early Church practice but also they can guide our way today, as our roots are more firmly planted within our inherited, living faith. With this in mind, we return to McKenzie, who offers helpful clarification regarding both proclamation and teaching in the early Church.

> In the New Testament the proclamation (*kerygma*) is distinguished from the teaching (*didache*). . . . Since the teaching was directed to those who had been baptized, it was not intended to convince them of the truth of that in which they already believed. The purpose of the teaching was not apologetic demonstration but a deeper understanding of faith.[14]

"Understanding" is a challenge in any era. Proclaiming and sustaining faith did not come without seeking to settle important issues in the first decades of the young Church. For example, in the mid-first century, the Council of Jerusalem (see Acts 15, Gal 2)[15] addressed the relation of the Mosaic Law to Gentiles. One significant matter was the practice of male circumcision. Was this also to apply to Gentiles becoming Christians? The Acts of the Apostles tells of Paul, Barnabas, and others heading from Antioch to Jerusalem to discuss the issue with the leaders there, including Peter and James. Peter tells those gathered that "God, who knows the heart, bore witness by granting them [the Gentiles] the holy Spirit just as he did to us. He made no distinction between us and them, for by faith he purified their hearts" (Acts 15:8–9).[16]

In Galatians we read of Paul's journey to Jerusalem with Barnabas and with Titus, a Greek not "compelled to be circumcised" (Gal 2:3). Paul's passion for "the truth of the gospel" (Gal 2:5) sustains the way for all coming to Christ, regardless of their origin. He recounts in this letter that "when they recognized the grace bestowed upon me, James and Cephas and John, who were reputed to be pillars, gave me and Barnabas their right hands in partnership, that we should go to the Gentiles and they to the circumcised. Only, we were to be mindful of the poor, which is the very thing I was eager to do" (Gal 2:9–10).

Acts 15 and Galatians 2 should be read in full, with accompanying commentary, for details and nuances surrounding the Council of Jerusalem. We can imagine the power of faith and depth of mission that drove these Spirit-led leaders, who drew many Jews and Gentiles to embrace Christ proclaimed. Living by the Way is not easy, a facile decision meekly applied, as Peter's own struggle attests (cf. Gal 2:11–14).

Some of the Church's early leaders, led by the Spirit, gathered to resolve important questions resulting from differences in existing practices. Wise catechists do the same. It can be difficult to discern what to do, to come to agreement, and to carry it out after we have given over our "right hands in partnership," but partnerships so formed can take us in many directions in living faith proclaimed. For example, they can strengthen the power and impact of merciful care for others. Belonging to and serving within and beyond the community of faith is essential for all the baptized. Being "mindful of the poor" can shape one's entire life in service of the Gospel, and it does not matter if persons in need are nearby or far off. The map of Gospel living knows no boundaries.

Growth, Catechesis, and Deepening Faith

The early Church grew beyond Jerusalem in the years and decades following Jesus' Death and Resurrection. Jerusalem fell to the Romans in AD 70, a devastation that encompassed the unthinkable trauma of the destruction of the Temple.[17] Emerging Church communities offered witness to the faith, taking on an evangelizing presence with the preaching and service of committed disciples. Over time, the Gospel spread around the Mediterranean basin, to such places as Antioch, Alexandria, and Rome, where both Peter and Paul would breathe their last in giving their lives for Christ. Paul, the apostle to the Gentiles, would make three missionary journeys that took him to such places as Philippi, Thessalonica, Athens, Corinth, and Ephesus. His last, long journey (see Acts 27–28) ended in Rome, where he ultimately died for the faith.

One catechetical foundation we receive from the early Church is a classic passage, proclaimed annually during the Liturgy of the Word at the Easter Vigil, from Paul's Letter to the Romans (6:3–11). In this text, part of which appears below, Paul speaks of union with Christ in both death and resurrection:[18]

> Are you unaware that we who were baptized into Christ Jesus were baptized into his death? We were indeed buried with him through baptism into death, so that, just as Christ was raised from the dead by the glory of the Father, we too might live in newness of life.
>
> For if we have grown into union with him through a death like his, we shall also be united with him in the resurrection. (Rom 6:3–5)

In the catechetical nomenclature of the last century, the terms *message, teaching, community, worship,* and *service* come to mind for exploring catechesis in the life of the Church. With Greek historical equivalents, they became easily recognized—though sometimes oversimplified—dimensions of a holistic framework for ministry and catechesis during the last half of the 1900s and early decades of the new millennium: message (*kerygma*); teaching (*didache*); community (*koinonia*); liturgy (*leiturgia*); and service (*diakonia*). Despite the potential hazard of "reading back" into history, it can be reasonably suggested that these descriptors can serve as reference points for reviewing dimensions of early catechetical history.

For example, we saw in chapter 3 much about the message and teaching of Jesus, now given to the Church. The cultural setting for this reception was the communal life formed by the followers of Jesus as they gathered together. Acts of the Apostles provides pertinent guidance for our reflection:

> They devoted themselves to the teaching of the apostles and to the communal life, to the breaking of the bread and to the prayers. . . . And every day the Lord added to their number those who were being saved. (Acts 2:42, 47)

We see here a community seeking to live according to the way of Christ, a way born of shared commitment to and mutual support in Christ. Morally rich, the combination of teaching and prayer within a communal setting certainly offers strong witness for such practice today, whereby our believing, praying, and belonging converge in community, formed not just for itself but in saving service to others, especially through the Catholic social tradition.

In the early Church, persons who had already expressed their belief in Christ and had passed through saving baptismal waters[19] were charged with living up to the demands of their newly established allegiance. Today, we may find ourselves welcoming back or quietly approaching formerly active Catholics by exploring with them what Baptism is and why it means what it does for the believer: implications, demands, commitments, and so on. The purpose of this effort runs deeper than increasing the numbers of Catholics; rather, it is a fresh opportunity for the New Evangelization in its most positive of forms.

Faith formation, including of those returning to the practice of Catholic faith and life, is not limited to verbal testimony alone. Our catechetical agenda is shaped, at least in part, by the recognition of baptismal grace, of faith already professed and Baptism already celebrated, with people who are less objects of our own dispositions and more, by the grace of God, agents of transformation. We welcome sisters and brothers back *through* and *in* faith to a refreshed presence within the Christian community that claims and shapes its identity through the Paschal Mystery.

The celebration of the Eucharist and the other sacraments is of great significance in this regard. For example, to live means to grow in the sustaining power and strength of the Eucharist, through which we continue to give thanks for all that God has done and continues to do for us. "Eucharist means first of all 'thanksgiving'" (CCC, 1360). The sacrament of Reconciliation, with emphasis on mercy and forgiveness, is a source of graced benefit for the entire community as people find their way, through the grace of the Spirit, to the love and mercy of the Lord. "For those who are led by the Spirit of God are children of God. For you did not receive a spirit of slavery to fall back into fear, but you received a spirit of adoption, through which we cry, 'Abba, Father!'" (Rom 8:14–15).

Today, *deepening faith* is a mantra of sorts for catechetical leaders, especially those whose principal work is adult faith formation. *Deepening*, a partner with *discernment*, remains an adult-friendly and active term, for it does not judge the faith of the believer. Rather, it assumes belief and invites the believer to enhanced understanding and response in faith. The call to believe, to a living through believing, is part of the dynamic of faith. Our ongoing response to this call, from the depths of our soul and sincerity of commitment, is an active quality that rises in harmony with verbal affirmations that move one to assert, though not in isolation, "I believe." And it is cause for great rejoicing as we exemplify and offer to others through catechetical witness "the attitudes of the Master himself" (GDC, 85). In Jesus there is fullness—of promise, of expectation, of redemption, of life. The Gospel we proclaim draws us back to the mandate for mission that Jesus gives his disciples, now handed on and carried out from generation to generation. The fundamental message of faith in Christ weaves through time and circumstance. Our ways of sharing this Good News benefit from centuries of historical, technological, and relational advancements.

I had a lengthy deepening faith experience as a member of a small prayer community during my air force service on the island of Okinawa in 1971 and 1972, not many years after the close of the Second Vatican Council, which impacted so many Christians and persons of other religious traditions worldwide. Decades later, I recall with vivid clarity the power and witness of Catholic faith and heritage carried forward through the wind of the Spirit on this beautiful island. The blend of cultures and Catholic practices helped shape a community linked at its core by prayer and gathering for the Eucharist. I recall the experience of Cursillo and other opportunities for renewing faith. Through their witness and the power of the Holy Spirit, this God-given amalgam of personalities and people, disciples all and Christian to the core, strengthened the Body of Christ and deepened my faith.

Proclaiming for All

In commenting on the early Church, Pope John Paul II notes that "very soon the name of catechesis was given to the whole of the efforts within the Church to make disciples, to help people to believe that Jesus is the Son of God, so that believing they might have life in his name, and to educate and instruct them in this life and thus build up the Body of Christ" (CT, 1). Early catechetical methods included both preaching and oral instruction (either one-on-one or group) intended to make the message clear and understandable to those coming to faith. Such were some of the tools of handing on faith to be passed on to others.

As we each draw from our own catechetical history and are enriched by our growing understanding of the nature of catechesis and the teaching of the Church, we may interpret our experience in a variety of ways. We may even sometimes assume, albeit unintentionally and unconsciously, that others' experiences are substantially the same as our own. Our natural tendency to focus first on our own experience can surface within any generation and can limit historical understanding. While a favorite teacher, childhood experience, or weathered textbook may reside at the center of our memory, we cannot forget the broader communal context for catechesis. "Catechesis is an essentially ecclesial act.[20] The true subject of catechesis is the Church which, continuing the mission of Jesus the Master and, therefore animated by the Holy Spirit, is sent to be the teacher of the faith. . . . The Church transmits the faith which she herself lives" (GDC, 78).

Catechesis is a boundary jumper, not to be contained exclusively within familiar settings. Chapter 7 of the *National Directory for Catechesis* provides clear guidance for addressing catechesis to a wide swath of constituencies and persons, including many who may be forgotten or whose needs may barely be met. At a time in the Church when new evangelizing efforts are moving forward rapidly, we need to ensure that Gospel-bearers do not find themselves saying, "We cannot attend to that need."

In the Church we find a religious body that, despite its age and growth, is no corporate monolith formed as a start-up organization that happened to expand beyond a predictable measure. The same proclamation of the reign of God—of salvation in Jesus Christ who suffered, died, and is now risen—that beat at the heart of the early Church continues to beat at the heart of the contemporary Church.

Today, we witness to the world as an evangelizing presence removed only by time from the first centuries.[21] Indeed, we are not a renewed twenty-first-century corporation whose mission may periodically be completely recast. In faithful discipleship, we live eagerly attentive to that unifying identity of "one body and one Spirit, as you were also called to the one hope of your call; one Lord, one faith, one baptism; one God and Father of all, who is over all and through all and in all" (Eph 4:4–6). We are the Church of the ages. No wonder we ask of ourselves, "What will Christians of succeeding generations say or know of us?"

We recall the scripture passage from the Gospel of John wherein the risen Jesus appears among his fearful disciples, offering them peace. He calms them, shows them his wounds, and again invokes the peace he brings, the peace he is: "'Peace be with you. As the Father has sent me, so I send you.' And when he had said this, he breathed on them and said to them, 'Receive the holy Spirit'" (Jn 20:21–22). They are sent, witnesses now driven by the Spirit to live and preach the Good News in Christ. An apostle, after all, is one who is sent.

Proclamation wrapped in peace is one way of offering belonging. We need to remember this as we enact our own varied ministries. It is Christ to whom we invite others to belong for a lifetime.[22] Our own experience of living by faith becomes a font of credibility for the Good News we proclaim. The depth of our belonging to Christ and his Church gives witness to the Gospel; word and action demonstrate to a cautious and perhaps doubtful inquirer what enthusiastic participation in the life of the Church can look like. At one point the Acts of the Apostles tells us that "the church throughout all Judea, Galilee, and Samaria was at peace. It was being built up and walked in the fear of the Lord, and with the consolation of the holy Spirit it grew in numbers" (Acts 9:31). For us today, we live evangelization made new: "Peace be with you."

Reflection Questions

1. Imagine yourself at the Council of Jerusalem. What might you propose? How might you try to see different sides of the issue? How might prayerful discernment impact such a discussion?
2. How might you describe catechesis in the early Church to a friend?
3. Why do you think belonging was so important to the growing Christian community?
4. What do you think makes people today stand up for what they believe in?
5. How does mission drive the Church today? How is mission central to your experience of parish life?
6. What does Christian discipleship demand of you today?
7. How does your experience of catechesis lend support to the Church's ongoing efforts in forming disciples and in strengthening belief?

Catechesis and Communication, Then and Now

Renowned scholar Mary Charles Bryce, O.S.B., offers sound guidance for probing catechesis within a historical framework. Citing the words *catechesis* and *catechize*, she indicates "that both the message and its communication are alternately involved in reaching an understanding of the word itself."[23] This insight helps to foster a dynamic sense of catechesis, especially when viewing the topic historically. Catechesis includes an active element that resides within the believer, bringing the message out of the communication itself. And the communicator—the catechist or similarly named promoter of the faith—is the activator (through the Holy Spirit) in handing on what has been received by the Church (see GDC, 238).

Catechesis must engage both the message and the communication of the message, guided by the informed wisdom of the Church. One way the *General Directory for Catechesis* and the subsequent *National Directory for Catechesis* speak to the diversity of catechetical responsibilities is by identifying and promoting the implementation of the six tasks of catechesis, "each of which is related to an aspect of faith in Christ" (NDC, 20). They are

1. Promoting knowledge of the faith
2. Liturgical education
3. Moral formation
4. Teaching to pray
5. Education for community life
6. Missionary initiation (GDC, 85–87; see NDC, 20)[24]

The six tasks call us to water deep roots of *kerygma, didache, koinonia, leiturgia,* and *diakonia.* The relation of the six tasks to these elements is no coincidence, for catechesis builds on historically rich foundations that serve the mission of Christ and his Church. "Every means that the Church employs in her overall mission to go and make disciples has a catechetical aspect" (NDC, 19C).

Harmonious reliance on these six interdependent catechetical tasks enables us to see beyond narrow images of "teacher, method, and text," and especially "instruction" (sometimes misunderstood as limiting catechesis or misapplied as the entirety of catechesis). Education in faith draws upon many areas, including the message and mission given by Christ to the Church, the life setting and experience of the individual, reliance on appropriate developmental approaches, and opportunities for reflecting critically on how the Word shared can come alive through the gifts of the individual and the community. The six tasks are not disparate but are interwoven elements for fulfilling the Church's catechetical mandate. "When catechesis omits one of these elements, the Christian faith does not attain full development" (GDC, 87). This inclusive understanding of catechesis encourages deeper comprehension of and heightened communal response to the truth that "the Word became flesh and made his dwelling among us" (Jn 1:14).

Some informative Pauline references identified by Bryce as relevant to catechetical understanding include 1 Corinthians 14:19, Ephesians 4:11, and Galatians 6:6.[25] The latter says, for example,

> "One who is being instructed in the word should share all good things with his instructor" (Gal 6:6).

The message communicated is, of course, the Good News of salvation in Christ. Early catechetical efforts focused not only on the necessity of coming to Christ ("being born of water and Spirit" [Jn 3:5]) but also on the implications and challenges ahead for those willing to move forward in faith and stand with others, now sustained by Christ, "mediator of a new covenant" (Heb 9:15).

Other New Testament references also inform our understanding of catechesis in the early Church. For example, Joseph Collins, S.S., S.T.D., PhD, notes that "the first kerygmatic proclamation of the Faith was enlarged and extended for those who accepted it by further instruction and explanation which St. Luke calls the *catechesis* or oral proclamation of the teaching of Christ."[26] He identifies Luke 1:4 (part of the gospel prologue) and Acts 18:25 (regarding Apollos) as examples.

Luke's gospel begins with a statement to Theophilus about his own informed account of events, already reported by others, "that have been fulfilled among us" (Lk 1:1). He tells Theophilus that he is writing his account "so that you may realize the certainty of the teachings you have received" (Lk 1:4).[27] We seek to live by faith with steadfast confidence in the Word of God as we uncover with the mind of the Church hidden depths of meaning that seize our hearts and swell our spirits. We may be prompted to examine how we understand, why we question, and what we offer to another—and to Christ—through the Church's ministries of evangelization and catechesis.

Acts 18:24–27 provides both a perspective on catechesis and the use of the term *the Way*, which this book relies on as a central metaphor. In these verses, Luke offers an account of Apollos, "an eloquent speaker" (Acts 18:24), highly skilled in the scriptures, who finds his way to Ephesus. "He had been instructed in the Way of the Lord and, with ardent spirit, spoke and taught accurately about Jesus, although he knew only the baptism of John. He began to speak boldly in the synagogue; but when Priscilla and Aquila heard him, they took him aside and explained to him the Way [of God] more accurately" (Acts 18:25–26).

Since Apollos's framework was the baptism of John, his rendering needed more instruction, which Priscilla and Aquila gave him. A married couple, they provide sound modeling for ongoing catechesis in our day. Sometimes we need the voice of another to clarify, enlighten, and persuade. Those among us who are "eloquent" and an "authority" in our field of service may be surprised by and even resistant to such opportunities. Yet by the grace of God, wisdom continues to surface through others' insight and support.

When I read that Paul was aided by both Priscilla and Aquila (see Rom 16:3–4), I am reminded not only of the historically grounded contributions of laypeople to catechetical ministry in general but particularly of the numerous benefits offered by the hundreds of thousands of women who have given their lives to catechesis. They have spread the Word of God, and continue to do so, in a multitude of ways as catechetical enactors and leaders, seeking no more from those in their care than faithful commitment to Jesus and the Church. Their tireless efforts, coupled with those of men who have responded to God's call as lay witnesses, enliven the Gospel of Christ and strengthen the Church beyond measure.

From Mary—mother of the Lord Jesus, his first disciple, Mother of the Church, and model for all—to Priscilla, Phoebe, and so many more women of faith, the Church today reaps the benefits of a distinctive ongoing historical witness, rich in belonging; believing; discerning and reflecting; and living, dying, and rising in Christ.

Passion born of faith, embedded with gifts of understanding, can lead us, as it did our forebears, to action on behalf of the Gospel. For catechists, that action may be teaching, explaining, or exhorting.

Another account from the Acts of the Apostles strengthens our sense of catechesis. Peter's interaction with the centurion Cornelius[28] in Caesarea is one between a devout Jew consumed with Christ and burning with mission and a "God-fearing man," a Gentile eager to hear with others "all that you have been commanded by the Lord" (see Acts 10:36–48). Imagine Peter addressing Cornelius and the others assembled. Unrestrained witness falls from Peter's lips in words that capture the power and the message of the One with whom Peter walked, prayed, and ate the sacred Supper of the Lord before Jesus' last steps to his sacrifice on Calvary.

Jesus' death neither contains Jesus (see Acts 2:24) nor steals Peter's voice: "You know the word [that] he sent to the Israelites as he proclaimed peace through Jesus Christ, who is Lord of all, what has happened all over Judea, beginning in Galilee after the baptism that John preached, how God anointed Jesus of Nazareth with the holy Spirit and power. . . . He commissioned us to preach to the people and testify that he is the one appointed by God as judge of the living and the dead. To him all the prophets bear witness, that everyone who believes in him will receive forgiveness of sins through his name" (Acts 10:36–38, 42–43).

We are drawn into the scene, where the mystery of faith deepens. As Peter speaks, "the holy Spirit fell upon all who were listening to the word" (Acts 10:44). But how could this happen to people who have not been soaked in the waters of Baptism? Peter asserts, "'Can anyone withhold the water for baptizing these people, who have received the holy Spirit even as we have?' He ordered them to be baptized in the name of Jesus Christ" (Acts 10:47–48). Belonging truly is for all; "God shows no partiality" (Acts 10:34). Indeed, our belonging is to Christ, who binds us together in the Spirit.

The First Letter of Peter[29] also contributes to our picture of the early Church. This letter is particularly appealing to both catechists and liturgists and is a source for the Liturgy of the Word (second reading) for the second to the seventh Sundays of the Easter season (cycle A). Directed to Gentile believers in different areas of Asia Minor, the letter sets a baptismal tone from the outset: "Blessed be the God and Father of our Lord Jesus Christ, who in his great mercy gave us a new birth to a living hope through the resurrection of Jesus Christ from the dead, to an inheritance that is imperishable, undefiled, and unfading, kept in heaven for you who by the power of God are safeguarded through faith, to a salvation that is ready to be revealed in the final time" (1 Pt 1:3–5; cf. 1 Pt 3:21).

The letter also brings forward such important themes as obedience (1 Pt 1:13–16), love for one another (1:22), compassionate and humble behavior (3:8), and avoiding whatever would lead one to drift from "the will of God" (4:1–2). Suffering "because of righteousness" is deemed a blessing; believers are enjoined to "sanctify Christ as Lord in your hearts. Always be ready to give an explanation to anyone who asks you for a reason for your hope" (3:14–15). The suffering we may endure—daily "dyings" or more serious life challenges, whether physical, emotional, or spiritual—is not in vain.

Christ is our hope: "By his wounds you have been healed" (1 Pt 2:24). This is not wishful thinking disguised as some sort of Christian naïveté, although it may appear as such to an observer who does not see beneath the surface.

The letter reminds us that "the stone which the builders rejected has become the cornerstone" (1 Pt 2:7), and so rejection does not free us from ongoing catechetical witness. Despite the pain of loss, especially loss of those among family and friends who may have turned away from Christ and the Church, we may find that positive efforts to evangelize and catechize sometimes stem more from what we do—supported always by prayer, a prayerful disposition, and a welcoming spirit—rather than only from what we say. The First Letter of Peter also reminds us, as it did believers nearly two thousand years ago, that we "have been born anew" (1 Pt 1:23). It informs both a first-century audience and a twenty-first-century Church that we "have received mercy" (1 Pt 2:10).

Indeed, the Gospel is to be offered to all, regardless of cultural background or heritage. "The Church must be a place of mercy freely given, where everyone can feel welcomed, loved, forgiven and encouraged to live the good life of the Gospel" (EG, 114). The Holy Spirit is strengthening the most unlikely among us for Christian witness. Might that be you today?

Reflection Questions

1.   What might Luke be saying to you in the prologue to his gospel? How might you "be" Theophilus?

2.   What leads you to continue to discern the Word of God as you embrace faith, especially when challenged by persons of no religious tradition or those who have chosen to leave behind the Church of their upbringing? How might this impact communities to which you belong? What might be dying? Rising?

3.   Have you had a recent experience of being "taken aside" for instruction or correction by another in your primary community of belonging? How did you receive the person?

4.   Do you recall when you last clarified some fundamental teachings of our faith for another? How did you harmonize believing with witnessing your faith? What words did not come to you at first but do now?

5.   When are you most inclined to listen to or for the Word? What voice does the Spirit draw you toward? How might you be more attentive to the homilist at Mass?

6.   What gets in the way of your maintaining a regular schedule for prayer and reflection as you live by faith? What happens when your prayer is interrupted? What "word" is the Holy Spirit offering you today?

7.   How might you raise up another, despite your own weariness, as an agent of mercy in Christ?

8.   How might you discern next steps for implementing the six tasks of catechesis in your life? What interactions with others offer you opportunities to witness to faith through one or more of these tasks?

Catechizing for a Lasting Identity

Catechesis in the early Church was linked, as were other ministries, to a holistic understanding of what it meant to be Christian. Being Christian meant living a Christian life. Identification came through the journey to and from saving baptismal waters and was sustained through regular gatherings that included the celebration of the Eucharist.

At the center of an emerging ecclesial landscape was the community's Sunday celebration of the Eucharist, the sacrificial meal and memorial of the Redeemer. "The Gospel and the Eucharist are the constant food for the journey to the Father's House" (GDC, 70). This is a constant not just for catechesis but for the Church's entire life and witness over the ages. From within the longstanding setting of a meal we derive important foundations for the celebration of the Eucharist in the early Church. For example, after telling the Corinthian Christian community "I hear that when you meet as a church there are divisions among you" (1 Cor 11:18), Paul repeats for them what he has received from the Lord. With great clarity, he asserts:

> For I received from the Lord what I also handed on to you, that the Lord Jesus, on the night he was handed over, took bread, and, after he had given thanks, broke it and said, "This is my body that is for you. Do this in remembrance of me." In the same way also the cup, after supper, saying, "This cup is the new covenant in my blood. Do this, as often as you drink it, in remembrance of me." For as often as you eat this bread and drink the cup, you proclaim the death of the Lord until he comes. (1 Cor 11:23–26)

The early Church saw a shift from "the house-church" to "the church hall" about halfway through the second century.[30] We can imagine our ancestors in faith seeking to live as faithful witnesses to their baptismal call as they gathered for prayer, worship, and fellowship. They faced their own life challenges. Surely, uncertain conditions as well as expectations born of the hope for Christ's return would have commanded their attention and strengthened their resolve.

Their gatherings confirmed their deepening identity as communities formed in Christ. And they would not fade into historical oblivion after a time of societal probation, for Jesus Christ not only redeemed them but also redeems us, inviting us into his redemptive presence through the gift of the Eucharist, the same gift offered to the early Church.

In the early centuries, the shared movement of the liturgical and the catechetical gradually developed into what might today be called a process approach for catechesis, with adjustments and adaptations as needed and as welcomed over time. As we will see, catechesis eventually evolved into a lively blend of scripture, symbol, creed, ritual, prayer, worship, and witness, all within a framework of communal support, participation, and discipleship. Replenishment, after all, is one lasting fruit of ecclesial renewal; we are the Church.

The experience of living and catechizing in faithful discipleship leads to and from the celebration of the Eucharist.[31] "In the Eucharist Jesus does not give us a 'thing,' but himself; he offers his own body and pours out his own blood" (SCa, 7). This life-giving nourishment sustains us along the way of catechesis. Reliance on this sacrificial memorial enables us to enter into the Paschal Mystery of Christ's Passion, Death, Resurrection, and Ascension, strengthening us for Christian witness. The Paschal Mystery is central to any catechetical effort faithful to the Church's mission and ministry. "The Church celebrates in the liturgy above all the Paschal mystery by which Christ accomplished the work of our salvation" (CCC, 1067).

Jesus' "multi-dimensional" (NDC, 28A2; see GDC, 140) pedagogy of signs, words, and works that summoned others to repent, listen, and act continues to inspire us and summon us to him in a relationship that knows no end: "As the Father loves me, so I also love you. Remain in my love" (Jn 15:9). As emissaries of the New Evangelization, we strive to keep faith alive as we encourage others to dwell in faith along with us. We are called to rouse and support others during crises of faith arising from life's tender or doubtful moments, pray with them, and accompany them to the celebration of the Eucharist. As we do this, we need not worry about filling Christ's shoes. He fills ours, and then he carries us as our catechist, our teacher, our Savior. Contemporary catechetical leaders know the significance of both our teaching and our perspective. We remember that "the Church was born of the paschal mystery" (EE, 3).

The growing Church of Antioch, southeast of Paul's birthplace in Tarsus, was where "the disciples were first called Christians" (Acts 11:26). In his letter to the Smyrnaeans in the early second century, Ignatius of Antioch (d. ca. 107) used the term *Catholic Church* in speaking of the intimate linkage between Christ and the Church: "Where Jesus Christ is, there is the Catholic Church."[32] Nearly two thousand years removed from Ignatius, an apostolic Father who would suffer martyrdom, we see that this is a lasting bond of identity and mystery, faith and redemption.

Unwillingness to express loyalty to the gods of the Romans may seem like a distant concern to Christians today. But the first Christians were our ancestors in proclaiming the kingdom of God. One scholar, Kevin Hughes, notes, "Christians were accused of atheism, cannibalism, and libertinism. The charge of atheism arose not simply from the theological differences between the Roman and Christian faiths, but from the practical consequences of those differences. . . . Christianity seemed to many Romans distasteful and unpatriotic."[33]

Committed Christian witness would sometimes lead to persecution (e.g., Acts 12), which would threaten the Church intermittently.[34] It was the great early Church theologian Tertullian (ca. AD 155–ca. 220) who would write in the late second century, "We become more numerous every time we are hewn down by you: the blood of Christians is seed."[35] Today this is commonly expressed as "The blood of Christians is the seed of the Church." Increasingly in our times, we see accounts of the torture and slaughter of Christian women, men, and children. Today's martyrs include witnesses to Christ whose response to God's call was marked by a vocation to religious life. The Church is one. Jesus' seamless garment is one. When one person suffers, the entire community of faith suffers. How often we hear of requests for prayer for persons halfway around the world, within our own parish, or just down the block. Suffering and violence can occur anywhere. As Christians, we offer ourselves in direct or indirect sustained and prayerful support, especially of children, emblems of innocence among us, as well as of others whose spirits are rent in two in a struggle for release from pain, shock, and, in some cases, betrayal. We are called not just to live alongside persons so burdened but to accompany them, even entering into the "dying" of the other and seeking to rise together in Christ.

With the identifying claim of membership in the Church and its accompanying Christian witness comes the responsibility to adhere to and live up to what the Church proclaims and teaches in the name of

Christ. By claiming Jesus as Savior and brother, we are putting forth no
small claim. Through the blood of martyrs—of which we are well aware
through events in our own time—the Church remains a life-bearing font
of Christian witness to the One whose own blood gives new life.

The Didache

One treasure from the early tradition of the Church is the *Didache,* or *The
Teaching of the Twelve Apostles.*[36] Theologian Richard E. McCarron quotes
distinguished scholar Paul Bradshaw in indicating that "scholars classify
the *Didache* as an 'ancient church order,' a type of manual for church life.
The church order genre was intended 'to offer authoritative "apostolic"
prescriptions on matters of moral conduct, liturgical practice, and ecclesiastical organization and discipline.'"[37]

　　With roots in Syria, the *Didache* evades any firm dating, though
scholars lean toward the first or second century AD.[38] From various
sources, it is oral teaching that eventually was put into written form,
"probably [for] a Greek-speaking Jewish-Christian community in a town
on the Syria-Palestine border, around 100–120 C.E."[39] The *Didache* is
not a lengthy document; it consists of sixteen short "chapters." A copy
of the document was found in Constantinople in 1873 and dates from
the mid-eleventh century;[40] there have been partial finds as well.[41] In
commenting on chapters 1–10, Aidan Kavanagh describes the *Didache's*
"pronouncedly Jewish character. . . . All its structural precedents are
Jewish—the two ways of teaching, the Kiddush-meal eucharist, and the
ablutionary baptism."[42]

　　Theologian and catechetical scholar Gerard S. Sloyan identifies
the *Didache* as "the earliest non-canonical handbook of instruction we
have. . . . There is no professedly dogmatic instruction in the *Didache*
but only Christian morality, an outline of liturgical conduct (baptism, Eucharist, public confession, fasting), and some indications as to
authority and the various ministries in the early Church."[43] The morality section appears in chapters 1–6, "a pre-baptismal catechesis";[44] the
liturgical section in chapters 7–10; and ministries in chapters 12–15.

A final chapter resounds with readiness for the end times and the coming of Christ.

The *Didache* begins with ethical teaching: "There are two ways, one of life, the other of death, and between the two ways there is a great difference."[45] Initial features given for the Way of life are love of God, love of neighbor as oneself, and a form of what is commonly known as the Golden Rule.[46] There follows a blended use of familiar teaching, including from the Sermon on the Mount and the Ten Commandments.[47] Richard McCarron identifies a contemporary connection to the *General Directory for Catechesis* (115), which brings together a number of these elements in an informative section on the Christian message.[48]

Of interest as well are the brief liturgical chapters, which introduce the reader to methods of baptizing (e.g., "in running water"[49]) as well as participation in the Eucharist. Only the baptized may partake of the Eucharist.[50] Liturgical scholar and theologian Maxwell Johnson observes that "chapter 7 of this important document provides us with the earliest description of the rites of Christian initiation we have beyond those given in the New Testament itself."[51]

Of interest in the third section of the *Didache* is the need to be alert to false teachers of doctrine (chapter 11); how to receive and treat traveling apostles and prophets (chapter 11) and anyone else "who comes in the name of the Lord" (chapter 12);[52] and the selection of bishops and deacons, offering care for them as would be given to prophets and teachers (chapter 15).[53] Notice is also given: "Assembling on every Sunday of the Lord, break bread and give thanks, confessing your faults besides so that your sacrifice may be clean" (chapter 14).[54]

The final chapter, set on the end times, teaches us even today to set our lives on Christ. None of us is ever fully formed in faith. The *Didache* urges, "Keep vigil over your life" and "be ready."[55] All the faithful are so charged today as we understand and apply what the New Evangelization calls us to be and to do. As a young Church—we are, after all, only two thousand years old—a question remains: Are we ready?

This extraordinary document strengthens our belonging to our catechetical tradition. Indeed, the *Didache* links oral and written foundations for catechesis, key elements of the Church's catechetical endeavor.

Reflection on the *Didache* reminds us of the great care involved in form-ing others in faith as the Spirit moves them toward the community of the Church and as the Spirit moves the community of the Church to worship and to live as faith in Christ demands. This is no limited or piecemeal effort. Rather, it is an opportunity and an honor: an opportunity to engage others in the encounter of living faith, despite our own trials and trib-ulations, and an honor to represent the Church's catechetical heritage, including our own vital witness.

"Jesus Is Lord"

Early Church catechesis was resilient with the power of Gospel witness, and faith was alive in various locales (e.g., we remember Paul's missionary journeys). As we would expect, professing faith in Christ was fundamental and foundational. "From the beginning, the apostolic Church expressed and handed on her faith in brief formulae for all" (CCC, 186). Berard Marthaler, O.F.M.Conv., writes that "the kerygma formed the nucleus of a christological confession that is summarized in the slogan, 'Jesus is Lord' (1 Cor 12:3). Brief formulas of this kind appear side by side with fuller and more detailed doctrinal formulas that echo the preaching of the apostles. . . . By the time of St. Justin (ca. 160), stock formulas seem to have come into use."[56]

The Church, beneficiary of scriptures handed on and develop-ing traditions and practices, resonated with creeds in summary form, "also called 'symbols of faith'" (CCC, 187). The term *symbol* is natu-rally linked to sacramental and liturgical experience, and deservedly so. Here, however, we are treating what may perhaps be a less-well-known understanding of the word: "The Greek word *symbolon* meant half of a broken object, for example, a seal presented as a token of recognition. The broken parts were placed together to verify the bearer's identity. The symbol of faith, then, is a sign of recognition and communion between believers. *Symbolon* also means a gathering, collection or summary. A symbol of faith is a summary of the principal truths of the faith and therefore serves as the first and fundamental point of reference for cat-echesis" (CCC, 188).[57]

Such symbols as the Apostles' Creed ("the oldest Roman catechism" [CCC, 196][58]) and the longer Niceno-Constantinopolitan, or Nicene, Creed (stemming from the Councils of Nicaea in AD 325 and Constantinople in 381) became the commonly expressed creeds that we profess today as we affirm faith and belief in Father, Son, and Holy Spirit. For the catechumen, receiving the Creed freely given, or handed over (*traditio symboli*), was only part of the equation; the other was "giving back" (*redditio symboli*) the cherished gift that penetrated one's lived experience through the appeal to faith.[59] Cyril of Jerusalem would encourage his listeners with this endearing expression of the joy and truth handed on: "This summary I wish you to commit to memory, word for word, and to repeat among yourselves with all zeal, not writing it on paper, but engraving it by memory on the heart. . . . Keep it as a provision for the way throughout the whole course of your life."[60] Emphasizing scriptural foundations, Cyril indicates a little later: "For not according to men's pleasure have the articles of faith been composed, but the most important points collected from the Scriptures make up one complete teaching of the faith."[61]

It is no mere footnote of history that our Way today is still sustained by the profession of faith: given, received, and given back. The terms *transformation*, *identity*, and *recognition* join with *symbolon* to invite us to reflect on who we are, why we take our catechetical mission so seriously, and how we celebrate such blessed communion. "The first 'profession of faith' is made during Baptism. The symbol of faith is first and foremost the *baptismal* creed" (CCC, 189).[62] To summarize: "The Creed is a Symbol, a representation or a summary of the whole Bible, and indeed of our whole faith."[63] We are "wholly" Catholic, formed as one in faith.

Imagine yourself as bearer of a broken seal. You seek the confirming identity of another, for without such verification your own identity is incomplete and difficult to affirm or even claim. It is not a typical sense of recognition (e.g., applause) that is your goal but mutual awareness of identities confirmed as you profess together faith shared and sustained. Somehow you sense that you are arriving in your history, ready for your own brokenness to be linked with that of another. Realizing the necessity of communion within the community of faith—people of faith in relationship with one another in Christ—you engage the "other" and approach together the table of the Lord. Your identity sealed, you are nourished at the altar of sacrifice, one in faith, one in life, one in the Spirit of Christ.

Together we live for the reign of God. The United States is home to people from many different heritages and family backgrounds. This is an indescribable blessing. People perhaps unknown to us yesterday become vital sources of faithful witness whose gifts and talents we cherish. Relationships formed in faith and held in common grow and prosper.

We need and rely on others who guide and challenge us and who, at times, may offer correction. Purification and enlightenment, we find, are not just for "other" persons or groups. Inculturation "involves, when necessary, the purification of the elements in the culture that may be hostile or adverse to the Gospel. And it involves an invitation to conversion" (NDC, 21C).

We may resist the notion that "my culture" is in need of conversion. But then, without fanfare and in the breath of the Spirit, we sense that we are already on the move, turning a corner together. Faces and markers along the way summon us to a renewal of conversion to Christ, for there is both witness and strength in the shared identity that we claim, profess, celebrate, and live. What "echo of the word of God" (NDC, 21C) are you hearing today?

We offer no static display of history buried in abandoned and hardened soil. Although our hands may at times become weakened and calloused, we invite the "other" into the life-giving mysteries of faith through life in Christ Jesus, the vine to whom we cling, as one.

As we will see, branches of catechumenal care are starting to grow. In the meantime, "let us hold unwaveringly to our confession that gives us hope, for he who made the promise is trustworthy" (Heb 10:23).

Reflection Questions

1. Persecution was a reality the Church sometimes faced during the first centuries. What might you and others do to support sisters and brothers in faith who face severe punishment or even death for their discipleship?

2. How might you explain to another why Christians undergo suffering?

3. How do you bring to life the words of the Creed? How does your life give voice to and complete the sentence "I believe in . . ."?

4. Since *didache* means "teaching," what teaching of the Church elevates your experience of faith and of life?

5. What topic does the source document called the *Didache* call you to explore? What piques your interest or curiosity?

6. Why do you think there is such strong emphasis on moral living in the *Didache*?

7. What motivates you to communicate the Gospel in word and action?

8. What are some characteristics of the early Church that you might like to study further? What makes you proud to belong to this historic Church?

5

FRAMING THE WAY
The Church and the Catechumenate

But you are "a chosen race, a royal priesthood, a holy nation, a people of his own, so that you may announce the praises" of him who called you out of darkness into his wonderful light.
Once you were "no people"
   but now you are God's people;
you "had not received mercy"
   but now you have received mercy.

—1 Peter 2:9–10

We now move to highlights regarding the development of the catechumenate and its accompanying communal witness,[1] which will broaden our perspective on catechesis in the life of the Church. In the first several centuries of the first millennium, catechesis benefited from the passionate resolve and theological insights of the Church Fathers, who served the theological, doctrinal, and apologetical development of the Church in distinctive ways and from within a diversity of era-driven challenges. Over the course of about seven centuries, they provided a wealth of theological development and insight, with accompanying impact on catechesis. First among them were the apostolic Fathers of the late first century AD and then the apologists.[2] Renowned theologian Johannes Quasten points out, "Whereas the works of the Apostolic Fathers and of early Christianity were directed to the guidance and edification of the faithful, with the Greek Apologists the literature of the Church addresses itself for the first time to the outside world and enters the domain of culture and science."[3] Succeeding Fathers, with their own gifts and talents, would continue to mold the still-developing Christian tradition in both East and West.

During the first few centuries, the work of such Fathers as Clement of Rome, Ignatius of Antioch, Justin Martyr, Irenaeus of Lyons, Tertullian, and Origen strengthened the faith foundations of the Christian community. They provided, each in his own way, reason for belief. For example, Irenaeus (d. ca. AD 202) observes in his *Proof of the Apostolic Preaching*:

> Now, this is what faith does for us, as the elders, the disciples of the apostles, have handed down to us. First of all, it admonishes us to remember that we have received baptism for remission of sins in the name of God the Father, and in the name of Jesus Christ, the Son of God, who became incarnate and died and was raised, and in the Holy Spirit of God; and that this baptism is the seal of eternal life and is rebirth unto God, that we be no more children of mortal men, but of the eternal and everlasting God.[4]

Although *Proof of the Apostolic Preaching* is represented as a catechetical contribution, it has more of an apologetic flavor since Irenaeus seeks to counter heretical teaching.[5] "The points on which he repeatedly insists are those which were denied by the heretics."[6] Irenaeus and other Fathers help to guide our understanding of who we are, what we need, and who we are called to rely on.

In the early centuries, the Church's catechesis grew from within formation for life in Christ through the strong voices and nurturing care of communities of faith. In fundamental ways, catechesis was "born" of the sacramental encounter: for example, it claims and shapes its identity with roots in and lives formed through the encounter with Christ in the Eucharist. Nearly two thousand years later, the Second Vatican Council would proclaim, "The Church has always venerated the divine Scriptures as she venerated the Body of the Lord, in so far as she never ceases, particularly in the sacred liturgy, to partake of the bread of life and to offer it to the faithful from the one table of the Word of God and the Body of Christ. She has always regarded, and continues to regard the Scriptures, taken together with sacred Tradition, as the supreme rule of her faith" (DV, 21).

An Emerging Catechumenate

It is beyond the scope of this work to offer a comprehensive analysis of the extensive historical details, nuances, and figures that informed the ancient catechumenal experience and early approaches to Christian initiation. However, some examples of initiation practice and related aspects are presented.[7]

Both continuity and differences in practice and perspective marked these early centuries, as new members were welcomed and formed in faith and discipleship within the Church in various geographic locations. Catechumenal scholar Michel Dujarier points out: "*During the first two centuries, the preparation of converts for the sacraments of initiation was very flexible. . . . There was no fixed organization of the catechumenate in the strict sense.*"[8]

Those seeking to be baptized needed to demonstrate willingness to live in accord with Christian tradition as lived within the Christian community. They were not alone in their progressive conversion of heart to Jesus Christ; the support and participation of the local community was an essential and significant part of formation. Discernment of and movement toward the Good News, the Christian message of hope and salvation in Jesus Christ, was bolstered by the living catechetical witness of the Christian community.[9] Justin Martyr of Rome (d. ca. AD 165), a Greek of Palestinian origin who would give his life for the faith, offers this perspective on Church initiation practice in the second century:

> Those who are persuaded and believe that the things we teach and say are true, and promise that they can live accordingly, are instructed to pray and beseech God with fasting for the remission of their past sins, while we pray and fast along with them. Then they are brought by us where there is water, and are reborn by the same manner of rebirth by which we ourselves were reborn; for they are then washed in the water in the name of God the Father and Master of all, and of our Savior Jesus Christ, and of the Holy Spirit.[10]

Dujarier points out that in mid-second-century Rome, those seeking Baptism needed to express repentance for their sinfulness, "faith in the Church as the teacher of truth," and a "transformation of life" consistent with Christian practice.[11]

The catechumenate eventually evolved into a formative initiatory experience with careful and deliberate incorporation of new members into the community of faith. Over time, the emerging catechumenate guided movement toward Baptism through such dimensions as scripture, community, fasting, and prayer, as well as instruction, moral formation, and witness to faith. A nurturing catechesis drew sustenance from deep wells of faith proclaimed, celebrated, taught, and lived.

Joseph Collins offers this perspective: "After the apostolic period, kerygmatic catechesis was mainly carried out by clerical and lay catechists during the period of the catechumenate. . . . The catechumenate was a school of doctrine and moral teaching which based its instruction on the Gospel message of Christ."[12]

Persons seeking membership in the community of Christian believers through Baptism needed to demonstrate "faith in Christ and conversion of life."[13] Conversion was not spiritually segregated from one's "real life" or from the community. The emblematic and gradual "turning" and demonstrated Christian way of living was characterized by a change of disposition and a new type of living witness, now bound to the lives of others of similar persuasion. Preparation within the community included coming together to pray and to ponder the scriptures.[14] There existed a close link between belief and practice, especially with regard to ethical conduct. The example of their lives was a significant factor in determining whether or not candidates[15] would advance toward Baptism. Clearly, they needed to demonstrate willingness to live by what they professed; witnesses would indicate the candidates' readiness to proceed.[16]

J. B. Xavier states that "by the end of the second century, owing to the ever increasing number of converts seeking admission into the Church, the organization of the catechumenate began to take shape in all its main lines. Faced with this new situation, the main preoccupation of the Church was to admit into her fold only those who gave the guarantees of a sufficient preparation and proof of courageous perseverance."[17] He also notes that the preparation for Baptism was "catechetical, ascetical, and liturgical."[18]

Entrance into the waters of Baptism and subsequent emersion confirmed the conversion to new life already underway, lived now through the community of the Church founded in and by Christ. Such would not be a life without struggle, but the struggle was underscored by the vigilant hope of life always in Christ.[19] "The kingdom of heaven is at hand" (Mt 10:7).

Regarding catechesis, the way one lived was in natural relation to one's developing faith in and relationship with Christ within the faith community. Generations of Christians of the first few centuries were not far removed from the Death and Resurrection of Jesus.

We do well to recall some baptism-related scriptural uses that help to guide understanding. With regard to the first two references, see especially the *Catechism of the Catholic Church,* 1225, in a section on the baptism of Jesus.

- "Can you drink the cup that I drink or be baptized with the baptism with which I am baptized?" (Mk 10:38).

- "There is a baptism with which I must be baptized, and how great is my anguish until it is accomplished!" (Lk 12:50).

- "Amen, amen, I say to you [Nicodemus], no one can enter the kingdom of God without being born of water and Spirit" (Jn 3:5).

- "Peter [said] to them, 'Repent and be baptized, every one of you, in the name of Jesus Christ for the forgiveness of your sins; and you will receive the gift of the holy Spirit'" (Acts 2:38).

- "We were indeed buried with him through baptism into death, so that, just as Christ was raised from the dead by the glory of the Father, we too might live in newness of life" (Rom 6:4).

- "Now you have had yourselves washed, you were sanctified, you were justified in the name of the Lord Jesus Christ and in the Spirit of our God" (1 Cor 6:11).

- "For all of you who were baptized into Christ have clothed yourselves with Christ" (Gal 3:27).

- "You were buried with him in baptism, in which you were also raised with him through faith in the power of God, who raised him from the dead" (Col 2:12).

In Baptism, one crosses the threshold of life and is wholly enveloped by the Savior, the one who calls, heals, carries, and lifts up all the baptized. Jesus reaches out to us, a point reinforced by scriptural images that never fail to enlighten us.[20] For example, we do well to remember John 3:5 and "being born of water and Spirit" as we seek baptismal understanding in our own day.[21] In Baptism, we enter blessed saving waters. Jesus never lets go as he continues to teach us through life made new in the Spirit, lived out in communion with the entire Church.

We catechize with vigor. Using the limbs of faithful believers, Jesus lifts us over the threshold of whatever might prevent us from becoming one with him, now lived through our shared witness with other believers. Through "the birth of water and the Spirit" (CCC, 1215) we are privileged to share in the freeing love of the Savior: we are freed from sin and whatever else binds us or clouds our vision. This is what liturgical catechesis offers us and all who respond to his call. This is liberation. "None of us lives for oneself, and no one dies for oneself. . . . We are the Lord's" (Rom 14:7–8).

As already noted, those seeking Baptism needed to demonstrate faith in Christ and conversion of life. Initiation into the sacramental life of the Christian community occurred over a period of time. Writing from North Africa near the end of the second century, Tertullian would say to Roman officials, "Christians are made, not born!"[22]

Southeast of Rome and across the Mediterranean Sea, Origen of Alexandria (ca. AD 184–253) indicates that

> as far as they can, Christians previously examine the souls of those who want to hear them, and test them individually beforehand; when before entering the community the hearers seem to have devoted

themselves sufficiently to the desire to live a good life, then they introduce them. They privately appoint one class consisting of recent beginners who are receiving elementary instruction and have not yet received the sign that they have been purified, and another class of those who, as far as they are able, make it their set purpose to desire nothing other than those things of which Christians approve.[23]

Subsequently, Origen writes that when those of the latter group "make progress and show that they have been purified by the Logos, and do all in their power to live better lives, then we call them to our mysteries."[24] Here we see that belonging was movement along the way of faith within the Christian community.

Coming to faith occurred within Christian communities whose evangelizing efforts were shaped in part by members' demonstrated discipleship. This formative way encouraged receptivity to the proclamation of the kerygma, the distinctive message of the Good News of salvation in Christ. Christian initiation included the participation of those already baptized as a vital component of the formation of those inquiring about joining the Church community. The laity were not added hands, waiting to be summoned; by virtue of their own Baptism and presence within the community, they were essential to catechumenal formation.[25] New life "in" community was new life "of" the community of faith, the Church. Thus were belonging and believing forged together along the way of conversion; for such do we continue to strive today. Conversion culminated in shared discipleship with others who believed in the saving Jesus and in what he had called them to become—witnesses to new life along the way of faith in Christ, a departure from what had been the previously accepted milieu. We remember, God's promise is eternal life (see 1 Jn 2:25, 5:11).[26]

Clement of Alexandria (ca. AD 150–ca. 215) called for a gradual catechesis leading to a deepening and strengthening of faith in those preparing for Baptism. Clement develops an agricultural image, noting that "after three years,[27] the firstfruits are to be consecrated to God after the tree has reached maturity. . . . Time is needed for strength in a catechumen. In a fourth year the four virtues are consecrated to God. The third stage touches the fourth place, where the Lord is."[28]

Clement is significant for his direction of the Catechetical School of Alexandria, which would eventually benefit from Origen's leadership. This school, which would become "a great influence upon theological development in the Church,"[29] was not what we would identify today as a "parish intergenerational catechetical center." It "was really a type of higher education."[30] The school is prominent for its interpretation of the spiritual sense of scripture (see CCC, 115–119).[31] Historian and catechetical scholar Berard Marthaler puts it this way when citing the work of the historian Eusebius (ca. AD 263–ca. 339) in relation to catechesis in Alexandria: "On the one hand it expounded doctrine through Scriptural exegesis and, on the other hand, it refuted opinions of heretics and philosophers."[32]

One might imagine that the cultural setting of the time made for an "easy" faith commitment during the first few centuries, lived out by the baptized in a spiritualized and idyllic land. However, this was no perfect time for the communities of believers. For example, in an age of Roman governance and demands for adherence to Roman religious practices, it could be risky to permit the effects of the weekly[33] gathering to linger in public. The choice for Christianity led to struggles and sometimes persecution. Eusebius records Dionysius's account of persecution in Alexandria during the time of Origen. After reporting on the stoning to death of the Christians Metras and Quinta by "heathen masses," Dionysius (d. ca. AD 265) states, "They all ran in a body to the houses of the Christians, charged in by groups on those they knew as neighbours, raided, plundered, and looted. . . . The Christians retired and gradually withdrew; like those to whom Paul paid tribute, they took with cheerfulness the plundering of their belongings. I do not know of anyone, except possibly one man who fell into their clutches, who up to now has denied the Lord."[34]

Mutual support, derived especially from their worship together, was an important part of life within the faith community.[35] The Eucharist was essential for living the Christian way. Liturgical-catechetical scholar Catherine Dooley, O.P. (1933–2015), notes that "in the early catechumenate there was almost no distinction between liturgy and catechesis. The classic catechumenate set out an integrated vision of coming to faith that wove together the biblical, liturgical and ecclesial signs within the human situation."[36]

For the contemporary Church, discipleship carried forward through the integration of liturgy and catechesis is one effect of the implementation of the baptismal catechumenate. While assisting with leading parish catechumenal formation, I witnessed firsthand catechumens' experience of Christian initiation. Formation incorporated Catholic faith and practice within a scripturally abundant, holistic approach to Christian discipleship. Liturgy did not "end" under the exit sign of a church door; catechesis did not conclude with the final segment of a faith formation session. The aroma of the applied *Rite of Christian Initiation of Adults* seemed to gradually permeate this time of life-changing decisions in openness to the Spirit of God (see RCIA, 4). The widening effect of this liturgical-catechetical blend, linked to evangelizing witness, was not limited to catechumens, who enjoyed the prayerful and visible support of the parish community. Catechumenal care seemed to become a *natural* expression of parish life. I can attest that my own expression of discipleship was enhanced by interacting and praying regularly with the catechumens. The Holy Spirit moves us, individually and communally, as people are formed or renewed in faith. Belonging and believing thrive as people discern next steps for lives of faith and witness.

A story of such a holistic Christian witness in the early Church comes from Bede the Venerable, early Church historian and author of the *Ecclesiastical History of the English People*. Bede (d. ca. AD 735) writes of Alban (d. third century?), a soldier in Britain who took in a priest seeking to avoid persecution. We see in this story a combination of observation, prayer, and teaching. Alban welcomed "this pious man" and was deeply affected by his guest's prayerful witness. "And when he saw him day and night busied in continual prayers and vigils, then was Alban suddenly visited by the mercy of God's grace. And he soon began to imitate the example of his belief and piety; and also gradually was taught, by his saving exhortations, to leave the darkness of idol worship and become with sincere heart a christian man." When the governor's servants sought to remove the priest from his care, Alban "put on the monk's dress, substituting himself for the stranger who was his guest, and gave himself into their hands."[37] Questioned about his background, Alban declared, "But if you wish to hear the truth as to my religion, know that I am a christian, and will devote myself to christian services. . . . I ever worship and pray to the true and living God who created heaven and earth and all creatures."[38] After Alban was tortured, the furious judge saw that he could not "turn him from the worship of the christian religion, [and] he ordered him to be beheaded."[39] The martyr Alban's story—which includes decisive faith witness before his executioner—gives vigorous testimony to two realities: the sustaining power of faith and the lasting power of Christian witness. Sincerity and integrity of heart go a long way.

A source often referenced with regard to the development of the catechumenate and of catechesis is *The Treatise on the Apostolic Tradition of St. Hippolytus of Rome,* also rendered as the *Apostolic Tradition.*[40] This church order treats of a number of matters of Church life, including catechumenal formation, Christian initiation, and related rituals. Witnesses (i.e., "sponsors"[41]) attest to the intent and readiness of those persons seeking to pursue the Christian faith. We see again that those seeking Baptism needed to be prepared to live as faithful Christians: "Let a catechumen be instructed for three years. But if a man be earnest and persevere well in the matter, let him be received, because it is not the time that is judged, but the conduct."[42] Catechumens benefited regularly from instruction, prayer, and the imposition of hands.[43] Liturgical and catechumenal scholar Paul Turner notes that "sessions included scripture, prayer and handlaying."[44] "After the prayer [*of the catechumens*] let the teacher lay hands upon them and pray and dismiss them. Whether the teacher be an ecclesiastic or a layman let him do the same."[45]

Discussion today about the ancient catechumenate sometimes focuses on the "three-year" length of the catechumenate, as if to suggest that the process was identical in every place and for every catechumen. From a historical perspective it is important not to generalize from the limited information available. Liturgical scholar and theologian Maxwell Johnson's important work in examining appropriate historical sources regarding length of time for early catechumenal formation is helpful in this regard. He indicates that "the exact length of the prebaptismal catechumenate in pre-Nicene Christianity, however, is not known with any degree of certainty."[46]

Observers and practitioners may assume that contemporary catechumenal and related catechetical efforts fall far short of those of our forebears, since contemporary preparation may not be as extensive when measured in years. Some parishes may design (for a variety of reasons) catechumenal approaches based on the academic year rather than more expansively on the rich preserve of the Church's entire liturgical cycle. The "National Statutes for the Catechumenate" indicate that "the period of catechumenate . . . should extend for at least one year of formation, instruction, and probation."[47]

Whatever methods are applied and whatever justifications are made, attention must be given to the diverse needs of catechumens all year long; these needs may be culturally, religiously, or generationally driven. As we have already seen, "it is not the time that is judged, but the conduct."[48] In addition, appropriate care must be given to the needs of baptized persons seeking full communion with the Catholic Church. The support and participation of the local community remains significant to the entire formation process. This is no simple appeal to history in order to reinvent it. Rather, it is a recognition of our responsibility as a community of faith, regardless of the century or cultural climate, to serve and catechize with vigor.

The term *commitment* helps to characterize the journey along the way of faith during these early centuries. But this commitment did not flow in one direction, for the community of faith demonstrated its own responsibility for catechumenal formation. Candidates for Baptism were called to express their adherence to Jesus and the message of the Gospel in order to become part of the faithful. A spiritual high point came during the week just prior to Baptism. For example, in North Africa, "they spent a certain period—probably a week—in prayer, vigils, and fasting."[49] In his homily *On Baptism* Tertullian says, "Those who are at the point of entering upon baptism ought to pray, with frequent prayers, fastings, bending of the knee, and all-night vigils, along with the confession of all their former sins."[50]

Living in accordance with the Christian faith was a serious expectation for the catechumens, an expectation that would not diminish with Baptism. Indeed, in Rome (and elsewhere) witnesses testified to people's "aptitude to become catechumens." Later, closer to Baptism, "they testified to the conduct of the catechumens during the instruction period."[51] Those seeking Baptism needed to demonstrate ongoing conversion, confirming that their lives had been changed and impacted along the way of faith. Those who did so were now closer to the gift and celebration of Baptism and sharing in the Eucharist. Professor of liturgics Leonel L. Mitchell points out, "At the end of the three-year catechumenate, those who are to receive baptism are chosen. This group of *electi* (chosen) are called by later Latin authors *competentes* (seekers), as opposed to the simple *audientes* (hearers)."[52]

We see in the *Apostolic Tradition* an expressive and meaningful ritual path marking the way of those to be baptized as the time came for entering the waters of Baptism.[53] Three questions drawn from the profession of faith were asked, each beginning the same way: "Do you believe . . . ?" The candidate would declare "I believe" three times, professing separately faith in Father, Son, and Holy Spirit, with each affirmation followed by Baptism in water.[54] The ceremony also included the bishop's laying his hand upon the candidates, anointing each of them with holy oil, and sealing each candidate on the forehead. The bishop would give each "the kiss" and say, "The Lord be with you," and the one sealed responds, "And with thy spirit."[55] The *Catechism of the Catholic Church* indicates that "in the first centuries Confirmation generally comprised one single celebration with Baptism, forming with it a 'double sacrament,' according to the expression of St. Cyprian" (CCC, 1290).[56] The way of initiation[57] would lead the newly baptized toward partaking of the Body and Blood of Christ with and within the Christian community for the first time.[58]

From earlier sources such as the Acts of the Apostles we see several references to the postbaptismal communal life (2:42; 9:9; 16:5, 34). In the early centuries, the period after Baptism was one of immersion into the Christian life. All during the spiritual journey of Christian initiation, the community had played an essential and constitutive role in the person's preparation for and ultimate participation in the life of the Church. The postbaptismal period, therefore, truly occupied the rest of the lives of the newly baptized. The *Apostolic Tradition* points out that each newly baptized was to "be zealous to perform good works and to please God, living righteously, devoting himself to the Church, performing the things which he has learnt, advancing in the service of God."[59]

Applying today's terms, we might say that evangelization and catechesis, immersed within a gradual coming to faith, were rich in ritual expression and nurtured by the support and witness of the baptized. With the support of the Church community, coupled with the extensive preparation that had preceded Baptism, the newly baptized, or *neophytes*, were well prepared to do their share in living and clinging firmly to the faith into which they had now been fully initiated. They would be integrated into the community of the faithful, the already baptized.[60] Catechesis lived *through* the catechumenal experience and the immersion of the baptized into the life and care of the community.

The catechumenate today calls for "a suitable catechesis . . . planned to be gradual and complete in its coverage, accommodated to the liturgical year, and solidly supported by celebrations of the word. This catechesis leads the catechumens not only to an appropriate acquaintance with dogmas and precepts but also to a profound sense of the mystery of salvation in which they desire to participate" (RCIA, 75.1). Essential are communal support and participation, well-formed catechists, the calming and guiding hand of sponsors, the embrace of prayer, ritual participation, and a developing Christian witness. All of these elements combine in the formation of persons coming to faith through engagement with the welcoming community of faith, now re-formed and renewed in service to the greater Church.

The blend of belonging and believing, coupled with discernment of and by candidates as they sought to enter saving waters of new life in Christ, provides a strong impression of early catechumenal practice. Our journey into history can refresh our understanding not only of believing and belonging to the community of the Church but also of discerning the depth and power of our baptismal call (even if we were baptized years ago), including when unexpected circumstances jostle us. Yet our "look within" is not a search for a "spiritual selfie," for God is our center.

Calming discernment may move us—perhaps for the first time in a long time for some of us—toward inspirited sacramental participation.

Even slight movement of the prism of life can alter one's perspective. Despite decades of serving and seeking to advance catechesis, I am drawn periodically to ponder anew what I am called to become rather than just what I am called to do. As the years have added up, making me more recognizable now by virtue of the distinguished title "senior," the former concern seems to have taken hold of me. Discerning future steps seems to occupy more of my prayer and conversation. It is almost too easy to assume my "belonging" to the Church after so many years of life within the community of faith, so I seek to guard against complacency. However, the fresh relief of sacred waters—whether experienced through sprinkling with holy water at Easter or making the sign of the cross with holy water upon entering a church—encourages ever-evolving discipleship, especially through reception of the Eucharist. Indeed, "drawing out the Gospel kerygma of Jesus" (GDC, 102) characterizes catechesis that lasts.

Accompanying this discernment is reliance on the assurance of faith, simultaneously gift and challenge. When I profess faith, what am I stating beyond (or, rather, from behind) words? Even with the inadequacy of words, how do I express and "hold fast to the hope that lies before us" (Heb 6:18) with people whose distance from the community of faith has grown over the years? What *is* my witness when I sense "dying" but others within my complex of personal relationships politely reject what the Church offers? A calm demeanor, nurtured by the whispering breath of the Spirit, can be a starting point for sustaining hope within these relationships.

What gift of wisdom might be making its way to you from the voices of others, offering witness to dying coupled with witness to rising—voices that reflect the Paschal Mystery in faith, hope, and love? The Paschal Mystery of Christ's Passion, Death, Resurrection, and Ascension sustains our belief and strengthens us in hope in the midst of life's changes. Jesus is with us. He is especially present to us in the sacraments, through which we encounter again and again his saving love, made present here and now. His invitation to participate in the saving mystery of his own Passion, Death, and Resurrection is treasure enough for us. The Spirit lives deep within us, the community of faith, beckoning us to come to Christ *and* to be Christ to others—others who yearn for wisdom through life's dyings and risings, humbly straining for the embrace that only God can provide.

Discernment can set us right on the way to sources that sustain us, especially within the Church's ministry of evangelization and catechesis. It is more than the historical record of the Church and some highlights of catechetical history that inform us. Respect for our past and perhaps curiosity invite us to enter into other ages alive through faith handed on. The blended cultural witness of generations to which we are connected through Christ and the Church helps to sustain our spirit as time goes on. Refreshed by the simplest of motions—approaching and touching blessed water in a font and then slowly making the Sign of the Cross in the name of the Father, the Son, and the Holy Spirit—may we "be zealous to perform good works and to please God, living righteously, devoting [ourselves] to the Church, performing the things which [we have learned], advancing in the service of God."[61]

Reflection Questions

1. Why do you think people of the early Church sought out belonging to the Christian community, despite the risks involved in doing so? What made Christianity so attractive?

2. Is there a scripture verse that you read here that might lead you to further reflection?

3. How do themes such as belonging, believing, and discerning, so vibrant in the catechumenate, foster your connection to these early centuries of Christianity?

4. How might an experience of your life offer to another an example of living, dying, or rising in Christ?

5. What does the growth of the early catechumenate imply about parish participation today?

6. What makes handing on faith such a rewarding and joyful ministry?

7. How might catechesis today be enriched by the Church's historical experience of the catechumenate?

8. What do you see as one of the primary benefits of the catechumenate in the early Church?

Changing Times, Changing Catechumenate

An important adjustment for the Church, now three centuries young, occurred during the time of the Roman emperor Constantine in AD 313. That year's Edict of Milan, to which his name is linked, offered religious toleration. Little more than a decade later, Constantine, who remained unbaptized until near his death many years later, would call the Ecumenical Council of Nicaea (325). Historian Christopher Bellitto states that "he initially presided over it, held the gathering in his own palace (in present-day Turkey), addressed the members, and at the meeting's conclusion confirmed and then promulgated its decrees."[62] The Creed of that council, coupled with the determinations of the later Council of Constantinople (381), produced the familiar creedal statement of faith professed by Christians to this day. Constantinople would become a major Church center.

Although Christianity could breathe more easily due to official toleration of the faith, this was an age of significant theological disputation. It was also an age of significant theological development. Such fourth-century figures as Athanasius (ca. 295–373) and Basil the Great (ca. 330–379) are examples of vigilant thinkers whose efforts left a longstanding imprint on theological understanding. Both vigorously promoted the teaching of the Council of Nicaea.[63] They and others introduced wellsprings of theological development that would undergird the faith for centuries to come.

One might identify the era as marked by an expanding diversity of heresies that challenged, modified, or rejected some of the Church's fundamental and still-developing understanding of the Trinity, the Incarnation, Jesus Christ, Mary (Theotokos, or God Bearer), and the Church. For example, the Council of Nicaea (325) dealt with controversy over the divinity of the Son of God. The Creed of Nicaea asserted and taught "that the Son of God is 'begotten, not made, of the same substance (*homoousios*) as the Father,' and condemned Arius, who had affirmed that the Son of God 'came to be from things that were not' and that he was 'from another substance' than that of the Father" (CCC, 465).[64]

Decisive judgments do not always signal the end of controversy or debate. Arian support continued, and in 381 the first Council of Constantinople condemned the heresy. "Under the inspiration of Basil, the Creed asserted that the Holy Spirit was equal in honor and glory to the Father and the Son, and thus fully divine."[65] This council offered "the first formal declaration of the doctrine of the Trinity."[66]

A half-century later, in 431, the Council of Ephesus, under the guiding hand of Cyril of Alexandria (d. 444), would refute the heresy of Nestorianism (Nestorius was bishop of Constantinople). This "heresy regarded Christ as a human person joined to the divine person of God's Son" (CCC, 466). But if that were the case, could Mary be Theotokos? The teaching of the Council of Ephesus affirmed "that Mary truly became the Mother of God by the human conception of the Son of God in her womb" (CCC, 466; cf. CCC, 495). Only twenty years later, another council would be called, this time in Chalcedon. In arriving at its own clarifications, this council looked back on the work since Nicaea.[67] Historian Christopher Bellitto offers this assessment: "The major doctrinal statement by Chalcedon reasserted a fundamental Christian mystery: Jesus is one person with two natures joined together in a hypostatic union."[68]

Other councils would follow over the centuries; however, the context here is the toleration the Church enjoyed after the Edict of Milan. But toleration would lead to something more. A 380 decree by Emperor Theodosius I essentially established Christianity as the religion of the empire: "We desire that all peoples who fall beneath the sway of our imperial clemency should profess the faith which we believe has been communicated by the Apostle Peter to the Romans and maintained in its traditional form to the present day."[69]

It is perhaps predictable that toleration combined with freedom may lead to relaxation. Dujarier notes that "defective motivation for conversion constitutes the most typical and most grave deviation of this period."[70] People might choose to seek membership in the Church for a variety of motives unattached to matters of faith.

Augustine of Hippo (354–430) tells us that a person might have "insincere intentions."[71] At the same time, this great theologian and friend of catechists sees questionable motives as an opening for inviting the person to move toward reshaping his or her intent. In his extended response to a questioner (about whom more will be said shortly), Augustine also advises that, depending on the circumstance, it may be necessary at some point "to reprove him, but courteously and gently as befits an inexperienced newcomer, and then . . . to give him a glowing account of the goal of Christian teaching and its truth."[72] In this way the perceptive guide can positively influence the interaction.[73]

Of course, new challenges emerged for the Church of the fourth century, not the least of which had to do with the meaning and experience of conversion and sustaining ongoing community support in an era functionally different from the preceding one of intolerance and periodic persecution. Earlier centuries had yielded the witness of many early martyrs and saints, a testimony to faith that would not be surrendered, regardless of potential dire consequences. But the landscape for catechumenal formation changed after the advance of religious toleration. People behave differently in freer times than they do when oppressed, when life is threatened and death may be near.

By becoming a catechumen, one could identify oneself as Christian.[74] We can imagine the kinds of challenges for evangelization that faced the Church. For example, what did belonging mean, now that it was less worrisome to adhere to Christ and the Church? How demanding would discernment about deciding to pursue membership in the Church (for the right reasons) and discipleship in Christ have been? Were people running with the tide and "signing up" for the catechumenate only to delay further participation? Sometimes people put off for some time the reception of Baptism, which came with "rigorous obligations."[75] A few weeks prior to their Baptism, John Chrysostom (ca. 344–407) exhorted catechumens in Antioch this way: "Put away from you all you have done up to now, and prove with your whole heart that you are through with the past."[76]

Changing times brought redirection from the established catechumenal discipline of the previous century toward formation within cultural environments now marked by religious freedom. Historically, the catechumenal discipline developed with emphasis on the symbolic nature of the movement in faith of the candidates (understood here as those catechumens who "had, before Lent, given in their names"[77]). An important observation is provided by Turner, who states that (in Jerusalem) "the long period of formation culminated with the inscription of names."[78] The indication of a lengthy formation reinforces the need to avoid broad generalizations about the duration and character of the catechumenal discipline. Turner notes that for the Church in Jerusalem, "formation may have lasted over a year."[79]

The season of Lent sharpened the task of providing faith formation meaningful in both breadth and depth as permitted within its limited time frame.[80] "Lent was a time of doctrinal and moral formation."[81] Both the Creed and (in some places) the Lord's Prayer were presented to the candidates during Lent.[82] Cyril of Jerusalem's (ca. 315–ca. 387) Lenten teaching consisted of eighteen catecheses,[83] primarily dealing with elements of the Creed. Preceding them is a *procatechesis*, a type of introduction that, among other purposes, welcomes the candidates. The hearts of catechists today might sing as they make Cyril's injunction their own: "Be eager to attend the catechetical classes."[84] Cyril would also say, "With Hope invincible for your sandals and with Faith the guest of your heart, you may pass through the enemy's lines and enter into the house of the Lord. Prepare your heart for the reception of teaching and the fellowship in the holy Mysteries."[85] Well north of Jerusalem, in Antioch, John Chrysostom would tell the candidates just a few weeks before Baptism, "We also appeal to our catechetical instructions because it is necessary that even in our absence the echo of our words resounds in your souls."[86]

During the time of the Second Vatican Council, theologian Walter Burghardt, S.J., addressed fourth- and early fifth-century patristic catechetics (with regard to adults) through the lenses of "doctrine, Scripture, liturgy, and psychology."[87] He writes that "when the Fathers of the Church are giving religious instruction, they are consistently concerned with doctrine. I mean, there is a message, an idea, a conceptual content that has to be communicated."[88] In his section on scripture, Burghardt says, "Doctrine is transmitted, and instruction is made effective, in a twin context and by twin instruments. The context and the instruments are Scripture and the liturgy."[89] Later, he pens an observation familiar to the experience of many catechetical leaders today: "Religious instruction leads to liturgy, and religious instruction stems from liturgy—this is basic to early Christianity."[90] In the psychology section, he concludes with an examination of Augustine, who "knows, above all, the revolutionary power of love."[91] This fundamental point must permeate all catechesis.

In writing about the catechumenate of the fourth century, scholar of initiation Edward Yarnold, S.J., notes, "Many of the teachings and practices of the Church were kept secret from outsiders; this cult of secrecy became known to later scholars as the *Disciplina Arcani*. It was not until the Lent preceding baptism that a candidate would begin to receive systematic instruction about these secret matters."[92] Egeria (ca. 380), a sister from Spain on pilgrimage, informed her community of some prebaptismal practices in Jerusalem in the late fourth century. She notes:

> Ladies, my sisters. . . . All those who are to be baptized, both men and women, sit closely around the bishop, while the godmothers and godfathers stand there; and indeed all of the people who wish to listen may enter and sit down, provided they are of the faithful. . . . In the course of these days everything is taught not only about the Resurrection but concerning the body of faith. This is called catechetics.
>
> When five weeks of instruction have been completed, they then receive the Creed. He explains the meaning of each of the phrases of the Creed in the same way he explained Holy Scripture, expounding first the literal and then the spiritual sense. In this fashion the Creed is taught.[93]

Lent offered a heightened spiritual context including rich liturgical and ritual expression for catechumenal formation in faith. With the benefit of exorcisms, prayer, instruction, godparents, the handing over of the Creed and in some places the Lord's Prayer, and more, those to be baptized continued on the way to the water bath.[94] Following the satisfactory completion of this intensive preparation, one was considered ready for Baptism and full sharing in the Eucharist, which took place during the Paschal Vigil.

The setting for Baptism in Jerusalem would have been the Church of the Holy Sepulchre. "Under that roof Egeria witnessed the baptisms over which Cyril very possibly presided."[95] Imagine the darkness of night and the bath to come, the water before you. Imagine being asked if you believed in the Father, and the Son, and the Holy Spirit. How firm might your answer be? A resounding "Yes, I believe"?

Cyril of Jerusalem, preaching about Jesus' Death and Resurrection, tells the newly baptized, "You dipped thrice under the water and thrice rose up again, mystically signifying Christ's three days' burial."[96] We are reminded of the classic passage of Paul's Letter to the Romans, which speaks of Christ's death and the resurrection (cf. Rom 6:5). Burkhard Neunheuser points out in his treatment of the Fathers of the West in the fourth and fifth centuries that

> we must observe above all that what a later period practised as two clearly separate sacraments, baptism and confirmation, constituted then a single structure of sacred acts—one single act of initiation, which is called "baptisma" in the most comprehensive sense of this word. It imparts fellowship with Christ, with his death and resurrection, and therefore regeneration. The dependence of baptism on the death and resurrection of Christ (cf. Rom 6) is mentioned again and again by the Fathers.[97]

The week following the Easter celebration was especially significant for the Christian community for probing the experience of the mysteries, or sacraments. This was a time of *mystagogy*, the postbaptismal catechesis directed toward the newly baptized (neophtyes). Hugh Riley, scholar of patristic mystagogy, puts it this way: "The instruction which is imparted to help the candidate understand the meaning of what is said and what is done in the liturgy of his initiation into the Christian life is called 'mystagogy,' instruction in the meaning of the mysteries."[98]

Two among several essentials of mystagogy are the liturgical celebration itself (not just information about what such a liturgy is) and the neophytes themselves (not just that they were physically present but their experience of the celebration itself, woven into their "real lives").[99] "The candidates themselves, their environment, the church's needs of the present moment against its sociological backdrop, these factors must be calculated by the mystagogue."[100]

Implications of the celebration of the sacraments do not dissipate under the exit sign of a church door; rather, they give shape to witness beyond brick and mortar, witness now residing within the lives of neophytes themselves as well as within those of the entire community of faith. The Advocate is with them.

Mystagogy does not seek seclusion. Today, the *Rite of Christian Initiation of Adults* paints a compelling picture of mystagogy as

> a time for the community and the neophytes together to grow in deepening their grasp of the Paschal Mystery and in making it part of their lives through meditation on the Gospel, sharing in the eucharist, and doing the works of charity. . . .
>
> The neophytes are, as the term "mystagogy" suggests, introduced into a fuller and more effective understanding of mysteries through the Gospel message they have learned and above all through their experience of the sacraments they have received. (RCIA, 244–245)

The liturgical experience is essential and foundational for any mystagogical enterprise.

A significant catechetical source, the *National Directory for Catechesis*, addresses mystagogy as well, stating that "in the broader sense, mystagogy represents the Christian's lifelong education and formation in the faith. By analogy it signifies the continuous character of catechesis in the life of the Christian. Conversion to Christ is a lifelong process that should be accompanied at every stage by a vital catechesis that leads Christians on their journey towards holiness" (NDC, 35D). Such a recognition encourages living the call of Baptism one's whole life long, with Word and sacrament shaping the way of faith for all the baptized.

Conversion does not come with rose-colored glasses. Mystagogical guides today are wisdom seekers and resurrection thinkers who see victory in the risen Christ, the One who conquers death.[101] "Death is swallowed up in victory. Where, O death, is your victory? Where, O death, is your sting?" (1 Cor 15:54–55).[102]

The mystagogical efforts of the fourth century solidified the neophytes' experience of Christian initiation. Homilies of several Church Fathers of the time were inspiring mystagogical presentations that enabled neophytes to relate their experience of sacramental initiation to the mysteries into which they had been initiated. Riley points out that these Fathers "are dead serious, and their catecheses are for concrete candidates wrestling with concrete problems of the Christian life."[103]

Such Fathers as Cyril of Jerusalem, Ambrose of Milan, John Chrysostom, and Theodore of Mopsuestia[104] guide the way of mystagogical reflection on sacred mysteries in the here and now, with a context for mystagogy in the community of faith. Their rich reliance on scripture accompanies the neophytes on their journey from the font (e.g., Cyril says, "'Baptized into Christ' and 'clothed with Christ,' you have been shaped to the likeness of the Son of God"[105]).

The term *mystagogy* and its inherited meanings are not new to the catechetical life of the Church.[106] In the late fourth century, Cyril of Jerusalem identified his preaching to the newly baptized as "these daily instructions on the mysteries."[107] These postbaptismal homilies form the "Mystagogical Catecheses,"[108] a series of five homilies he delivered during Easter week in the Church of the Holy Sepulchre. In speaking of the anointing with chrism after Baptism, Cyril notes that those baptized "have become anointed ones by receiving the sign of the Holy Spirit. Since you are images of Christ, all the rites carried out over you have a symbolic meaning."[109]

The second mystagogical catechesis concludes this way: "I urge you to keep it in your memory that I, too, though unworthy, may be able to say of you: 'I love you because at all times you keep me in mind and maintain the tradition I handed on to you.' [Cf. 1 Cor 11:2]. God, 'who has presented you as those who have come alive from the dead,' is able to grant to you to 'walk in newness of life,' because His is the glory and the power, now and forever. Amen."[110]

The mystagogies of Ambrose of Milan (ca. 339–397), the only one in the West of the group named above, are found within his *De sacramentis* (*The Sacraments*) and *De mysteriis* (*The Mysteries*).[111] In his second mystagogical sermon, Ambrose says this (and more) to the newly baptized of the experience of Baptism:

> You were asked: "Do you believe in God the Father almighty?" You said: "I do believe," and you dipped, that is: you were buried. Again you were asked: "Do you believe in our Lord Jesus Christ and in

His cross?" You said: "I do believe," and you dipped. So you were also buried together with Christ. For who is buried with Christ rises again with Christ. A third time you were asked: "Do you believe also in the Holy Spirit?" You said: "I do believe," you dipped a third time, so that the threefold confession absolved the multiple lapse of the higher life.[112]

Also of interest in Ambrose is the inclusion of a ritual of foot washing. His reference is Jesus' exchange with Peter over the washing of his feet (see Jn 13:6–10). Ambrose notes that

> the Roman Church does not follow this custom, although we take her as our prototype, and follow her rites in everything. . . . You must know that this washing is a mystery and sanctification. . . .
>   We follow the apostle Peter himself; it is to his devotion that we cling. . . . Consider his faith. When he refused at first, this was because of his humility. The submission he made afterwards came from devotion and faith.[113]

Ambrose guides his hearers, elevating awareness and understanding of the way of life in Christ. At one point he urges his hearers to "open your ears and enjoy the good odor of eternal life which has been breathed upon you by the grace of the sacraments."[114] Ambrose probes, for example, the neophytes' Saturday vigil "Opening" experience before Baptism,[115] recalling the scriptural account in Mark 7 in which Jesus heals a man who is deaf and has a speech disorder. Jesus "looked up to heaven and groaned, and said to him, '*Ephphatha!*' (that is, 'Be opened!')" (Mk 7:34). In our own day the celebrant's symbolic touch of the elect's ears and unopened lips is accompanied by these same words that linger within lives spiritually touched. "Opened" lives formed in faith echo God's saving Word.

The RCIA reminds us that the newly baptized "have truly been renewed in mind, tasted more deeply the sweetness of God's word, received the fellowship of the Holy Spirit, and grown to know the goodness of the Lord" (RCIA, 245). These words do not define a distant static memory, now safely stored. Rather, there is more to the movement of living faith. "Out of this experience, which belongs to Christians and increases as it is lived, they derive a new perception of the faith, of the Church, and of the world" (RCIA, 245). We live as a community woven together around the table of the Lord, a field of well-rooted seedlings, watered and fed as one.

These mystagogues strove to encourage their listeners to live according to the way of Christ.[116] They provided mystagogical interpretations during a time "when people were so sensitive to symbols that the liturgy could be left to speak for itself, even before the preacher had given any explanation."[117] Indeed, one might identify this era as the Great Age of Mystagogical Catechesis.

What we see here and benefit from today is a rich embodiment of holistic catechesis, firmly rooted and plentifully watered over time. Mark Francis, C.S.V., observes that "there is an increasing interest in returning to an ancient form of catechesis known as mystagogy in order to recapture the power of ritual and symbol."[118] In addition, we recall the six tasks of catechesis identified in chapter 4: (1) promoting knowledge of the faith, (2) liturgical education, (3) moral formation, (4) teaching to pray, (5) education for community life, and (6) missionary initiation (GDC, 85–87; see NDC, 20).[119] All are important not only for defining but also for refining the expansive catechetical agenda, including during catechumenal formation. The catechumenal discipline provides a clear opportunity for informed doctrinal understanding along with the lasting support of sponsors, catechists, and the broader parish community.

We might apply the ancient phrase *lex orandi* (the law of praying), *lex credendi* (the law of believing) to help us summarize the rich liturgical-catechetical experience briefly treated here: "The law of prayer is the law of faith: the Church believes as she prays. Liturgy is a constitutive element of the holy and living Tradition" (CCC, 1124). There is a unity to Catholic faith and life, one to which we give witness by carrying out *lex vivendi* (the law of living) in our daily interactions and activities, regardless of how insignificant they may seem to be, for it is neither recognition nor momentary prosperity that we seek. "Children, let us love not in word or speech but in deed and truth" (1 Jn 3:18).

A Lasting Voice: Augustine

A persistent voice for catechesis in the late fourth and early fifth centuries was that of Augustine of Hippo (354–430). Augustine, who was baptized by Ambrose of Milan, is considered one of the preeminent theologians in the history of the Church. Also a philosopher and catechist, he is widely known for his *Confessions*, *The City of God*, and numerous other works. He is held by many to be without peer as a theologian in the first millennium, and his contributions to the Church's theological development rest alongside those of Thomas Aquinas, who lived about eight centuries later.

Augustine preached in a homily to the newly baptized in the fifth century, "Yet faith does crave instruction."[120] His impact on catechumenal development is carefully presented and assessed by William Harmless, S.J., in his *Augustine and the Catechumenate*, which offers fresh perspectives on Augustine's vast contributions to the life of the Church. He writes that "Augustine's mystagogy, like that of his contemporaries, drew together various threads: (1) liturgical actions and words, (2) scriptural images and themes, (3) analogies drawn from nature or culture."[121] He points out that Augustine "stood closer to Chrysostom both in timetable and in emphasis" than to the other mystagogues named here.[122]

For the catechist, no less a contribution is Augustine's classic work on catechesis, *De catechizandis rudibus* (*Instructing Beginners in Faith*, also identified as *The First Catechetical Instruction*).[123] *De catechizandis rudibus* consists of twenty-seven chapters and is no more than about seventy-five pages of standard book length. When placed alongside Augustine's library of works and those of so many others, this brief practical guide from the early fifth century may disappear on shelves bursting with patristic teaching, preaching, and moral discourse. However, as Gerard S. Sloyan notes, "No one, actually, who teaches religion can afford to be unfamiliar with Augustine's uncanny analysis of this apostolate."[124] *De catechizandis rudibus* invites us to explore and apply Augustine's advice to Deogratias, a deacon from Carthage; Deogratias sought Augustine's assistance in understanding how to deal with persons inquiring about coming into the Church who were not yet catechumens.[125]

At the core of *De catechizandis rudibus* is the constancy of God's love,[126] a point that is woven through the work and that cannot be overstated. It undergirds all that Augustine sets out to do in advising Deogratias. God's gift of love, given in Christ, is foundational to Augustine's response and essential to the spirit of the catechist. Here are three examples:

- "Now, what stronger reason could there be for the Lord's coming than that God intended to reveal his love among us and prove it with great force?"[127]

- "For there is nothing that invites another's love more than to take the initiative in loving."[128]

- "Thus, before all else, Christ came so that people might learn how much God loves them, and might learn this so that they would catch fire with love for him who first loved them, and so that they would also love their neighbor as he commanded and showed by his example."[129]

Indeed, the core theme of God's magnanimous love offers a context for what Deogratias and all who catechize are to be and not just what they are to do. So we should not be surprised when Augustine proposes that one should find joy in offering her- or himself to another, even when self-assessment would tend to make one think poorly of his or her own efforts.[130]

Augustine advises Deogratias about making adjustments in consideration of people's backgrounds.[131] *De catechizandis rudibus*, as an original "guide" (a term commonly used in today's parish and school catechetical programs for children), had no reduced or colorful pages surrounded by teaching suggestions. Rather, the "guide" was a living witness to faith who was formed in Christ and supported by the gift of Augustine's wise and lasting counsel. One guides, alive in Christ and afire in faith.

Augustine's response to Deogratias in *De catechizandis rudibus* would impact catechesis and catechetical development for centuries to come, and one can still see today its underlying influence on contemporary catechetical methodologies. Augustine deals with the "how" and the "what" of catechesis: method and content. One sees Augustine's passionate faith and catechetical experience within this brief work, which is set out in two parts. The first part deals with a variety of essentials: for example, dealing with one's own limitations, dealing with different types of candidates (including nonresponsive listeners), probing the motivations of the inquirer, and looking out for the welfare of the inquirer.

The second part includes two catecheses of different lengths through which Augustine shares the story of salvation in Christ. Augustine tells Deogratias to begin with creation, move through the Old Testament, and to include the history of the Church.[132] He weaves a scripturally rich tapestry that moves through "six ages of this world,"[133] reaching a climax in the sixth age, that of Christ, now and forever. Augustine identifies, as Tertullian did before him, "the blood of martyrs"[134] in treating the Church. His words ring true 1,600 years later.

Augustine notes that a "newcomer" who asserted belief in what had been shared and willingness to live accordingly should "without doubt be marked with the sign of the cross in the usual way and treated according to the custom of the Church."[135] Turner points out that "catechumens were also given salt, either as a symbol of preservation or as a foretaste of the eucharist."[136]

Catechetical scholar Anne Marie Mongoven, O.P., identifies Augustine's method this way: "(1) Tell the story. (2) Explain the doctrine in the story. (3) Ask questions to check understanding. (4) Exhort to right behavior."[137] Mongoven's clear descriptors are a substantial aid to any catechist in any age. Years earlier, Joseph Collins stated that Augustine's approach had "three main stages: *narration* of biblical and historical events, *explanation* of the doctrines therein contained, and the *exhortation* or application to life and conduct."[138] Although it is tempting to view Augustine's contribution as merely a methodological approach (however it is described), we would do so at great loss. For Augustine continues to invite us into the Christ moment.[139]

Perhaps one way of restating Deogratias's question of Augustine for today could be: "What am I to do? I am unsure of how to proceed and even of what to say. I am concerned that whatever I do falls far short of what is needed. Those before me seem so bored. Please, help me!" This may sound all too familiar to many of us. It is wise, then, to return to why we do what we do.

The context for what concerned Deogratias concerns us still today. "From evangelization, completed with the help of God, come the faith and initial conversion that cause a person to feel called away from sin and drawn into the mystery of God's love" (RCIA, 37). Perhaps we need to be reminded of the many ways to live as witnesses to this mystery, especially through the celebration of the sacraments with and within the community of faith, the Church. Your witness may be the salve through which a newcomer begins to be drawn to God's love and care, for grace abounds.

Perhaps we need to consider our own motives in identifying ourselves as Christian. Key questions for us become: What moves us to continue to stay faithful to Christ and the Church? What value or benefit is there in such a faith affirmation? How might you imagine your challenge to remain faithful in discipleship if you lived in a society that offered no religious toleration? What keeps you Catholic? In other words, what influences your continuing to belong to the Catholic Church?

Reclaimed at the Table of the Lord

One compelling feature of reflection on sacred mystery—of mystagogical reflection—is its extraordinary blend of elements that reach beyond the familiar. Through the grace of God, these elements come together within the community's expressed faith via active liturgical expression, leading to a heightened sense of sacred mystery and, within that experience, well-rooted understanding. Think of the power of scripture and faith professed. Think of sign and symbol, movement and gesture, ritual action and silence, song and more.

Whereas mystagogy incorporates "my" memory of a powerful experience, it is more than that and more than the collective memory of my fellow parishioners. Rather, it offers to all the faithful the opportunity to embrace anew the Word proclaimed in scripture and the sacramental events in their lives. We sense a communal convergence—in Christ, our home, present in his Spirit—lived now through the sacramental experience of persons gathered as one. The participation of the believing community, gathered in the worshiping assembly from a diversity of cultural (see CCC, 1204) and experiential milieus, is a key element here. The invitation to enter into the Paschal Mystery of the Risen Lord leads to discovery of what is expected of us. Our yes propels us to the vigor and rigor of discipleship as we are reclaimed at the table of the Lord.

Mystagogy resists passivity as it discloses deepening faith not for one or a few but through the ongoing witness for all the faithful, stewards of God's love. Our words and actions of praise and thanks to the Father continue to center us in the Eucharist, "a sacrifice of praise in thanksgiving for the work of creation" (CCC, 1359). Lives that "say" amen confirm such a posture. Mystagogy invites our continuing surrender to Christ as we forge a path with others (belonging) and assert enthusiastic acceptance of what we profess (believing). Our decision-making in this regard is neither aimless nor mindless. As Pope emeritus Benedict XVI wrote, "The mature fruit of mystagogy is an awareness that one's life is being progressively transformed by the holy mysteries being celebrated" (SCa, 64.). The experience of mystagogy leads us to Eucharist and leads us from Eucharist, "the heart of Christian life for the whole Church" (NDC, 36A3).[140]

We carefully discern and reflect on challenges to faith and to life (to "faith-life") not only for ourselves individually but also within and for the Church, the community of faith. Prayer, meditation, and conversation help us to forge new paths of allegiance and alliance. Daily doses of the realities of life (life changed and seen through paschal lenses of living, dying, and rising) contextualize for us why we seek to live in the first place as we move beyond compartments of inner security that offer only seclusion. In dying with Christ we find that life is not without purpose, for that would be no life at all but only momentary existence. In our daily "rising" we live in hope, faithful to the One who never abandons us: "It is Christ in you, the hope for glory" (Col 1:27).

Mystagogy moves us to witness to this reality, which becomes a norm over time within hearts seized by the Word of God and relationships formed in Christ. We praise with unmuted voices the one true God of all creation. Christ the Redeemer lives! The Spirit—the Advocate—abides! Mystagogy secures new depths of meaning when limited understanding might seem at first sufficient but clearly is not. Craig Satterlee offers an important clarification of the meaning of the term *explaining* in relation to mystagogical preaching: "probing, deepening, intensifying, and illuminating rather than defining and making plain."[141]

The bottom line: Cherish the sacramental encounter within the community of faith, especially as you experience the Cross of Christ as your joy and his Resurrection as your hope. Do not resist entering into the experience of sacred mystery through the sacraments. Strengthen and stretch the Church through new layers of witness; make your life a testimony to the Word of God visited anew through the experience of sacred mystery.

Our expressed commitment to catechetical ministry confirms reason for belief and ultimately gives voice to our creedal profession that carries us through familiar words into the life-changing power of the Gospel and the sacraments as we catechize. Verbal explanation alone is insufficient; hearing alone is insufficient; liturgical nonparticipation as a "Sunday observer" is clearly insufficient. Rather, the declarations of the heart—"I believe" and "We believe"—are part of the sturdy fabric of our spoken and unspoken witness to Christ and his Church. Catechesis, and liturgical catechesis especially, weave information and intellectual meaning with the benefit of many "languages" of faith. This movement is often a first step in reclaiming Catholic identity through the New Evangelization as people probe their memories for what they may have left behind years ago. Although conscious awareness of our forebears in faith may at times escape our testimony, we can be confident that lives formed today through sacred mystery become their own faithful witness. This is one essential source of our hope for the future.

Catechesis invites us to embrace images of hope across a wide swath of generations and cultures. We are not alone as we seek to see Christ in others. "Hope does not disappoint," Paul tells us, "because the love of God has been poured out into our hearts through the holy Spirit that has been given to us" (Rom 5:5). A few centuries later, Augustine of Hippo would write to Laurence the wisdom seeker that "love cannot exist without hope nor hope without love, nor can either exist without faith."[142]

As we look to the coming ages, we remember with humble spirit the timeless words of 1 Peter: "But you are 'a chosen race, a royal priesthood, a holy nation, a people of his own, so that you may announce the praises' of him who called you out of darkness into his wonderful light. Once you were 'no people' but now you are God's people; you 'had not received mercy' but now you have received mercy" (1 Pt 2:9–10). Thanks be to God!

Reflection Questions

1.   What does our history teach you about what you believe and how the New Evangelization might benefit from your faith witness?

2.   What does our history teach us about inviting Catholics who are distant from the Church to find their way back to this community of faith? About discerning active reengagement within the Church?

3.   What do you think might have been the response of young adults in the early Church when belonging seemed too difficult? What worries might they have had?

4.   Do you ever imagine how you might have "come to faith" as an adult in the early Church? What might your discernment have been like?

5.   What do you see as the benefit of a gradual approach for seeking membership in the Church?

6.   Why does the Church need you? Why do you need the Church?

7.   What is "new" this week about the New Evangelization in your life?

8.   What do you do between celebrations of the Eucharist? How does the Eucharist "carry" you all week long?

9.   What societal pressures or opinions of others close to you make you uneasy about discussing matters of faith? What catechetical topics silence you? Why?

10. What "deaths" might be surrounding you today? Who encourages you by their witness to living faith? How?

6

SPANNING THE WAY
Catechesis through the Middle Ages

Beloved, let us love one another, because love is of God; everyone who loves is begotten by God and knows God. Whoever is without love does not know God, for God is love. . . . No one has ever seen God. Yet, if we love one another, God remains in us, and his love is brought to perfection in us.

This is how we know that we remain in him and he in us, that he has given us of his Spirit.

—1 John 4:7–8, 12–13

What is there to talk about? A thousand years of medieval history? Let's move along."

These questions hint at how catechesis during the Middle Ages might be viewed: as sands descending through a scarred old hourglass on the way to storage in a locker named "Footnotes of Catechesis." However, our catechetical timepiece is running still; what we make of this time along the way is up to us. I cannot help but wonder how our catechetical heirs a thousand years hence might assess our era. What would we want them to hold as distinctive about catechetical efforts of our age? Our high points and low points? Will our age even matter?

It seems to me that the period from about AD 500 to 1500 is sometimes considered as a broad valley resting between the catechumenal peaks of earlier centuries and the mountains of printed resources that emerged from the time of the Reformation and the Council of Trent. These Middle Ages[1] do not provide us with a continuously rising scaffold of ecclesiastical-catechetical high points. Some might even suggest that these centuries offer no more than a rickety catechetical bridge to be traversed along the way to better locales.

Let us look beyond the limitations of such images. We belong to the Church of the ages behind us, here now, and to come: cherished children of God, alive in the Spirit. Try as we might, none of us can bypass the flow of God's gift of time. As we will see, movement through these thousand years did not come without changes for catechesis.

In his assessment of catechesis from *before* the Middle Ages, Josef Jungmann, S.J., renowned scholar of liturgy and catechesis, points out a close link between catechesis and liturgy: "An active participation in the liturgy was on the whole the most desirable way in which the individual Christian and the Christian community were able to acquire the necessary religious knowledge. The liturgy, the forms of which were clearly recognized and the language of which was understood, was in a certain sense a continuation of catechesis and a substitute for those who had already been baptized as infants." Jungmann also indicates that "for the children of Christian families the parents were the catechists in the true sense of the word."[2]

I hold up for commendation in this chapter adults who kept the fire of faith alive, including parents and others who looked after children and their many needs during often unpredictable times. Love for children shone through work and the wisdom that home (however that is defined) can provide.

My mother worked for years at home and later for a local town. My father worked for decades in a large New York City bakery. I remember him worrying more than usual about providing for our family during a lengthy strike. I recall my mother's endless struggle to care for my father during his (and our family's) years of affliction with Alzheimer's disease. Neither realized it, but they were my informal catechists for "adult faith formation." Their lifelong spoken and unspoken lesson plan of Christian discipleship was of love, faith, family, community, and steadfast resolve. Perhaps this is one reason why I claim relation to "commoner" families of centuries gone by.

The interpretation for catechesis that I offer here is informed by both historical understanding of the Middle Ages[3] and the reality that people of any age are shaped and formed as human beings made in the image and likeness of God: "Then God said: Let us make human beings in our image, after our likeness" (Gn 1:26; see also Gn 5:1).

Each of us lives through and builds on common human experiences: for example, of birth and our first belonging; of nurture; of learning and teaching; of trial and travail; of correction; of joy. Whether raised by married or single parents, guardians or stepparents, siblings or godparents, grandparents or other caregivers, we experience human interaction from our earliest days. As time goes on, our experiences demonstrate even more how and why we belong to the Church and what and why we believe. These are often our first catechetical lessons. Gripped by faith, we may find ourselves discerning life changes as we live, die, and rise through times of rejoicing and adversity. Our experience of adversity may occur in the midst of another's rejoicing, or vice versa, including during shifts in the catechetical life of the Church.

For example, a groundswell of factors contributed to catechetical renewal both before and after the Second Vatican Council (treated in chapter 8). Shifts during the past half-century continue to impact catechetical understanding and practice; some are a direct result of the council, and others reflect more recent and related emphases drawn from the New Evangelization. Some were (are) related to theology and doctrinal understanding, others to developing intergenerational approaches for forming adults, families, and children in faith as agents of mission and evangelization.

Significant lay engagement in catechetical ministry and leadership during the last third of the twentieth century reflected the pronouncement of the Second Vatican Council regarding the laity. The laity "to the best of their ability carry on the mission of the whole Christian people in the Church and in the world. . . . They live in the world, that is, they are engaged in each and every work and business of the earth and in the ordinary circumstances of social and family life which, as it were, constitute their very existence" (LG, 31).

Changing the verbs of the last sentence to the past tense gives us a type of summary view of life in the Middle Ages. My modest proposal is that faithful Christian people, guided by the Spirit of God, served before us and serve today as carriers "into" and along the way of faith. This carrying occurs along available pathways for catechesis as shifts occur in the ecclesial environment, regardless of era, including the ups and downs of the centuries that occupy our attention here. Societal and cultural shifts occur periodically and even unexpectedly. Catechesis may have seemed to light up a "faith superhighway" in some centuries, while during others weary wicks of light seem to have struggled to stay afire along windy and winding pathways.

Growth of Infant Baptism

The Middle Ages offer a variety of catechetical topics to explore. The era played host to a number of shifts, linked to the experience and culture of the times, that affected the Church's catechetical landscape. For example, we see reference to dissolution or decline of the catechumenate[4] and to numerous conversions of Germanic and Slavic peoples with limited baptismal preparation.[5] One writer notes that during the medieval period "scripture was completely overshadowed by the minutiae of doctrinal and moral syntheses."[6]

Theologian Charles Gusmer references the efforts of prominent scholars of Christian initiation in addressing the temporal separation of the celebration of the sacraments of Initiation from "a continuum at the Easter Vigil." He identifies "the shortening of the interval between birth and baptism," "the lengthening of the interval between baptism and confirmation," and "the separation of communion from initiation altogether."[7] This change happened over time, not suddenly.

One significant shift that began to settle in midway through the first millennium was the growth of infant Baptism and the resulting impact on sacramental initiation. As Berard Marthaler writes, "After infant baptism became the norm in the West (sometime during the fifth century), the catechumenal structures gradually fell into disuse."[8] However, we are wise to avoid assuming that the Baptism of infants was new in Christian life and practice.[9] The *Catechism of the Catholic Church* indicates that "infant Baptism is an immemorial tradition of the Church. There is explicit testimony to this practice from the second century on, and it is quite possible that, from the beginning of the apostolic preaching, when whole 'households' received baptism, infants may also have been baptized" (CCC, 1252).[10] See, for example, Acts 16:15 and 33, Acts 18:8, and 1 Corinthians 1:16.

In the fifth century, Augustine, who is frequently cited in conjunction with the doctrine of original sin, argued against the teaching of the monk Pelagius, who "held that man could, by the natural power of free will and without the necessary help of God's grace, lead a morally good life; he thus reduced the influence of Adam's fault to bad example" (CCC, 406). Within its presentation on original sin, the *Catechism* references the teaching of St. Paul from his Letter to the Romans. For example, in Romans we read, "Just as through one transgression condemnation came upon all, so through one righteous act acquittal and life came to all" (Rom 5:18; see CCC, 402). A few paragraphs later, the *Catechism* goes on to say that "although it is proper to each individual, original sin does not have the character of a personal fault in any of Adam's descendants" (CCC, 405).[11] We bear an inclination to sin, but we are not forever deprived of God's grace and life, for we place our hope in Christ, Redeemer and Savior.

By Baptism the newly baptized is freed from original sin and personal sins and is made "a new creature" (CCC, 1265; see 2 Cor 5:17), born to "newness of life" (Rom 6:4; see CCC, 1227), now "an adoptive son of the Father, a member of Christ and a temple of the Holy Spirit" (CCC, 1279). He or she "is incorporated into the Church, the Body of Christ, and made a sharer in the priesthood of Christ" (CCC, 1279). When weakened in our personal or work life or when we doubt God's nearness, we can lean on the words of Paul: "Where sin increased, grace overflowed all the more" (Rom 5:20).

During its early centuries the Christian faith was worth pursuing, despite real and perceived risks ranging from periodic persecution in the first three centuries to fear of social rebuff after the Edict of Milan. We look back in admiration at those early evangelization efforts and at households turning to Christ and embracing faith, harboring the not unreasonable assumption that children of these households would grow, along with their parents and siblings, in the habits associated with living as Christians. Although we can reasonably assume that many people strove to live the Way, we may be tempted to imagine an idealized intergenerational atmosphere for "forming disciples." However, another not unreasonable assumption can be made about these early Christians: that among motivators for parents to have infants baptized may have been fear of what was understood to be the dire consequence of failure to pursue Baptism for them—an eternity of life without God.[12]

The expansive growth of infant Baptism came about in the midst of changing religious, cultural, and political conditions. Creeping and sustained barbarian invasions, the fall of the Roman Empire in 476 (less than fifty years after the death of Augustine), the expanding influence and reach of the Church and its leaders, and the rise and growth of monasticism are just some of the factors that helped to define the early Middle Ages. During the late sixth century, St. Gregory the Great (ca. 540–604), a monk who became pope and is revered as a Doctor of the Church, led and served the Church through turbulent and changing times, meeting ecclesial and other needs with a deft and firm hand. Jungmann notes that "his influence on the definitive form of the Roman liturgy was most pronounced."[13]

Less than a hundred years after the mystagogical Fathers, we meet St. Benedict of Nursia (ca. 480–ca. 547), the father of Western monasticism. The Rule of Benedict continues to inspire and shape the lives of many Christians to this day. From Celtic roots we find the practice of developing a "soul friend" relationship. These and other approaches have had lasting impact on many people's spiritual formation in the years since, offering an enriched context for their own catechetical understanding as they experience what it is to be the Church.

Weaving a Tapestry of Life and of Faith

With the advancement of infant Baptism, what became of catechesis?[14] At the end of the fifth century, according to sacramental scholar Joseph

Martos, "Most children were baptized at the yearly Easter celebration but in some places they were baptized soon after birth."[15] We see a shift in perspective with an adjustment in catechetical practice as the role of sponsors/godparents changed from "guarantors of the candidate's faith before baptism," to "guardians of the child's faith after baptism."[16] Godparents bore the important duty of ensuring religious education and moral formation for the child, all in due consideration of the child's salvation.[17]

However, the mother was a key part of the catechetical equation, and not only through oral means, which were standard for catechesis in the early Church. Medieval scholar Didier Lett emphasizes the mother's distinctive responsibility within the family: "The mother took the children to church, showed them the sacred images and statues, taught them the gestures for the prayers."[18] Formation for Christian living was promoted at home. Guy de Bretagne wrote many years ago, "The child lived in a society in which, as Maritain says, the sacral order prevailed. Its first religious initiation was made on its mother's knees."[19]

As for fathers, Didier Lett indicates several examples of their taking on a nurturing role; he makes a comparison at one point to duties that are today regarded as those of fathers.[20] Twenty-first-century fathers actively engaged in their children's daily welfare and nurture can trace roots for such devotion to centuries past. Lett convincingly presents grounds for the presence of "the nuclear family in the earliest medieval centuries."[21] Yet he also points out that for many children, relationships were formed in other ways: "More than a third of all children lived in reconstructed families. This 'circulation' of children in the Middle Ages was reinforced by placement in foster homes, with nurses, or in apprenticeships, by couples separating, and by abandonment."[22] As medieval scholar Shulamith Shahar states, "There is no place for idealization of the life of children in the Middle Ages. . . . Nor was the lot of most adults a happy one."[23]

We can imagine many people—adults and children—experiencing the rhythm of life, seeking to survive day by day, perhaps with little account taken of what is called today "human dignity." Historian Christopher Bellitto notes, "Because their own lives were so fragile, medieval Christians looked to Jesus' passion for consolation, knowing he had suffered, too."[24] As I see it, the cultivation of life was blended with the cultivation of the soil and the cultivation of the soul, "culture" breathing in and out with each motion of bending toward the land and straightening, perhaps a prayer or brief recitation on one's lips. Hardened skin of wearied flesh, with soil lodging under nails affixed to fingers that nurture but do not strike, symbolizes for me the resolve and love of disciples "made in the image and likeness of God," who is, after all, both Lord and landowner. I imagine many unassuming disciples, looking to place one foot ahead of the other, offering experiential witness to the words of Paul to the Corinthians: "For we who live are constantly being given up to death for the sake of Jesus, so that the life of Jesus may be manifested in our mortal flesh" (2 Cor 4:11).

Sacramental formation for children would ordinarily be provided at home or in schools.[25] Esteemed scholar John Elias indicates that "the first distinctively Christian school was the monastic school in the fifth century."[26] And Aubert Clark, O.F.M. Conv., points out that, over time, monastic schools and cathedral schools took the place of the Roman educational system, which succumbed to barbarian invasions.[27] Access to schooling was limited to those fortunate enough to be able to pursue such opportunities.[28] Reed and Prevost state that "in the Middle Ages . . . a woman's best educational opportunity was the convent."[29] They add, "A craftsman's daughter rarely studied at the nunnery, and a serf's daughter almost never. Money, more than social class, was the major reason."[30] Elias notes that "by the eighth century virtually all education in the West, including the conduct of the schools, had become centered in the churches and monasteries. Monasteries were the principal centers for the preservation of learning."[31]

The sixth century saw reliance on parish schools and cathedral (episcopal) schools, which provided pathways to clerical formation for some (not all students chose such a direction).[32] The priest was central to education beyond the home, and common teaching tools used by priests in parish schools were "the psalter and the sacred texts."[33]

More is known about the education of children of the aristocracy, and within the aristocracy, more about that of boys than of girls.[34] Children of the aristocracy had more opportunities than did the far more numerous peasantry, who learned basic foundations in faith from parents and the priest.[35]

Family Engagement and Care

In my estimation, the lay faithful, often hidden in the shadows of the centuries, lived and handed on the gift of faith woven through a sometimes frayed tapestry reflective of the social, political, religious, and cultural tenor of the times. It was not uncommon to rely on family and godparents for formation in faith.

Those whose names are not recorded in history constituted the majority of the population when medieval family structures were taking shape.[36] Illiteracy and difficult living conditions notwithstanding, parents and children continued to belong to the community of faith. Through toil and soil, aristocracy and peasantry, and periods of dramatic change within and beyond the Church (sadly, often for worse rather than for better), Christians carried on.[37]

Generalized assumptions of parental disengagement and neglect of children may sometimes be assumed of this era, especially when one considers the difficulties of the age. Although the complexity of the matter prevents generalization in an opposite direction, it seems to me that some reassessment is in order. Consulted sources[38] provide important information, analysis, and insights about the Middle Ages. However, the interpretation here is derived from my catechetical understanding and related sense of perspective.

In their well-researched book *Children in the Middle Ages*, medieval scholars Danièle Alexandre-Bidon and Didier Lett offer enlightening perspectives in addressing "misunderstanding that has led to the belief in an absence of love and tenderness with regard to children in ancient times."[39] They provide supporting documentation and a realistic look at childhood and the difficulties of the era. Their conclusion includes the statement that, "despite often difficult living conditions, the great majority of children, within their families, at school, in monasteries, with a patron or a lord, in the street or in the fields, were surrounded with affection and carefully educated."[40] Perhaps these limited observations lend themselves to consideration of the possibility of a type of redemptive affirmation for parents who may have been judged inattentive to the needs of their children during this era.

I am drawn here to Jesus' words: "Let the children come to me; do not prevent them, for the kingdom of God belongs to such as these" (Mk 10:14). For us today, how might we speak of our coming together in Christ, of belonging to him? "Belonging," however it is lived, demands serious and caring commitment. The broadening sense of community brought about by families' own witness to faith is an important consideration not only for the era under review but also for us. But might belonging become limited to the parent-child relationship?

In writing about Baptism some years after the Second Vatican Council, distinguished theologian Julia Upton pointed out: "The faith that is described in relation to infant baptism is regarded as being three-dimensional. Thus we have the incipient faith of the child, the matured faith of the parent, and the corporate faith of the community."[41] All of these factors relate to the formulation of a sustained and comprehensive catechesis that broadens the catechetical agenda in service to mission. Defined groups (e.g., of children, of the elderly, etc.) *exist within* and *contribute to* the larger community of faith, not as self-serving, independent subcommunities (entities ideally foreign to contemporary catechetical witness) but as interdependent parts of the whole. The parish, which looks beyond itself, is the priority.

A sustained corporate witness is the *established* context from within which the community welcomes and stands up on behalf of others along the way of catechesis within numerous constituencies.[42] Of particular significance is the catechesis of adults. Adults bear "the greatest responsibilities and the capacity to live the Christian message in its fully developed form" (CT, 43). Adult catechesis serves a critical purpose as "the *organizing principle*, which gives coherence to the various catechetical programs offered by a particular Church. . . . This is the axis around which revolves the catechesis of childhood and adolescence as well as that of old age" (GDC, 275 [italics in the original]).[43] Opportunities for an evangelizing catechesis cannot be set aside for "a rainy day" when major programs may be winding down. For example, children's sacramental formation does not "stand alone"; parish-wide approaches to sacramental and liturgical formation are essential, especially for parents, other adults, and siblings.

Pope Francis urges us: "Let's keep moving forward!"[44] We take seriously the urgent appeal that "for all the baptized, children or adults, faith must grow *after* Baptism" (CCC, 1254 [italics in the original]). This involves not only the comfort of belonging but also the wisdom of believing. "Effective adult catechesis relates the content of the faith to life experience. It enables the Christian to read the signs of the times in light of the Gospel" (NDC, 48A4). We may resist going forward along a road of discernment cluttered with obstacles. But "the joy and hope, [and] the grief and anguish" (GS, 1) of people awakening in faith summons us to keep moving.

Catechesis is for all, even in settings that are at best informal, and often with nonverbal witness as its calling card. This applies as well to the "Church of the thousand years" (500–1500), as irregular and informal as that catechesis may have been at times, including for adults.

Even a quick glance at the *National Directory for Catechesis* informs the most casual of readers of the breadth and depth of the ministry of catechesis. Its chapters on divine and human methodology, diverse catechetical settings, and catechists and their formation bear witness to the refreshing reality that no single approach to catechesis, to learners, or to catechists suffices.[45] The joy of diversity comes in meeting multiple needs and expectations in a variety of ways. Hard "Gospel work" often yields tired joy, but joy nonetheless. Solid apprenticeship yields committed discipleship from within varied cultural realities.

In writing about the history of catechesis from 600 to 1100, scholar James Campbell notes that memorizing both the Lord's Prayer and Apostles' Creed was a basic catechetical expectation. Preaching, emphasis on saints and their prayerful intercession, and pilgrimages also formed part of the overall catechetical picture.[46] "As rudimentary as these catechetical efforts seem, they were strong enough for Christian life to survive and later flourish."[47] The Apostles' Creed and the Lord's Prayer (and eventually the Ave Maria[48]) provided much of the sustenance of catechetical resources for parents and godparents.[49] The scholar Lucinda Nolan seems to summarize when she states, "There is no evidence of any organized system of catechesis for children in the early middle ages for this was to be accomplished by the parents in the home and the pastor during the liturgy."[50]

It is tempting, of course, to judge the era's shortcomings. Despite catechumenal decline and the residual decline in initiatory catechesis, "instruction in the basic concepts of Christianity continued to be given and to be a primary concern of the leaders of the church."[51] The centuries-long practice of "handing on the faith" continued along through complex and changing times. Historian of catechesis and scholar Berard Marthaler points out: "In the Middle Ages, *catechismus* referred to oral teaching, both the act of instruction and the doctrine taught."[52]

An indication of what is called today the sacrament of Reconciliation comes to us from the early Middle Ages. To assist the penitent, "Confession' booklets became popular some time after the seventh century, when annual confession became the rule." In question-and-answer form, these booklets typically identified many sins.[53] Manuals for the clergy included a multitude of sins along with "penalties" and would eventually become resources for literate laypeople.[54]

This was a time when "formal"[55] catechesis waned. In contemporary catechetical usage, *formal* implies planned, systematic, and organic elements in relation to those catechized, the catechist, the message, and the means of engaging the message (the "what" and the "how" of catechesis). (Today such catechetical resources as religion texts for children and young people can be reviewed for authenticity and completeness.[56] Such approaches guide catechetical priorities and progress.) In the Middle Ages, "what formal catechesis there was . . . revolved around set formulas, especially the Creed. The traditional approach, teaching Christ by means of a biblical narrative, continued."[57]

Bishop G. Emmett Carter, writing on the eve of the Second Vatican Council, addressed an adult catechetical focus during the medieval era: "The Creed and the Lord's Prayer continued to be the 'course of instruction' and priests were required to explain them to the faithful (especially during Lent) in the vernacular and have them occasionally recited. This recitation led by the priest ordinarily followed the sermon given after the Gospel at Mass. . . . While the Creed and the Lord's Prayer served as excellent patterns for the explanation of faith and morals, succeeding centuries added to the instruction the Ten Commandments, the Hail Mary, the teaching upon the capital sins, the works of mercy, and the beatitudes."[58] We see here not only a predictable formulaic context but also a liturgical one.

Clearly, practices of the time reflect a catechetical narrowing from the more robust formative and educative practices of previous centuries when catechesis, especially for adults, flowed through a cohesive blend of scriptural, creedal, doctrinal, liturgical, evangelizing, and catechumenal realities. One may ask if *catechesis* of the era is now synonymous with *information*. Joseph Collins appears to summarize when he states of the era, "There was much *instruction* from many and varied sources, but very little *education*."[59] Further catechetical contraction would arrive after the invention of the printing press in the mid-fifteenth century. How fortunate that catechesis today benefits from the blending of the interdependent six tasks of catechesis.

Activities and Works of the Era

Charlemagne (742–814), who would be crowned emperor by Pope Leo III in 800, sought out the brilliant scholar Alcuin of York (735–804) to lead the palace school.[60] With Charlemagne came organization; the Carolingian Renaissance was on, and Alcuin, a scholar and teacher of no little repute, impacted education and learning in broad and lasting ways.[61] John Elias states that "as would be expected, religion was the hub of the education that the monk Alcuin proposed for the schools of the empire."[62]

The strong witness of women of faith characterizes catechesis and religious education today, and the written record of such contributions is well established. Mining women's contributions from the centuries under review is more difficult. Still, as Katharina M. Wilson observes, "However much outnumbered by men and however much excluded from the literary canon, women did write in the Middle Ages and did offer their perceptions of reality both secular and religious."[63]

One compelling treasure is the mother Dhuoda's handbook, known as *Liber manualis,* for her son William. Medieval scholar Carol Neel's translation, *Handbook for William: A Carolingian Woman's Counsel for Her Son / by Dhuoda* provides an inviting doorway into this important piece.[64] The work includes a prologue and eleven "books"[65] and addresses topics we would expect to see: the Trinity, prayer, morality, the Beatitudes, and more. What I find especially appealing is the manner and tone of the work. Written in the early 840s,[66] this guide from the hand of a strong and loving mother is, in my estimation, a gem of the era, a notable source of parental commitment to handing on the treasure of faith and lessons for life to a teenage son. Through her written witness, she is, as Christ is, "with" William despite worry and the pain of separation.

The words of this committed noble laywoman bring reassurance, challenge, and support during difficult times. Three samples follow:

- "You and I must seek God out, my son; we take our existence from his approval, *we live, and move, and are.* Even I, unworthy and frail as a shadow, seek him as best I can and unceasingly call upon his aid as best I know and understand it."

- "Pray with your mouth, cry out with your heart, ask in your deeds that God come to your aid always, day and night, in every hour and every moment."

- "So be merciful. . . . Show mercy as much as you are able even to the least of men, to those subject to you, and to those in need. Then you too may be found worthy to be treated mercifully by our good and merciful God."[67]

It seems reasonable to dismiss the notion that these centuries were no more than a catechetical placeholder biding time until a later age; Dhuoda's words bear testimony to a lasting faith commitment. I see here a holistic type of catechesis of and for life, where, in the midst of painful separation, belonging and believing converge. Her words speak of forming a discerning attitude of life and of faith, especially as William lives in real time and through real circumstances of life under the authority of those whom he is required to serve.[68]

Eminent scholar Gerard Sloyan provides a summary review of a work of the era known as the *Disputatio puerorum.* It includes twelve chapters in a question-answer format and treats a wide variety of topics (e.g., biblical information, the Mass, faith and the Apostles' Creed, and the

Lord's Prayer).[69] However, Sloyan calls into question the impression that this precise work is portrayed as a handbook for the student. He states, among other critical observations, that "in it the Bible is taught about rather than taught from."[70] Another commentator, Aubert Clark, indicates that the *Disputatio* "is not a homily nor intended as an aid to preaching, but a real lesson book. It is for school work. It . . . helped to set the pattern for succeeding ages."[71] Scholar Liam Ethan Felsen indicates that both cathedral school students (who might eventually teach) and the general laity could rely on this work, "and even adult converts from conquered lands could learn the catechetical information necessary to be baptized and enter the Christian faith."[72]

Another resource of the era that draws our attention is the *Elucidarius*. Evelyn Scherabon Firchow, translator and distinguished scholar of the Old Norse *Elucidarius*, indicates that the *Elucidarius* was a "popular medieval Latin work, probably written in the early twelfth century by a monk called Honorius Augustodunensis."[73] The source consulted here displays a familiar question-and-answer structure, with the "disciple" asking the questions, and the teacher, or "master," often responding at greater length.[74] Many topics are treated in this widely translated work.[75] Firchow states, "Its simple and naive explanations of theological questions were used to teach elementary Christianity to medieval Christians. Its audience consisted chiefly of the unlearned laity who esteemed the work for the straightforward and authoritative answers it contained."[76]

In his own assessment of the *Elucidarius*, Gerard Sloyan sharply observes that "surely it marks the death and burial of the patristic tradition in catechetics."[77] He notes "the brevity of its responses and its directness"[78] as benefits.

Although the *Elucidarius* is not a book for children,[79] the approach seems to anticipate a later age characterized by extensive reliance on an interrogative approach coupled with recitation of "correct answers" but with little opportunity beforehand for understanding.[80] Accordingly, I would propose that the expected response became of itself an endpoint rather than a doorway to further exploration for many Catholics in later centuries. One may hear today of adults who, relying principally on approaches and learnings from their own childhood experience, have yet to benefit from robust adult faith formation.

Challenge and Change

The intermingling of the Church and the political sphere is one character-istic of the growth of "Christendom"; ecclesial and secular rule were inter-twined. The Middle Ages were characterized by challenges and changes within Church and society in an atmosphere considered Christian, one influenced by a combination of family, liturgy, and community.[81] The Church would gain broad authority and wield powerful political influ-ence. For some, clerical privilege and advancement and a thirst for power shaped life's priorities. However, reform, including monastic reform, also played an important role in the life of the Church. Bernard of Clairvaux (1090–1153), reforming monk and "virtual pope of the western Church,"[82] impacted both monastic and ecclesial development. This abbot's far-reach-ing efforts ranged from theological and spiritual writing to the founding of many monasteries to vigorous opposition to clerical abuse of power.

Ecclesial prominence and governmental rule were often indistin-guishable as the Church's political and societal engagement eventually became a standard. These centuries also witnessed the long-simmering and painful schism between the Church of the East and the Church of the West; the complex march of the Crusades (bent on securing the Holy Land); and, over a period of nearly a century, four Lateran councils, the last of which occurred in 1215. Among issues of the time were author-ity over ecclesial appointments and opposition to heresy.[83] Marthaler states that "the Fourth Lateran Council (1215) institutionalized several changes and reforms that impacted on catechetical practice, namely, its disciplinary decrees on preaching and reception of the sacraments."[84] Ongoing oppression of Jews was a reality of this era that can be neither dismissed as the tenor of the times nor forgotten as no more than a detail of history.[85]

In addition, the devastating plague of the mid-fourteenth century decimated the population of Europe. Imagine the effect on catechesis of such an extended experience that must have grown to seem normal. Yet faith, and people, lived for another day.

Sermons constituted a foundational aspect of catechesis at the turn of the first millennium in England, especially so during Lent and Easter.[86] The monk and homilist Aelfric (ca. 1000) is considered by the renowned scholar Milton McC. Gatch as "the greatest of the Anglo-Saxon sermon writers."[87] Gatch holds that Aelfric was no reluctant catechist but an exemplar of catechetical commitment: "He is conscientious, conservative, orthodox, and clear in his teaching."[88]

In the West the liturgy of the Mass was prayed in Latin, a language not familiar to most of the population.[89] In his classic work *The Good News Yesterday and Today*, Josef Jungmann writes, "Even the most fervent hardly dared to receive Communion several times a year. Hence a desire sprang up to see the Sacred Host. Not satisfied with the fleeting glance at the Elevation, the faithful yearned for more and more exposition, even during Mass, in order that they might adore and from this gaze gain grace and blessings."[90]

Artistic images of saints and other religious topics served as catechetical pathways for many of the faithful. Morality and miracle plays, pilgrimages, and other devotional practices were identifiable elements of Christian faith, life, and practice. In discussing a work of the era known to us as the *Lay Folks' Catechism*, Thomas Frederick Simmons and Henry Edward Nolloth state, "It is certain that dogma, as well as history, was illustrated by miracle-plays, strange though it may appear."[91] In the thirteenth century, Francis of Assisi (ca. 1181–1226) provided a devotional and catechetical visual experience recalling the birth of Christ. His nativity scene was of faith and of life, joyfully celebrated together with the faithful.[92] The celebration of Corpus Christi traces its roots to the thirteenth century.

Renowned historian David Herlihy (1930–1991) writes, "One possible window onto the emotional world of the medieval family is religious practice, as distinct from formal doctrine and admonition."[93] Pious practices of the era included devotions to Mary, the child Jesus, and Joseph.[94] Writing of the late Middle Ages, Herlihy states, "The Holy Family itself was viewed as a trinity, which in some ways replicated on earth the Blessed Trinity in heaven."[95]

According to a twelfth-century homily, "three things there are that each man must have who will lead a Christian life: the first is right (true) belief, the second is baptism, the third is fair (good) life; and he is not fully a Christian that is wanting in any of these three."[96] The tenth canon of the Fourth Lateran Council held that bishops who for any reason could not preach were to "choose men effective in action and speech, suitable for executing the office of sacred preaching to advantage, to visit zealously the peoples committed to them in their place when they themselves cannot and edify them by word and example."[97]

A period of renaissance[98] and political engagement[99] characterized the centuries following the turn of the first millennium, an era that saw the emergence of a move toward a "humanistic" sense of personhood.[100] Universities[101] were central to the later Middle Ages, which also saw the birth and expansion of mendicant (begging) religious orders (e.g., Franciscans and Dominicans), with their particular charisms of preaching, teaching, and service. The determined, influential, and lasting Christian witness of such mystics as Hildegard of Bingen (1098–1179) and Julian of Norwich (1353–1416) and the persuasive and firm guiding hand of Doctor of the Church Catherine of Siena (1347–1380), to name only a few personalities, helped to carry the heart of the Church during the first half of the second millennium. They are reminders for us of the importance of belonging, the power of believing, and the necessity of discernment within the community of faith.

An approach to theological and philosophical study that emerged in the later Middle Ages was Scholasticism (i.e., relating to "school"). Reliance on logic and reason in matters of faith greatly influenced theological understanding. "It had as its goal a greater understanding and exploration of revealed truth and Church doctrine through the application of reason, analogy, and careful analysis of faith."[102] As Marthaler indicates, catechesis became more systematic in keeping with the scholastic theological emphasis of the times.[103] The number seven became a key identifier. Today many Christians can easily cite this number when describing areas of belief (e.g., deadly sins, virtues, etc.).[104] Marthaler also cites the enumeration of the articles of the Creed by such theologians as St. Bonaventure (1218–1274) and St. Thomas Aquinas (1225–1274).

For these scholastic theologians, there are "seven [articles] pertaining to the majesty of the Godhead and seven to Christ's human nature." Marthaler goes on to point out that "their efforts to organize the Creed into a theological framework blurred its trinitarian structure and further detached catechesis from baptismal liturgy."[105]

Among the theological giants of the time were Anselm of Canterbury (1033–1109) and Thomas Aquinas. Anselm would write his famous argument for proving the existence of God "in the person of one who strives to lift his mind to the contemplation of God, and seeks to understand what he believes."[106] The notion of "faith seeking understanding" was destined to have lasting theological import. I have often considered catechesis as a vehicle for making this "seeking" a reality. Catechesis—with scriptural, theological, doctrinal, liturgical, communal, methodological, cultural, developmental, and educational emphases—retains a distinctive place for bridging understanding and witness born of faith. Today, at a time of New Evangelization, this is both necessity and reality.

Thomas Aquinas (1225–1274), known principally for his monumental *Summa Theologica*, gives us a glimpse of his catechetical inclinations through his sermons on the Apostles' Creed, the Ten Commandments, the Lord's Prayer, and the Hail Mary.[107] "Students and townsfolk" gathered in Naples during Lent of 1273 to hear Aquinas preach "sermons [that] never took longer than half an hour, some of them only fifteen minutes."[108]

The sermons are straightforward and organized and, in the words of Gerard Sloyan, "he shows himself a master of sources, employing both Testaments of Scripture and the Fathers with ease and unerring appositeness. . . . There is abundant illustration out of daily experience but it is never developed further than is required for immediate application."[109] These sermons add another layer to our catechetical heritage. In a homily on the Fourth Commandment, Aquinas states, "Children, therefore, receive from their parents birth, nourishment, and instruction."[110] I see here signs of the interwoven elements of belonging and believing from birth forward. Other teachings on the sacraments[111] also provide us with catechetical insight into the way of the "Angelic Doctor."

Another scholar, Rudolph G. Bandas, proposes: "Of him [Aquinas] it may be said that he wished to know in order that he might love; then, because he loved, he wished to scrutinize ever more closely the object of his affections."[112] The scholar Mark Heath, O.P., writes that "Thomistic religious education is systematic, theocentric, and doctrinal" and "is the work of student and teacher."[113]

The clergy were charged with explaining fundamentals of faith and belief to the faithful. Guidebooks were developed over the centuries to aid these preachers, whose training was commonly deficient.[114] Archbishop John Pecham (d. 1292) of Canterbury was concerned with improving the poor state of education among clergy in his care (and the resulting inadequacy of preaching and teaching). Gatch indicates that "the foundational document for all later medieval English legislation and handbooks on the subject of catechetical instruction is the canon *Ignorantia sacerdotum* promulgated at a council at Lambeth in 1281 by John Pecham."[115] Pecham, a Franciscan, "directs that every priest shall explain to his people simply and clearly, four times a year, the Creed, the ten commandments, the two precepts of the Gospel, viz. love to God and man, the seven works of mercy, the seven deadly sins, the seven cardinal virtues, and the seven sacraments of grace."[116]

Less than one hundred years later, during the episcopal service of John de Thoresby (d. 1373), Archbishop of York, "the morals, the learning, and the piety of the clergy were at a low ebb. They were held in but little estimation by the laity."[117] Thoresby was intent on the reform of the priesthood and the formation of the laity. He was well aware of the need to provide necessary assistance for the clergy.[118] Thoresby "put forward to his clergy in convocation a plan for the improvement of sacerdotal instruction to the laity."[119] One outcome of his concern was the provision of clear guidance for preachers, directing priests to teach weekly on Sunday and not just four times a year.[120] Historian W. A. Pantin states, "In 1357 he issued a Latin 'catechism' or summary of religious instruction, which was to be expounded in English by parish priests throughout the province of York."[121]

Thoresby's instructions are known as the *Lay Folks' Catechism*. The English form is "of the simplest character, so as to be understood by the most uncultured of the laity."[122] Thoresby was apparently so eager for the laity to benefit from his work that he directed the translator, a monk named John de Taystek, to rely on verse to aid memorization.[123] Pantin observes: "As a scheme of religious instruction put forward officially by a bishop it may be regarded as a belated survival of thirteenth-century methods; while the official publication of a version in English links it with the vernacular literature of the period."[124]

Thoresby had the benefit of Pecham's prior work in developing his own.[125] Topics included "the fourteen articles of belief"[126] (i.e., creedal), the commandments, the sacraments, the corporal and spiritual works of mercy, the seven virtues (faith, hope, charity, justice, prudence, fortitude, and temperance), and the seven deadly sins (pride, envy, anger, gluttony, avarice, sloth, and lechery). "And these all curates are bidden to teach, and require all within their cures, to teach them to their children."[127] With reliance on the vernacular, a confessor could check on people's progress: "none may plead want of learning."[128]

Most of the fourteenth century saw several successors of Peter primarily housed in Avignon, France; space does not permit our entering into those historical details here. Thoresby died a few years before the return of the papacy to Rome and five years before the start of the Western Schism (1378–1417), which at one point witnessed three claimants to the papacy. A notable reform-minded person[129] of the time was Jean Gerson (1363–1429), theologian, chancellor of the University of Paris, and a scholar credited for his contributions to catechesis. We will engage Gerson in chapter 7 as we transition to the deep fracture in the Church called the Reformation and explore its accompanying impact on catechesis.

Writing a few years before the Second Vatican Council, Josef Jungmann identified the lack of extensive formal catechesis ("extremely sparse") in the Middle Ages. However, rather than dismiss the era, he specifies three important points for his readers to consider regarding this lengthy period of Church history: the value of the home as an essential setting for catechesis; the value of living from within the experience of Christian community; and "the timeless value" of "set formulas" for "formal catechesis."[130] For now, I am drawn to a statement of James Campbell that seems to summarize well catechesis during these last few centuries: "Catechesis in

Western Europe during this time was a catechesis of immersion. People born into this world entered a community life that was entirely formed by the language of Christianity. All the stages of life, beginning in Baptism and ending in death, were marked and celebrated in Christian ritual."[131]

Belonging, Believing, and More

What might we make of these thousand years? This chapter has sought to affirm a Spirit-filled people who carried the lantern of faith and kept it burning from field to hearth, home to church, and back again. Such an image reminds us that the powerful voices and identifiable and memorable figures of Christendom were not its only witnesses to the Gospel. While not named in the annals of history, the subjects of untold stories of faith coming to life within Christian communities are no less important than those whose names we know. We may not know all the details, but we do "know" the players. I would propose that it is during these centuries that we see families of the Church nobly carrying on without fanfare or fame, with faith sustained through tightly woven strands of identity bound up in such traditional elements as the Creed and the Lord's Prayer,[132] both of which characterized part of catechumenal formation in previous centuries.

In the end, catechesis as represented in this era played an essential role for growth in faith regardless of setting (e.g., in the home), approach or technique (e.g., preaching, memorization, reliance on handbooks), or limitation (e.g., plague). However, as we will see in chapter 8, a recovered understanding of the depth, potential, and meaning of catechesis, especially in the decades leading up to and following the Second Vatican Council, provides a firm foundation for today and for the future for people of all ages and states of life.

As informal as catechesis may have been during the Middle Ages, families continued to travel the way of faith from generation to generation. Pope Francis repeatedly reminds us that lived discipleship is a significant expression of faith. Catechesis lives in the echo of faith handed on, incorporating, for example, the sustaining reality and beauty of our scriptural, doctrinal, and sacramental heritage from within the community of the Church. The New Evangelization engages people in reclaiming the reality and experience of belonging to Christ and the Church. Indeed, our joyful and faithful service is indicative of *living* witness. A smile, a moment of empathetic response to a troubling family situation, an invitation to clarify a challenging text, or merciful outreach to another may actually signal to those whose vision is not dimmed opportunities of grace. The Spirit abides. Catechists are living signs along the way of faith within all of these moments.

Despite catechetical shortcomings of the era, we can look back with admiration at the efforts of faithful Christians who kept the fire of faith alive during centuries that swelled in turn with unrest, stability, uncertainty, and days of glory. Faithful laity (including adults and families), clergy, and religious continued to embrace the faith tradition into which they had been baptized. I would submit that belonging and believing were reinforced as expressions and values of Christianity, including within the domestic church of the family and the broader community of faith.

What might happen if we imagine ourselves alongside our ancestors who lived during these centuries? Speculation can lead us to an informed "feast of the imagination." Imagine people's discernment of "life steps" (even of limited scope) in the midst of disease, turmoil, or separation; think of, for example, Dhuoda's message to her son or a commoner's daily grind. Survival of any sort is instinctual.

Imagine living and dying moments turning to hours, days, and months for people graced with "the firstfruits of the Spirit" (Rom 8:23) and anchored to hope: "For in hope we were saved. Now hope that sees for itself is not hope. For who hopes for what one sees? But if we hope for what we do not see, we wait with endurance" (Rom 8:24–25).

In putting forward this brief interpretation I have sought to demonstrate that "looking back" not only enriches our information base but also strengthens our appreciation of the people of the era, now cherished in memory. Perhaps this look back can sharpen our perspective for engaging people today in a New Evangelization marked by vigilance and vitality.

Yes, my imagination is at work as I think of these past centuries, but neither foolishly nor without a foundation rooted in hope.

I am imagining a steadfast "rising" that nurtures the Church with hope through challenges old and new.

I am imagining a people for whom "ongoing conversion" was more of a sustained reality than a familiar term.

I am imagining committed adults affected by a piece of art that locked their gaze.

I am imagining a yearning by some for the Bible to be "taught from" and not just "taught about," leaving one yearning for more.

I am imagining a pensive and deliberate recitation of the Creed and prayerful encounter through the Lord's Prayer.

I am imagining expressions of love for the Eucharist as confident hope in Christ's continuing presence among his people.

I am imagining women of faith, within and beyond the family, buttressing the Church.

I am imagining adults seeking and searching faith.

I am imagining the gifts of young adults, enlivening the Church.

I am imagining inspired adolescents and youth ministry thriving even more.

I am imagining caring adults looking after the catechetical needs of children, not as a narrow slice of life (e.g., seventy-five minutes a week to fulfill a program expectation) but as a revived standard through experiences imbued and sustained by faith alive through the witness of the family and other caregivers.

Pope Francis tells us, "Let us go forth, then, let us go forth to offer everyone the life of Jesus Christ" (EG, 49). I am imagining the broad and expanding net of a New Evangelization. This moment incorporates, for example, sacrificial commitment, Catholic social teaching, faithful witness to the Gospel, and caring stewardship of the earth God has given us. It relishes catechetical formation through the living Word of God and eager embrace of our tradition and doctrinal heritage. And it resides within a sacramental frame that gives life to both proclamation and teaching.

And so I am imagining a Church on pilgrimage, belonging as it believes and believing as it belongs, with leaders and other witnesses in shared discernment as "a Church which is bruised, hurting and dirty because it has been out on the streets" (EG, 49). Faith calls us to the joy found along pathways of uncertainty *and* stability. Sustained by hope, we remember, "No one has ever seen God. Yet, if we love one another, God remains in us, and his love is brought to perfection in us. This is how we know that we remain in him and he in us, that he has given us of his Spirit" (1 Jn 4:12–13).

Reflection Questions

1.   Situate yourself anywhere in the Middle Ages. What would be your first catechetical entrée to others? Why?

2.   What person from this era (named or unnamed) would you like to engage in conversation? What might you ask him or her?

3.   What does this era say to you about the significance of ongoing adult faith formation?

4.   What aspect of catechesis during this era might lead you to further study? Why?

5.   It is the twelfth century, and you are asked what you rely on for your developing faith. You reply, "The Bible is essential for me because . . ."

6.   Does anything about catechesis in these centuries frustrate you? Why? Is there something from this era that reinforces your sense of catechesis? What and why?

7.   How might your daily interactions become "signs of the New Evangelization" in Church and society?

8.   How might infant Baptism enrich the parish community's outreach of welcome and faith witness?

9.   What do you think enables families today to maintain a faith commitment? What challenges them?

10.   What worries seem to consume families today? What are some risks taken today by families coming to faith and Baptism? Or of remaining faithful to Christ and his Church?

7

SUSTAINING THE WAY
Fracture and Reform

I pray not only for them, but also for those who will believe in me through their word, so that they may all be one, as you, Father, are in me and I in you, that they also may be in us, that the world may believe that you sent me.

—John 17:20–21

It was a cold and icy December Friday, about halfway through Advent. Leaving campus late in the afternoon, I carried my briefcase along with a small box. With skies beginning to darken, I walked briskly through a large parking lot, confident that new shoes would ensure safe passage to my car. Though it was Advent time—when "waiting" makes more sense than usual—there was much to do before Christmas.

Without warning, black ice sent me reeling. Flat on my back, I lay on the cold asphalt surface, looking up at the world, severe pain now settling into my right arm.

Caring colleagues eventually came by and summoned help. Emergency personnel, despite my objections, cut through my coat, a family gift. Medication administered during the ambulance ride to the hospital did not "take." I would soon see the extensive discoloration on my torso resulting from an upper arm fracture.

"My strength fails in my affliction; my bones are wearing down" (Ps 31:11b). Months of demanding physical therapy followed. At home, basic functioning required assistance. Elevating my arm was out of the question; sustained immobilization became my reality. My wife, who had recently undergone unexpected, lengthy surgery, was my principal caregiver, as no other family members live nearby. Many people became instruments of healing during this time of waiting. Local parishioners and university colleagues provided accompaniment in the form of prayerful support and a constant flow of healthy meals.

Physical healing took far longer than I had anticipated or planned ("controlling," I saw, was not the same as self-control). Frustration set in, with daily reminders of the gradual and painstakingly slow knitting going on within my body. God is a deliberate artist.

More than a year would pass before I would feel close to "normal" (whatever that means). But the team of physical therapists whose healing ways supported both body and spirit into the spring, even in the midst of discomfort and lingering thoughts of a dim light at the end of the tunnel, rendered a lasting benefit.

A traumatic fracture had changed my life. Along the way of recovery I ruminated about my overall physical condition—might that have contributed to my being a candidate ripe for brokenness? Had my pace of living contributed to what had stopped me in my tracks? Perhaps I had already been immobilized, a fracture in the making, a child of God who had slipped and fallen, now in need of reforming my ways, ongoing conversion in the offing bringing comfort amid affliction: "Let your face shine on your servant; save me in your mercy" (Ps 31:17).

Wholeness and holiness weighed on me, disturbed and then challenged my spirit, buoyed not by lifeless idols of abandonment but by the God of nearness. "Be strong and take heart, all who hope in the LORD" (Ps 31:25). I learned new lessons about healing, patience, and accompaniment. Reforming some of my ways became my reality as gradual recovery took hold—all stemming from the experience of looking up at the world from the surface of a cold and hardened parking lot.

"On the Horizon"

A deep fracture would leave its mark on a surface of another kind—the life of the Church—during the middle of the second millennium. Sadly, Christianity had already experienced significant brokenness in the Great Schism between East and West centuries before. Ecclesial history bears witness to a variety of disputes over the ages. Cries for reform have come in different ways and from an assortment of voices while professing faithfulness to and love for Christ, and reform has occurred periodically during the life of the Church. "Reformation" is the term most identifiable with the era under review here; it is often more precisely specified as the Protestant Reformation and the Counter-Reformation.

Without people there is no reforming. One of the Church's significant voices in the century before the Reformation was Jean Gerson (1363–1429), who lived during the time of the Hundred Years' War. A priest and scholar of no small repute, Gerson served in a variety of roles, including chancellor of the University of Paris. He was a contributing voice to resolving the great dispute over the papacy during the Western Schism.[1] A prolific writer, he took great interest in the catechetical world of his day. He offers us a bridge from the Middle Ages to the time of the Reformation, which is linked to Martin Luther and the year 1517.

A need already identified over the course of the centuries was proper formation of the clergy. The same can be said of later times. For example, according to distinguished scholar and historian Brian Patrick McGuire, one of Gerson's sermons (*Bonus Pastor*) "provides an excellent overview of Gerson's program for improving the quality of parish life and the education of the clergy. Some of his proposals were not carried through until the Council of Trent in the middle of the next century, in a quite different Church."[2]

Gerson was passionate about handing on the faith and nothing short of serious about the importance of such teaching. He was an accomplished contributor to catechetical development and was not put off by the preferences of theologians who thought otherwise of such involvement.[3] Gerson's significant work, the *Opus Tripartitum*, is a good example of his contributions.[4] McGuire indicates that Gerson included among potential beneficiaries "those who care for the sick and work in hospitals."[5] Its parts include one with fundamental beliefs and teaching on the commandments, a second on readiness for confession, and a third on assisting those who are dying.[6]

Another work, *Leading the Little Ones to Christ*, was cited in a 1921 article by Roderick MacEachen as "an excellent plea for the religious education of children." MacEachen suggests that "Gerson might be called the modern apostle of religious teaching for children."[7] More recently, the scholar Francis Oakley uses the phrase "deep concern" in citing the importance Gerson attached to "the religious education and moral formation of children. It was with the young, he believed, that the task of reforming the Church and society at large must begin."[8]

A blend of faith formation constituencies would benefit from Gerson's work.[9] For us today, the broad sweep of catechesis enlivens and challenges us, especially as part of the New Evangelization. I am thinking here, though not exclusively, of categories of persons identified in chapter 7 of the *National Directory for Catechesis*. These include people with disabilities, adults, elderly people, young adults, adolescents, children, infants, and the many other groups of people whose special circumstances necessitate caring and careful catechetical formation. Surely, the way of catechesis has been traveled by countless persons, many with undiscovered needs, reminding us of the importance of catechesis for all.

As we have seen, many who have gone before us offered their own creative gifts to the task at hand as the gift of wisdom seemed to carry them through unpredictable times. As with our own efforts, often inspired by that same gift, some moves of our ancestors succeeded more than others. Much more could be said of the personalities mentioned in these chapters and about what from the outside may appear to be no more than a composite of successes and failures. Yet this ministry that seizes us is greater than any such measure. We seek to remain faithful to God, who calls us to himself. And we remember, "Jesus Christ is the same yesterday, today, and forever" (Heb 13:8).

In our own day we may hear of reform "on the horizon." My sense of the need for reform starts with a look in the mirror. What do I see that needs to be addressed? What within, perhaps residing just beneath the surface, is gnawing away at a fragile or weakened exterior? As I take in the image of self before me, I realize that my singular view is incomplete without the community of faith alongside me. Only a mirrored surface of far greater size can accommodate such a body, an expanse of people so broad that my imagination captures mere hints of its breadth, for this communal "look" represents a broad diversity of cultures and peoples.

Much catechetical history represents European experience (the source of my own roots), but that is only part of the incomplete story told through selected highlights here. More informed voices from other geographic homelands and centers of culture tell their own stories and trace other important steps. According to the *National Directory for Catechesis*, "The Gospel is intended for every people and nation; it finds a home in every culture" (NDC, 17A).

As members of the Church, we are reminded of the One to and through whom we belong, the One in whom we believe, the One who guides us in our struggles for clarity of life, the One who lived and died and rose for us. Jesus Christ, the Word of God, is our hope, giving us the gift of his Spirit in love beyond measure. "His voice continues to resound in the Church and in the world through the Holy Spirit" (GDC, 94). The Advocate is with us, helping us to believe, strengthening us in faith (see CCC, 179).

Reformation

As the Church, the People of God, we are not only agents of reform but also objects of reform. This perspective guides our probing of some catechetical undertakings during the sustained experience of Reformation that engaged much of Christianity halfway through the second millennium.

Space here cannot accommodate detailed analysis of factors leading up to this time in the life of the Church. Nevertheless, we can imagine how challenging the experience of belonging to the Church became for many and how some practices contributed to troubling and troubled times, despite emerging signs of reform[10] within the Church. Ignorance of scripture was not the only limitation to which people were exposed.

Corruption within the clerical ranks, simony, and the sale of indulgences all affected and wounded the Church.[11]

The principal reforming voice belonged to Martin Luther (1483– 1546). An Augustinian friar,[12] Luther lived his vocation as fully as possible in the midst of his own trials. Campbell states of Luther, "In his spiritual quest he discovered the saving love of Jesus Christ as a free gift to all who believe."[13] Luther sought reform, not ecclesial separation. Historian Christopher Bellitto points out that Luther's "goal was simple: to move the Church forward by recovering her ancient glory."[14] Reading Luther's *Ninety-Five Theses* (from 1517), which dealt with the sale of indulgences and through which he invited debate,[15] leaves no doubting his passion and resolve. Indeed, the abuse of indulgences had become a scandal in the life of the Church.

One of the major issues of the time, and for which Martin Luther was a central figure, had to do with the matter of justification. The 1999 *Joint Declaration on the Doctrine of Justification* by the Lutheran World Federation and the Catholic Church states, "Opposing interpretations and applications of the biblical message of justification were in the sixteenth century a principal cause of the division of the Western church and led as well to doctrinal condemnations."[16]

Catechists today can draw from several sources in seeking to understand the doctrine of justification, including scripture and the *Catechism of the Catholic Church* (e.g., CCC, 1987ff.). Contemporary efforts constitute a bright light for both Lutheran and Catholic communions. In light of history made and history shared, this is no minor matter. A very brief excerpt from the *Joint Declaration* encourages us to consult this source in its entirety: "We confess together that sinners are justified by faith in the saving action of God in Christ. By the action of the Holy Spirit in baptism, they are granted the gift of salvation, which lays the basis for the whole Christian life."[17]

Martin Luther was a scholar, professor, and expert on the Bible. However, "the nature of authority" was to become a crucial issue.[18] In discussing the disputation involving the Catholic theologian John Eck and Martin Luther in 1519, Kevin Hughes states that "Luther was forced to concede that he considered the authority of Scripture superior to the teaching of the Church and that his only resource for his interpretation of Scripture was the 'testimony of the Spirit' as he read it."[19]

Martin Luther, theologian and scripture scholar, was excommunicated by Pope Leo X, himself a controversial figure, in 1521, the last year of his pontificate.[20]

Catechisms, Small and Large

Luther's commitment to faith handed on was captured by his preaching and teaching. His written materials, including catechisms, became principal and practical tools that bear witness to his catechetical fervor. A 1520 work of Luther indicates:

> The ordinary Christian, who cannot read the Scriptures, is required to learn and know the Ten Commandments, the Creed, and the Lord's Prayer; and this has not come to pass without God's special ordering. For these three contain fully and completely everything that is in the Scriptures, everything that ever should be preached, and everything that a Christian needs to know, all put so briefly and so plainly that no one can make complaint or excuse, saying that what he needs for his salvation is too long or too hard to remember.[21]

The last part of this statement, regarding the duty of the believer, reminds me of the *Lay Folks' Catechism* from less than two centuries before, in which mention is made that the penitent could not "plead want of learning" during confession.[22] We do well to remember that the scriptures were inaccessible to most of the population of the time. One of Luther's great achievements was translating the Bible into German, an effort that took him more than a decade.[23]

Luther's *Small Catechism* and *German Catechism* (which came to be known as the *Large Catechism*[24]) came out in 1529. Later editions of these works in English consulted for the present work display a sequence of the Ten Commandments, the Apostles' Creed, and the Lord's Prayer, followed by other sections (e.g., Baptism, Confession, and the Sacrament of the Altar).[25]

The *Small Catechism* (which appeared first in poster form) proved to be very popular.[26] An older edition consulted for the present work addresses the Ten Commandments, followed by the Creed in three articles (creation, redemption, sanctification) and the seven petitions of the Lord's Prayer. Then come Baptism, Confession, and the Sacrament of the Altar, along with such topics as prayer, a scripturally based "table of duties," and some questions and answers.[27] The *Small Catechism* appears in question-and-answer form, with the question "What does this mean?" appearing regularly after a teaching, followed by a brief explanation. Some editions include this advisory before the major topical areas: "As the head of the family should teach it in a simple way to his household."[28]

The *Large Catechism*, which relies on Luther's sermons,[29] takes the form of a teaching commentary. Pastors and preachers in particular are among its beneficiaries; they are advised not to become comfortable with what they already know.[30] Luther held that it fell to "every head of a household to examine his children and servants at least once a week and ascertain what they have learned of it, and if they do not know it, to keep them faithfully at it."[31] The principal content areas are the three noted above (i.e., Ten Commandments, Creed, Lord's Prayer). As Luther begins a subsequent section on Baptism, he writes, "We have now finished with the three chief parts of our common Christian teaching."[32]

The source for the "shorter preface" of the *Large Catechism* is a sermon preached by Luther in 1528.[33] After identifying "children and uneducated people" as beneficiaries of his preaching, Luther uses the term *catechism* in relation to "instruction for children. Its contents represent the minimum of knowledge required of a Christian."[34]

Luther was not the first, of course, to identify the need for the faith development of children; previous chapters have addressed the matter, and more than a century earlier, Jean Gerson addressed the needs of these little ones of God's own creation. Perhaps both Gerson and Luther foresaw a time when "catechesis/message" and "catechism/instrument" would become synonymous, setting the stage for succeeding centuries.[35]

Luther sought a well-informed community, which would include childhood exposure to Christian teaching. He expected adults to ensure adequate preparation of the young. After referring to uninformed "old people," he says, "As for the common people, however, we should be satisfied if they learned the three parts which have been the heritage of Christendom from ancient times, though they were rarely taught and treated correctly, so that all who wish to be Christians in fact as well as in name, both young and old, may be well-trained in them and familiar with them."[36] Presumably this effort includes guiding the formation in faith of those who were uneducated.

Consider the phrase "both young and old": it is brief and to the point, seemingly symbolizing the breadth of the community. In his discussion of Luther's *Small* and *Large Catechisms*, scholar and historian of the era William Haugaard points out that those adults who work with the young have needs relating to their own catechetical formation. He states, "The church's education of the young is inextricably bound up with adult education."[37]

All need to be fed by the Word. This reality has already been recognized in this book. We may regularly hear of contemporary approaches, programs, and resources that promote the faith formation of children and young people. These positive developments, often born of extraordinary hard work and sacrifice, are worthy of recognition and, when possible, expansion. Amid the complexities of parish life, experiences of other committed faithful may demonstrate that other catechetical needs require more vigorous attention, especially in view of the progression of ecclesial sources about or related to catechesis.[38] The more a parish maintains a catechetical superhighway for one constituency, the more it is obliged to ensure that the Gospel path for others is not in disrepair.

Each of us begin life as an infant who is held up and nurtured by others. To foster and sustain partnerships of discipleship within a parish, seamless engagement in catechetical opportunities from early childhood on needs to be geared to advancement along a *continuing* path of lifelong faith formation. Yes, even for little children who will advance to adolescence and then on to young adulthood.

In our own day, fresh opportunities can arise from family-based or intergenerational approaches. The family, after all, is foundational.[39] No child rides on its wings alone but is borne aloft by the outstretched arms of the entire parish community. This includes persons who may hear God's call to married life, to the single life, to service as consecrated religious, or to Holy Orders. All belong.

Within the blessing of a growing multicultural environment, active engagement and *ongoing* faith witness need to become natural and systemic realities long before individual programs reach their conclusion. Programs may end, but formation for ongoing discipleship does not. Indeed, with all that is known about adult life, adult learning, and how adults welcome (and struggle with) challenges of lived faith in home and marketplace, the present time of New Evangelization is ripe for creative and sustained efforts for holistic faith formation.

It bears repeating that none of us is ever sufficiently formed as a Christian. Looking through a lens shaped by contemporary catechesis, we may be jarred by what appears to be an expectation of minimal competency in matters of faith (e.g., the "three parts" from Luther noted above). Yet we must reasonably ask, "What is the competency among today's believing community regarding awareness and understanding of creed, commandments, and prayer?" For all its advances, our catechetical era struggles to maintain a consistent, appealing, and abiding aroma of Christian persuasion.

Rather than judge another era by today's standards (which could unfairly cast judgment on reasons for reform in the first place), I propose that we mine the benefits to be derived from the wealth of contemporary approaches, especially through the inspired convergence of liturgy, catechesis, and evangelization in the Church today. Fresh words of welcome and nurture, "spoken" through eyes of care, may be just what an inquiring senior, young adult, adolescent, or even young child yearns to hear. This is especially important for welcoming strangers or "returning seekers" who, through the limitless grace of God, hear God's call through the New Evangelization.

As a result of the Reformation, religious bodies representative of various perspectives and priorities offered distinctive ways of rendering

Christian witness. In addition to Luther, a number of other people worked for reform (e.g., John Calvin in Switzerland). The *Heidelberg Catechism*, which dates from 1563, remains an important source; Marthaler states that it "has the force of an official creed in Reformed churches."[40] And the Church's widely known conflict with Henry VIII, not many years after the dispute with Luther, resulted in a sad and dramatic rift in England. For the English Reformation, "educational goals and methods evolved along with church doctrine and practice."[41]

The painful reality of separation had to be acknowledged along with the conditions that had led to such division.

The promotion of reform in both attitude and action is a powerful dynamic, especially when dealing with a diversity of understandings of faith and of life. Reform does not always result in separation, of course. The Church had experienced reform in centuries past: in monastic life, in efforts put forth for the review and reform of the clerical life, and in efforts directed to the advancement of a well-formed laity. But none of those efforts would come without challenges. The community of faith suffers when the human spirit is distracted, disjointed, and detached from the demands and realities of daily discipleship. No reality-show snapshot is needed to make the point. "Splintered belonging" is painful in any era. Fractures take time to heal. We continue to learn and understand as we live by what we profess and hand on what we believe in faithful discipleship. Sacred scripture and sacred tradition are foundational for the Church.

Pathways of hope can be forged by religious bodies doing hard work together. For example, the 2015 "*Declaration on the Way: Church, Ministry and Eucharist,* is a declaration of the consensus achieved by Lutherans and Catholics on the topic of church, ministry and Eucharist as the result of ecumenical dialogue between the two communions since 1965. It is a consensus 'on the way' (*in via*), because dialogue has not yet resolved all the church-dividing differences on these topics."[42] A key part of the declaration is its Statement of Agreements. The declaration is not an endpoint but a marker on the way of ongoing efforts toward Christian unity.[43]

For us today, witness often surfaces through faith lived and expressed in life's trenches. Trust reinforced by good and holy people can inspire us as children of God find their way home to the Father, the giver and sustainer of life.

The Catholic Church Responds

The cascading series of events that constituted the Reformation impacted the Catholic Church at its core, especially with regard to papal authority and ecclesial identity.

One can imagine the power of discernment coming to life five centuries ago as the Catholic Church "looked in the mirror," an image introduced earlier in this chapter. With only one person, a single image "looks" back. But when a community crowds together, various impressions surface; not all who squeeze together may look, speak, or behave in the same way (anyone who has tried to take a photograph of a family or group has experienced this firsthand!). Amid the communal view, strong strands of wholeness remain, the ongoing mystery of faith and of life present still. We believe and we need to belong.

Martin Luther died in February 1546. By then his work had advanced substantially, buoyed and accompanied by a variety of supporting printed resources. Just a few months before, in late 1545, the Council of Trent began and met periodically before concluding in 1563. Clearly, there were many needs for the Church of the Counter-Reformation.

Among the significant areas addressed by the Council of Trent were "the authority of scripture and tradition, the role of bishops, doctrines and sacraments, and reforms."[44] The decree on justification would come from the sixth session in 1547.[45]

Effort and attention were given to clarity of doctrinal teaching and the formation of clergy by means of seminaries, which "in their modern form date back only to 1563."[46] The ongoing formation of clergy would aim to help guide attempts to catechize the faithful. Celebrated in Latin, the "Tridentine Mass" would become the norm for eucharistic worship in the West until the liturgical reform of the Second Vatican Council.

The reforming efforts of the Catholic Church incorporated the development of and reliance on printed resources, as the printing press had been invented in the previous century. One of the outcomes of the Council of Trent was the *Roman Catechism*, also known as the *Catechism of the Council of Trent*. The idea of this catechism, conceived originally as a "tool for children and uninstructed adults"[47] (but subsequently envisioned as a resource for parish priests), was raised in 1546. Much time passed, however. It has been proposed that St. Charles Borromeo (1538–1584) raised the matter in 1562, the year before the conclusion of the council.[48] In his twenties at the time, he would eventually become the leader of the committee preparing the work. Under his leadership work on the document progressed significantly toward becoming a reality. It was finally printed in 1566 under Pope Pius V.[49]

It is through Borromeo that we see the advancement of what is known as the Confraternity of Christian Doctrine (CCD). The CCD was originated in 1536 by the Italian priest Castello de Castellino, who "gathered together a small group of men and women in Milan, Italy, to conduct schools of Christian doctrine for children, youth, and unlettered adults."[50] Collins reports on its impressive growth, which included as a result of Cardinal Borromeo's subsequent efforts: "at the death of the saint in 1584, 740 schools had an enrollment of more than 40,000 children and adults under the direction of 3,040 teachers and fishers."[51] Pope Pius V, a strong advocate of catechesis for all, had already given approval to the CCD. Children would receive instruction from family members who belonged to the confraternity.[52]

The *Roman Catechism* was a clear response to the moves of the Protestant reformers. Distinguished scholar Anne Marie Mongoven indicates that "the authors intended this text for the use of the clergy to help them in their sermons and their instruction of children and youth."[53] It would serve as a necessary resource in the formation of priests, who bore the responsibility for catechesis in the parish.[54] Preaching to and catechizing those in their care was no small responsibility; Jungmann reports that Sunday afternoon became a time for adults to gather for catechesis.[55] And religious communities also provided catechetical support.[56]

The original *Roman Catechism* appeared as continuous text, though its manner of presentation would change under Pope Pius V, who saw the need for a more clearly organized resource.[57] This catechism would influence the catechetical world for several hundred years.[58] Its sequential structure of four parts (Creed, Sacraments, Commandments, and Lord's Prayer) is recognizable in the "four pillars"[59] of today's *Catechism of the Catholic Church*, the first major[60] catechism of the Catholic Church since the Council of Trent's *Roman Catechism*. (Today's catechism, while promulgated less than three decades after the close of the Second Vatican Council, was prepared after a proposal made during the 1985 extraordinary synod marking the twentieth anniversary of the end of the council.)

Writing about Trent's *Roman Catechism*, Mary Charles Bryce observes that "biblical sources were sought and cited to prove the veracity of the formulae but no concentration on the Bible as a whole was included."[61] In our day, we are fortunate to benefit from the distinctive insights offered by distinguished theologian and scholar John C. Cavadini in his discussion of scripture in the *Catechism of the Catholic Church*. Giving examples of *Catechism* paragraphs that have scripture "not only cited but actually woven into the text of the *Catechism*," Cavadini identifies "a *scriptural catechesis*, a catechesis carried out not simply with the support of the words of Scripture but *in* the words of Scripture. It is a catechetical narrative that *relies* on the words of Scripture to speak its main points, so that it almost becomes a kind of glossed scriptural proclamation rather than a scripturally corroborated dogmatic statement. We find this strategy employed again and again in the *Catechism*."[62]

The preface to the *Roman Catechism* of Trent acknowledges the situation of those coming to understand matters of faith: "Their natural ability, cultural background and particular circumstances must be given attention."[63] A similar thrust appears in the *Catechism of the Catholic Church*, which quotes from the *Roman Catechism* in a brief section that identifies the importance of making adaptations for the catechetical enterprise. The *Catechism* clearly states what it does not claim to do and cites the need for "indispensable adaptations" (CCC, 24). Adaptation is not to be taken to mean randomly selecting a doctrinal topic or catechetical approach. The *National Directory for Catechesis*, in a section on inculturation, reminds us that it is a task of catechesis "to maintain the integral content of faith and avoid obscuring the content of the Christian message by adaptations that would compromise or diminish the deposit of faith" (NDC, 21C).

I would propose that Borromeo's achievement in the *Roman Catechism* not only demonstrates his gift of discernment in navigating the way forward but also witnesses to his sense of belonging to Christ and his Church. As mentioned above, Borromeo, a patron saint of catechists, was a young man during his engagement with the Trent catechism project. Yet imagine what he might have been doing when the idea of a catechism first surfaced at Trent: young Charles was only seven years old at the time. Little did he know then what role he would play and the impact he would have in serving the catechetical needs of the community of faith to which he belonged.

Belonging grips us, even subconsciously and perhaps even without language, as the Spirit rests upon and within us. This can happen at any age. We may come to "know" and understand what resides deep within through our intellectual faculties, a great gift. Yet the journey is also taken by the way of the heart. A sense of believing and belonging sustains us and calms us, especially during times of uncertainty.

While in my twenties and discerning a catechetical vocation, I served as a catechist at air force bases in Colorado and Ohio and overseas; the thought never crossed my mind that I would be getting a call formally seeking my advice about this ministry that would eventually become such an important part of my life. I recall being in great need of ministerial formation. As I will describe in the next chapter, this was a few years after the close of the sessions of the Second Vatican Council. Despite professional uncertainty, I could not resist "wondering forward" through challenging days, weeks, and months: "I say I will not mention him, I will no longer speak in his name. But then it is as if fire is burning in my heart, imprisoned in my bones; I grow weary holding back, I cannot! . . . But the LORD is with me, like a mighty champion" (Jer 20:9, 11).

The point of age in relationship to maturity in faith is a critical one. Do young adult leaders in their twenties and thirties struggle to be heard within the catechetical world? Are more fresh opportunities emerging to make use of their gifts of leadership, or do some remain hidden "under a bushel basket" (Mt 5:15)? What vehicles exist for sharing the distinctive witness of young leaders whose faith memories and life stories are born of diverse cultural backgrounds? I am imagining here a wide swath of existing and potential young adult leaders from an array of backgrounds interacting, planning, praying, leading, and serving.

Much is written these days about young adults and others who no longer self-identify as Catholic. Perhaps some are comfortable with the designation "Nones." However, this classification does more than dismiss ecclesial identity, even when self-applied; such a declaration strikes at the God-given gift of life awaiting awakening.

Wisdom is not limited to the insight of elders (although sometimes "elder wisdom," like younger wisdom, may seem to be at rest). The way of communication between generations, especially for leaders, is the way of mercy. This is a concrete and doable sign of a New Evangelization. "The mercy of God is his loving concern for each one of us" (MV, 9). "Loving concern": a simple phrase, but strong in substance. Works of mercy, carried out across generations, provide limitless opportunities for sustained Christian witness as part of the Good News we proclaim (cf. GS, 42).

Shaping a Pattern in Print

It is understandable that we would expect the *Roman Catechism*, the first for the entire Catholic Church, to have been the initial catechism prepared from a long line of Catholic catechetical responses. However, that was not the case. We find a link to the Society of Jesus for an explanation and for sustenance along the way.

Ignatius of Loyola (1491–1556), who founded the Society of Jesus (the "Jesuits"), was eight years younger than Martin Luther. The Jesuits became an essential arm of Church reform, including the advancement of catechesis. Some in the society served in advisory roles to the bishops of the Council of Trent; "Ignatius instructed them to take time each day to teach children."[64]

Ignatius's classic and beloved *Spiritual Exercises*[65] continue to inspire, form, and direct not only Jesuits but also numerous other Christians in offering themselves to Christ. "The Ignatian retreat always looks to the past but with the future in mind."[66] The oft-repeated phrase "finding God in all things" captures a central aspect of Jesuit spirituality through which active and formative discipleship progresses. "The daily examen (examination of conscience) . . . is an exercise in surrender to God and discernment of God's leading."[67] Of particular interest here is the work of the Jesuits Peter Canisius (1521–1597) and Robert Bellarmine (1542–1621). The work of distinguished Jesuit scholar Paul Begheyn, S.J., helps to guide understanding of the catechetical contributions of Canisius.[68]

The first and most demanding catechism of the esteemed Dutch theologian Peter Canisius, the *Summa doctrinae christiana*[69] ("Summary of the Christian doctrine"), was "ordered by Ignatius himself."[70] It appeared in 1555, the year before Ignatius died and about a decade before the publication of the *Roman Catechism* of Trent (a council in which Canisius participated[71]). It "was written in Latin and directed to undergraduates and pupils in classes comparable to our advanced high school years."[72] The catechism had more than 200 questions, with responses often of much greater length.[73]

To our benefit, Begheyn provides access to Canisius's own voice: "We may call this book the 'large Catechism' to properly differentiate it from the 'small Catechism' and also from the 'smallest Catechism'. The latter books I published later for the benefit of the less educated. Both proved so dear to the Catholics that they have been used by nearly all the catechists."[74]

Canisius's *Summa* treats a predictable body of teachings. Atop the list of contents of a copy in English (one which includes many scriptural references) consulted for this work is the sentence "Christian Doctrine consists in Wisdom and Justice."[75] Within the category of Wisdom are such elements as faith and the Creed, hope and the Lord's Prayer, and charity and the Ten Commandments. Treatment of the sacraments connects wisdom and justice.[76] Under "Christian Justice" appear such topics as sin, the seven deadly sins, good works, fasting, prayer, alms, works of mercy, virtues, gifts and fruits of the Holy Ghost, the eight Beatitudes, the evangelical counsels, and last things.

The *Smallest Catechism* appeared in 1556, and the *Small Catechism* in 1558.[77] The former, for younger children, was not limited to a question-and-answer format but included a variety of prayers. His "most widely acclaimed manual" was the *Small Catechism*, prepared for "children in the middle years."[78] It, too, was rich in substance as well as serving as a resource for prayer.[79] The work of Peter Canisius would leave a lasting imprint on catechesis for centuries to come.[80]

Before leaving this arena of printed resources, we must mention the contribution of the Italian Jesuit Robert Bellarmine (1542–1621), a brilliant theologian and skilled catechist. Bellarmine's voice, heard through his catechetical sessions, would become the foundation for his *A Short Catechism* (*Dottrina christiana breve*), first published in question-and-answer form (suitable for memorization) in 1597.[81] This highly favored work, "his most popular book, . . . remained in use for three centuries and . . . was translated into sixty-two languages."[82] A second catechism authored by Bellarmine appeared a year later; in that one, the questioner was the student, with the teacher providing a suitable answer to assist the learner.[83]

A copy of a 1614 edition of Bellarmine's *A Shorte Catechisme* consulted for the present work displays, in general, the format of a question by the "Master" and an answer by the "Scholar," along with illustrations.[84] Doctrinal presentation and engagement are central. We see in his work an organizing principle of faith, hope, and love, a pattern familiar to many catechists today. This catechism begins with a section on faith and twelve articles of the Creed (the given reason for twelve is the number of apostles). The next section, regarding hope, treats the seven petitions of the Our Father followed by the Ave Maria. A third part deals with what "*we must do to love God and our neighbor*,"[85] treating here the Ten Commandments, the six commandments of the Church, and the "Counsels of Perfection"[86] (poverty, chastity, and obedience). There follows a section on the sacraments, "*by whose means we obtain the grace of God*."[87] Subsequent sections cover the theological and cardinal virtues, the gifts of the Holy Ghost, works of mercy, original sin and mortal and venial sin, the capital sins and other sins, and the last things. The catechism concludes with a brief section on praying the Rosary. Regarding the sacraments, Bryce points out: "It was a long way in time and ideal from the early church when the mysteries (sacraments) were understood as participatory events in the saving acts of Christ's passion, death, and resurrection."[88]

Bellarmine, a patron saint of catechists, was a significant contributor to the catechetical renewal of the time. Yet perhaps his most significant characteristic was that Robert Bellarmine *was a catechist*.[89] He belonged to the community of catechists to which we belong today; we are in good company. As any writer does, he had to determine how best to proceed in response to the expressed need for his work; how fortunate he was to be able to rely on his catechetical experience in this discernment.

Changing Times

In reporting on practices in European urban centers, Carter indicates that the 1600s and 1700s saw children coming together by age for parish catechetical sessions held in church. The catechetical plan was a simple one: the catechist (who had a manual) explained the young person's text and then put forth questions and answers.[90] However, the era would gradually witness advances in education and other disciplines that would influence learning and teaching for centuries to come, including the environment for catechesis.

One approach came from Jean-Jacques Olier (1608–1657), the French founder of the Sulpicians.[91] His approach assisted children and young people who were lacking in "formal religious instruction in school."[92] It was not limited to a question-and-answer technique (though this was retained in a vigorous way). It incorporated prayer, hymns, and "recitation" spoken from memory by the students. Included, too, were instruction and questions from the catechist. "Questioning students was not intended to be a dry or barren exercise, fitted to small and unimaginative minds, but quick, lively, and animated."[93] Awareness of differences among those in their charge would guide the catechists' interactions with them individually.[94] The approach also capitalized on Bible reading by the students and a homily by the catechist pertinent to the lives of those being catechized. The prayer of the Church was a part of this approach as well; "the spirit of the liturgy developed in the children through attendance at Mass and Vespers."[95]

This brief look at the "Method of St. Sulpice" may not excite readers who are used to the veritable explosion of approaches that are available today. Still, Olier's contribution cannot be underestimated, nor can those of others of the era such as John Baptist de la Salle (1651–1719) and Claude

Fleury (1640–1723). "In the seventeenth century the educational genius of St. John Baptist de la Salle made available the classroom or simultaneous method of instruction which by the eighteenth century (when compulsory education was introduced in Europe) was common practice in all education."[96] Founder of the Christian Brothers, the Frenchman de la Salle was especially attentive to the educational needs of poor people. His catechetical approach included "carefully prepared questions," pertinent explanation, and identifiable relation to everyday life.[97]

Another person eager to improve the catechetical experience was the French Church historian Claude Fleury (1640–1723). He took seriously the need for Christians to become more engaged in the catechetical endeavor. In his *An Historical Catechism*[98] he provides many lessons on sacred history and Christian doctrine. One can see the passion behind his commitment to solid catechesis in this work, in which he vigorously expresses the fundamental importance of scripture.[99] Others also joined the effort to enhance catechesis with printed resources.

Over time, prominent educators and theorists developed and promoted what would become advancements in education. One such figure was John Amos Comenius (1592–1670), a foundational figure for modern education and a bishop[100] of the Moravian Church. He was a strong supporter and advocate of the child, though his thinking penetrated all of education. In his classic *The Great Didactic*, he proposes four grades with corresponding schools—infancy (the mother's knee), childhood (the Vernacular School), boyhood (the Latin School or Gymnasium), and youth (the university and travel): in all, a period of twenty-four years. For Comenius, reliance on such capacities as internal senses, external senses, imagination, memory, and will is essential along the way.[101]

Over decades and centuries, the movement of change in education would leave its mark. In some quarters, the way of society was to become a way of revolution. Change had settled on the doorstep of Europe, and the land across the Atlantic was rumbling. Revolution in England in the late seventeenth century is one case in point. Movement toward independence in the British colonies on the North American continent and revolution in France are other prominent examples, both from the late 1700s.

During the late seventeenth and through the eighteenth century, "enlightenment" catapulted societies into new ways of thinking. The nature of society was changing, and the nature of the person was seen in a new light: the freedom of the individual was strongly asserted during this time. Scholar John Elias writes that "Enlightenment thinking was a continuation of the thrust of Renaissance humanism. Its manifesto made individuals the centers and creators of meaning, truth, and value."[102]

One characteristic of the new age of openness was deepening reliance on the use of reason and scientific analysis, which superseded the embrace of perspectives and positions that heretofore had found their home in faith and religion. Collins writes, "Clarity in expression of theology with a purely intellectual approach left the catechesis dry, tasteless, and unattractive. The warm effulgence of the Good News of salvation was possibly felt only through the recurring feasts of the liturgy."[103] We might say that catechesis had become a tenant in a society driven by rational thought and systematic analysis.

Handbook and Heart

Both faith and reason guide our way to the One who seeks us out first. It is a clear benefit of the present day that faith and reason are understood as complementary elements in matters of Christian belief and practice. Today's digital age is characterized by an avalanche of developments in information delivery. Might this result in catechesis finding its way to narrower enclosures than in times past? Or might these pathways broaden and expand the catechetical enterprise?

Whatever system or approach is employed, how might an evangelizing catechesis maintain and strengthen that which is reasserted in our day through its firm identity with and derivation from scripture and tradition, liturgy and sacraments, Catholic social teaching, and new avenues of merciful accompaniment? How might gifts of inculturation be embraced even more as catechetical plans are formulated? Catechesis does not operate in seclusion. A complex, changing, and violent world surrounds and challenges the catechetical enterprise during an age that is often blind to witness and lacking in mercy.

Catechetical resources can encourage us to go beneath our sometimes fragile surface, challenging us to seek out the heritage imprinted within and the home that is our faith. Along these lines, reference points, which catechetical resources provide with precision, are important for catechesis, whatever the age. Among the conclusions of a groundbreaking international study week on catechetics in 1960 was one that affirmed, in part, "good textbooks are an absolute necessity for catechetical work."[104]

Authentic and complete catechetical resources enrich and inform our understanding. They open new doorways for explanation *and* exploration. And they provide helpful guidance as we interact with persons who may be curious about what Catholics believe. The *United States Catholic Catechism for Adults* is one fine example of such a helpful resource.[105] In addition, for many years a USCCB process has been in place for reviewing texts for children and young people for conformity to the *Catechism of the Catholic Church.* This opportunity for review is another benefit of the contemporary scene.[106]

Yet a pertinent question regarding the era under review is, "Was catechesis so changed during these centuries that it became a mere shadow of its own mission and purpose?" With the use of the printing press, catechesis seems to have drifted into a centuries-long identification with the printed resource. Simple generalization might suggest that catechesis moved from task to tool and people to product, equating (albeit unintentionally, I suspect) text with teaching and method with mission. It strikes me as not unreasonable to suggest that for some people, "believing" came to be seen as no more than the act of reciting words on a page or questions and answers from a chosen resource.[107]

Narrow emphasis on any ministerial area can cloud our vision. A resource poorly used can inadvertently draw attention away from the One who is more foundational than the printed or digitized manual, book, pamphlet, or guide: Jesus Christ, "the energizing center of evangelization and the heart of catechesis" (NDC, 1). He is "the first evangelizer" (NDC, 1); he is the One whom we proclaim and teach. Although words help, they are not the endpoint for what a catechist is or does. For that we must look to Jesus Christ, who *is.* Jesus Christ lives. He is key to our catechesis. He is neither defined by a brief historical entry on a page nor identified merely by placement on a list of prominent religious figures. He is the Son of God. "Catechesis unfolds the fullness of God's eternal plan entirely in the person of Jesus Christ" (NDC, 1). He is present with us, not just "by the ready" but rather calling us to *be* ready. Jesus sustains us, calling us now as he has called others before us.

Lay catechists bear witness to the reality of Christ among us through an evangelizing and boundless discipleship (see LG, 31; cf. AA, 2, and CCC, 873). This may sometimes come to fruition through the art of catechetical adaptation. You may remember catechists from your own life who personified Gospel commitment through insightful awareness (e.g., "Woe to me if I do not preach it!" [1 Cor 9:16]). They knew what was needed and the nature of those whom they sought to nurture in faith. They themselves learned how to adapt. I remember lay catechists and leaders, men and women, with whom I have served over the decades. They have helped to form me in faith, especially as I have witnessed firsthand how they have put Gospel care and catechetical needs of others before their own. Their tireless and faithful witness confirms their commitment to Christ and his Church.

Efforts and motivations of religious communities, families, and the limited number of figures we have seen here confirm the Church's catechetical commitment. We remember with special gratitude women and men religious and many married and single lay faithful who greatly influenced the flow of catechesis in our lives and in service to others. From my own childhood, I remember with fondness the Sisters of Charity–Halifax, the Franciscan Brothers of Brooklyn, and the Marist Brothers who staffed the Catholic schools I attended. Little did I know that so many Catholic school teachers, including from among the ranks of consecrated religious, also served as catechists after the regular school day concluded.

As we approach the conclusion of this chapter, we return to the era under review. Bryce addresses the distinctive contributions of the Ursulines, who were named for St. Ursula and whose founder was the exemplary catechist St. Angela de Merici (1474–1540). During their beginning decades, their lives intermingled with the families with whom they lived, the Ursulines advanced catechetical access for girls as they promoted moral

living and doctrinal understanding.[108] In the century that followed, more
communities of women religious would be formed, heeding God's call.[109]

Francis Xavier (1506–1552), the Jesuit missionary and saint, also
informs our understanding of the era of the Reformation. In a letter from
January 1544 (just a few years after the approval of the Society of Jesus
by Pope Paul III), Francis wrote "To His Companions Living in Rome" of
his evangelizing activity in India. His letter states, in part, "On Sundays I
brought all the villagers together, both men and women, young and old,
to recite the prayers in their own language. They were obviously pleased
and very happy to come."[110] He would focus first on the Sign of the Cross,
which expresses belief in the Trinity, and then would follow recitations
of the twelve articles of the Creed, each of the Ten Commandments, and
multiple recitations of the Our Father and Hail Mary (one of each for
each article of the Creed and each of the commandments), as well as the
Confiteor and the Salve Regina.[111]

Francis Xavier's evangelizing spirit, which included reliance on the
gospels[112] along with those who supported him, provides a look at the posture he took in encouraging others to embrace the Christian faith and be
baptized.[113] The letter referenced above also indicates that because so many
of those who were sick desired Francis's presence, he delegated boys[114] to
represent him. One can almost read his lips as his zeal pierces and moves
our catechetical heart, reminding us where discernment of God's call might
lead: "Many fail to become Christians in these regions because they have
no one who is concerned with such pious and holy matters." Lamenting a
preference (e.g., of university students) "for learning than desire to prepare
themselves to produce fruit with it," he fervently urges a resetting of priorities: "Taking means and making spiritual exercises to know the will of God
within their soul, they would say, conforming themselves to it rather than
to their own inclinations: *Lord, here I am! What would you have me do?
Send me wherever you will, and if need be, even to the Indies!*"[115] St. Francis
Xavier reminds us, living nearly five hundred years later, of the necessity of
establishing priorities in the "making" of Christians.[116] Catechesis remains
a matter of love, hearts bursting with the Spirit of Christ.

I am imagining quite natural personal interactions among members of the early Church as well as efforts of families and others during

the Middle Ages. Yes, we may treasure a copy of a favorite catechetical resource handed down. That is fine; we realize that such resources come with both possibilities and limitations. However, as we build a perspective informed by our history, it would be no small loss to forget what ultimately sustains us. Turning back the clock—just for a moment—to Augustine puts in front of us again the compelling context for formation in faith. In a work of doctrinal beauty, Augustine writes to Laurentius: "So let us return to the three things by which we have said God must be worshiped, faith, hope, and love: it is easy to say what must be believed, what hoped, what loved. But to defend this against the criticism of those who hold a different opinion demands fuller and more laborious teaching: for this it is necessary, not that your hand be filled with a brief handbook, but that your heart be set on fire with great love."[117]

Catechesis is sustained by this fire of love. Today, from within deepening and expanding dimensions of catechesis formed in love, there is a tightening interaction between our belonging to Christ and our believing in Christ as interplay with evangelization and liturgy continues to thrive.

"Voices of fire" of the Reformation era, such as those of Teresa of Avila (1515–1582) and John of the Cross (1542–1591), also continue to sustain us. These giants of Christian spirituality, saints, and Doctors of the Church followed Augustine by more than a thousand years: take note of the sustaining power of the Gospel! Teresa was two years old when Martin Luther wrote his *Ninety-Five Theses*, and John was just three when the Council of Trent began. They not only grew up during reforming times but also were destined to suffer through their own reforming efforts. In her classic *The Way of Perfection*, the Carmelite reformer Teresa would write to her sisters, "since water flows from the earth, don't fear that it will extinguish this fire of the love of God; such a thing does not lie within its power."[118] And one of the best-known poems of John of the Cross, Carmelite priest, is "The Living Flame of Love."[119]

The point here is that catechesis is no end in itself; it moves us along the way to the fire of God's love that burns deep within, never to be extinguished. We are part of an evangelizing faith community that "belongs as we believe and believes as we belong."[120] We are grounded in the love of Christ. Our hearts seek, know, and experience what it is to belong to him and to the Church, the community of faith. They are hearts that demonstrate firm faith foundations of believing along with the power of prayerful discernment as discipleship unfolds and as the Spirit leads and guides us, not alone but in concert with others of the Church, seeking to enact an evangelizing catechesis. And they are hearts that live the way of faith in life shared through times of challenge and change, formed by living witness to Christ through his Church. May our prayer for unity summon us before the one Cross as arms from every corner of the globe reach out to carry it together—and through it one another. "For if we have grown into union with him through a death like his, we shall also be united with him in the resurrection" (Rom 6:5).

St. Francis Xavier's *Doctrina Christiana* (*The Short Catechism*) begins with this prayerful entreaty: "Lord God, have mercy on us. Jesus Christ, Son of God, have mercy on us. Holy Spirit, have mercy on us."[121] May his words take us to a deeper place, to a hope that stirs the soul, sweetens the spirit, and moves the heart. God lives, and we live because God lives! Christ lives in us as we trust the Spirit to guide the Church and all of our catechetical undertakings. May we keep the fire burning!

Reflection Questions

1.   What more do you wish to know about a person or event of this era? To whom might you turn for information or conversation?

2.   "Enter" the era under review here. What do you see as limitations? Benefits? Concerns?

3.   Imagine you are in conversation with a person from a faith tradition different from your own. You are asked to explain why you believe as you do and why you belong to the community of the Church. How might you begin your reply? What facial expression might enhance your story?

4.   How might today's catechetical environment benefit from understanding of this era? How might the community of faith's evangelizing efforts be enhanced going forward?

5. What scriptural passages or verses guide your discernment as you reflect on the experience of "living, dying, and rising" through the emerging portrait of your life?

6. What community or person in the present era is a reflection for you of faith, hope, and love? What is it that draws you to that community or person?

7. How might God's gift of mercy be realized even more effectively through your faith commitment and catechetical outreach to others? How might your reflection enrich your ministry?

8. How might you encourage young adults as they discern God's call for their lives? What encouraging signs of discipleship do you see around you?

9. Think about a time when you relied on a catechetical resource to support your ministry, perhaps a book or a web-based resource. Why did you select it? What did you learn from it?

10. Why do catechetical resources remain important supports for ministry? How might they be used more effectively as part of a comprehensive catechesis?

8

REIGNITING THE WAY
Catechesis Bridging a Millennium

Let the word of Christ dwell in you richly, as in all wisdom you teach
and admonish one another, singing psalms, hymns, and spiritual
songs with gratitude in your hearts to God. And whatever you do,
in word or in deed, do everything in the name of the Lord Jesus,
giving thanks to God the Father through him.

—Colossians 3:16–17

For several decades my pen has welcomed the darkness of night as
a peak time for writing.[1] The practice emerged when my children
were very young; I would wait until they were asleep. The quiet of
night—a distinctive time of God's nearness—is calming as I probe the
joy of catechesis, a gift of "great bounty, till the moon be no more" (Ps
72:7). Sometimes I drift from the moment at hand and "see" through the
darkness, memories hidden yet present.

Memories linger. I see myself as an altar server in high school in
1961. Checks on my Latin responses during weekly group meetings assert
the joy of my tender age: *Ad Deum qui laetificat juventutem meam*[2] (To
God, who gives joy to my youth). The wonders of youth! If memory serves
me correctly, in the early fall of that year a group of us would head to

Yankee Stadium as guests of the parish priest responsible for our formation. Seated in a section behind home plate, we watched in amazement
as Roger Maris swatted his sixty-first home run. Could life get any better
for a young boy from New York?

Four days before my high school commencement, "Good Pope John"
died, several months before the start of the second session of the Second Vatican Council. The date was June 3, 1963. I would ultimately learn
that belonging can hurt. The class yearbook, *Recordare* (Remember), was
dedicated to him. Its opening lines remain fresh: "Courage, enthusiasm,
daring are the characteristics associated with youth. Because this is so,
young hearts leap to the recognition of these qualities in Our Holy Father
Pope John XXIII."[3]

I do not recall having a distinctive "faith seeking understanding"
moment regarding the council while I attended college in the 1960s. However, the notion of Church as servant seemed to come naturally. Serving
Christ, "the light of humanity" (LG, 1), and on behalf of Christ and the
Church seemed to be a family and parish expectation. My understanding
of the Church as sacrament emerged gradually as I began to experience
what it meant to profess and live faith within diverse settings, confirming
the reality that "the Spirit dwells in the Church and in the hearts of the
faithful, as in a temple (cf. 1 Cor 3:16, 6:19)" (LG, 4).

Surf and Turf

My formal entry into this ministry came during college, soon after the
council, while serving as a catechist assisting a young person with special
needs. That formative experience, along with coordinating and leading
faith-based college events, led to my serving as a catechist at military
installations in the United States and on Okinawa, part of an island chain
along the East China Sea. There, surging reminders of Baptism surrounded
me for sixteen months. It was the early seventies.

I was on unfamiliar turf, a world stadium of cultural awareness destined to challenge and enliven my faith in new and discomforting ways.[4]
Living within the cultural blend of this island community scarred by
war, I grew through the love and witness of others. In some ways, this

time represented belonging at its height for me. What we know today as discipleship was, at least for me at that time, in that place a standard expectation of Christian living. We are each other's keepers, after all. Extraordinary, powerful faith all around me seemed the norm.

Something deep within kept drawing me to Christ through the way of catechesis. The *National Directory for Catechesis* says it better: "The object of catechesis is communion with Jesus Christ. Catechesis leads people to enter the mystery of Christ, to encounter him, and to discover themselves and the meaning of their lives in him" (NDC, 19B).

The call to catechize had seized my heart. God had called. I could not say no, despite occasional resistance. The impact of the Second Vatican Council rested gently and solidly upon my shoulders, awaiting my response. It was as if I were already living the charge of the council document *Apostolicam Actuositatem* (*Decree on the Apostolate of Lay People*): "No less fervent a zeal on the part of lay people is called for today; present circumstances, in fact, demand from them an apostolate infinitely broader and more intense" (AA, 1).

Married and the father of a small child, I concluded my active air force service in 1972 to seek a ministry position in the United States. Armed with predictable naïveté and guided by the Spirit, I experienced the convergence of believing and belonging through the call to discern next life steps.[5] After an anxious period of unemployment, a position as a parish coordinator of religious education became my entrée into full-time ministry.

Some readers may claim with me that we lived the council as we learned the council and learned the council as we lived the council. According to Johannes Hofinger, S.J., "Not only did the Council ratify and approve what the leading catechists had been saying about the need to harmonize teaching and life, but it went far beyond their visions and opened up new horizons and perspectives."[6]

There is much to probe in the conciliar fall sessions from 1962 to 1965, a speck of time in the life of the Church. But the council did not end there. Fifty years later, we hear from Pope Francis that "the Church feels a great need to keep this event alive. With the Council, the Church entered a new phase of her history" (MV, 4).

The Second Vatican Council would change my life, enabling me to write much of this chapter from personal experience. My impressions of catechesis of the past half century are formed by a decades-long walk through Vatican II, whose sessions began less than twenty years after the end of World War II and concluded during a time of growing debate over the war in Vietnam.

We will return to catechesis in light of the Second Vatican Council later. For now, we ask, "What are some developments that brought us to the council's doorstep?"

A Slice of History

We enter recent history via the past two centuries. Highlights and personalities are numerous, and one investigator's preference for study may not be another's. What holds events and perspectives together is our experience of belonging and believing as a type of template for faith coming alive. Christians of any era need to discern next steps as they seek to live in Christ through the Church. We look back to this age and its stages of catechetical development with sincerity and an eager spirit.

The Enlightenment had yielded new ways of looking at our fundamental understanding of life itself, finding its way to "the person." We might apply the well-known aphorism of the Greek philosopher Protagoras: "Man is the measure of all things." The appeal to scientific analysis and reason reigned; the person was at the "center." What place was there, then, for faith?

Past missteps within Christianity had led to a mixed catechetical environment. Missionary scholar Alfonso Nebreda, S.J., writes, "The emphasis now shifted from the divine element in religion and salvation history to the human element. . . . The Roman Catechism stressed first what God has done for our salvation; whereas the catechisms of the Enlightenment stressed what *man* must do to save himself."[7] This way of thinking left its mark on catechism lessons; the sacraments were seen as "helps to preserve morality in man."[8] Nebreda says of the sacraments: "They were not considered as memorials of the Passion nor as signs of faith that justify. They were merely means to help man keep the commandments."[9]

A catechism sequence of Creed followed by sacraments became Creed followed by commandments.[10]

It is important to remember that "the *altar* of the New Covenant is the Lord's Cross, from which the sacraments of the Paschal mystery flow" (CCC, 1182 [italics in the original]). No wonder we are awed by the gift and impact of the sacraments, "efficacious signs of grace" (CCC, 1131) given for us.

We may sometimes hear people talk about Christians who "live a life of grace," one's life formed by and situated within Christ. God continues to call us to himself. The *Catechism of the Catholic Church* teaches, "Grace is first and foremost the gift of the Spirit who justifies and sanctifies us. But grace also includes the gifts that the Spirit grants us to associate us with his work, to enable us to collaborate in the salvation of others and in the growth of the Body of Christ, the Church" (CCC, 2003).[11] No one collaborates "alone"; it is a movement of the community of living faith, graced by God.

Among other developments, the nineteenth century witnessed the continuing preparation of catechisms. In some ways they served as a type of self-definition of the ministry, "tools of the trade" and upfront expressions of the trade itself. Over time, catechesis would see more deliberate moves in a direction informed by both scripture and sacred history.[12]

The young United States had already faced a war of independence and a second war with Great Britain during the lifetime of the country's first bishop, Baltimore's John Carroll (1735–1815). Although the First Provincial Council of Baltimore, meeting in 1829, ordered the preparation of a catechism, no "common catechism" would soon follow.[13] Many details and twists mark a pathway to the printing press that took more than five decades. Bryce reports that the catechism of Robert Bellarmine was held up as an example by authorities in Rome. The issue of "uniformity" would become a significant point of discussion.

During the next six provincial councils held after the 1829 gathering, "no attention was given to the subject of a single catechism for use throughout the entire United States."[14] But catechesis continued to be addressed during the intervening decades.[15] Other catechisms were written by bishops or others (with approval) during these years for use in local dioceses.[16] And Bryce also notes reliance on the form of a joint pastoral letter from the bishops after the councils that included guidance on catechetical matters for the faithful.[17] The *Baltimore Catechism* came out in 1885, more than a half-century after the First Provincial Council.

Two persons from among many who form part of *Baltimore Catechism* history were Bishop John L. Spalding of Peoria (the nephew of Bishop Martin John Spalding, who presided over the Second Plenary Council of Baltimore) and Januarius de Concilio, a New Jersey priest and theologian. They brought the project to completion after the close of the Third Plenary Council of Baltimore. It bore the title *A Catechism of Christian Doctrine, Prepared and Enjoined by the order of the Third Plenary Council of Baltimore.* The original contained 421 entries in question-and-answer form.[18] It drew, at best, mixed reaction.[19]

In my judgment and despite its mixed reception, this catechism would eventually be viewed over time by scores of people as *the* most influential catechetical source for Catholics in the United States. Renowned historian Jay Dolan indicates that "up until the 1960s, the Baltimore Catechism remained the staple of the Catholic Sunday school and of children's religious instruction in general."[20]

The original edition placed the sacraments before the commandments as the *Roman Catechism* had done.[21] However, it was not unusual to find revised Baltimore editions with sacraments and commandments reversed.[22] Tests and exercises for students to complete were sometimes included within the book itself.[23] A 1949 edition stated that the *Official Baltimore Catechism No. 3* incorporated "considerable additional matter in the form of Scriptural quotations and more extensive doctrinal explanations."[24] The preface to a 1962 version said, "It is usually the practice to have the children memorize the answers in the text, but this is of comparatively little value if the children do not understand well what they are memorizing. The explanatory material has been adapted to the age and general intelligence of children in the upper grades of grammar school."[25]

It is reasonable to suggest that for many adults, the *Baltimore Catechism* represented their last regular exposure to teaching in written form.

Perhaps for some it seemed to reduce "faith" to a set of questions and answers and, as life went on, limited "understanding" to what they had learned as children.[26]

Three years after the Second Plenary Council of Baltimore of 1866, the First Vatican Council was held. Called by Pope Pius IX ("Pio Nono"), the council lasted less than a year (1869–1870).[27] Faith, reason, and revelation were major topics for this council, which is well known for its teaching on papal infallibility. Another topic was that of a "small catechism" for the entire Church. The topic received great attention during about a three-month period;[28] viewpoints and preferences varied considerably. Issues included "the relationship of uniformity to unity"; reference to adults occurred "only rarely."[29] When the proposal was finally put to a vote, it was approved by a very large margin. "Implementation, however, . . . did not come to pass. The council fathers dispersed, and no particular commission was assigned the task."[30]

A little more than two decades later, in 1891, Pope Leo XIII promulgated his landmark encyclical *Rerum Novarum* (*On Capital and Labor*) during dangerously unsettling economic times. "Grafting itself onto a tradition hundreds of years old, it signals a new beginning and a singular development of the Church's teaching in the area of social matters."[31] The encyclical dealt with many issues and would become a foundation for what we know today as the "Catholic social tradition." The Holy Father writes of "truth and justice" (RN, 1) with great urgency in addressing the severity of the times. He states, for example, "Some remedy must be found, and quickly found, for the misery and wretchedness which press so heavily at this moment on the large majority of the very poor" (RN, 2).

In my judgment, catechetical efforts in our day on behalf of the Catholic social tradition are the strongest of my lifetime and a standard expectation for contemporary catechesis. Whether across the street or across the globe, challenges confront people of good will. Sustained catechetical efforts from our Catholic social teaching prompts our participation in justice and peace initiatives rooted in the Gospel, for "the Gospel of life is at the heart of Jesus' message" (EV, 1).

Into the Twentieth Century[32]

Methodological advances followed a conglomeration of factors over the course of the nineteenth century.[33] Bryce calls attention to the second half of the nineteenth century in parts of Europe, where "a ferment developed which questioned the doctrinal question-and-answer approach to catechesis."[34] Lucinda Nolan indicates that the typical approach used "at the end of the nineteenth century was one of text explanation followed by memorization."[35] Jesuit catechetical scholar Johannes Hofinger (1905–1984), while giving high praise to those who taught him as a child, tells of a "kind of catechism [that] excelled in its faithful concern for correct doctrine together with a deplorable, unintended neglect of children's psychology."[36] The period around the turn of the century was the first part[37] of a move toward improvement, with a focus on catechetical method.[38]

Method was "in." For example, roots of what became known as the "Munich Method" are traceable to the German scholar Johann Herbart (1776–1841), whose work in educational psychology would eventually impact (through adaptation) religious instruction.[39] Three verbs summarize the approach: present, explain, apply.[40] As Nolan points out, the Munich Method "was based on the educational theory that learning proceeds from observation to understanding to application."[41] The teaching matter relied on "the locally accepted catechism."[42] The emphasis on methods "sought to improve religious instruction by relating it more closely to daily life."[43] The early decades of twentieth-century catechesis would bring innovations in approaches to learning, with accompanying methodologies.

Within the Catholic Church, the early twentieth century witnessed significant catechetical activity in Vienna and Munich, places of vibrant and sustained development. Across the Atlantic what we know today as the National Catholic Educational Association (NCEA)[44] would see founding roots established in St. Louis in 1904. Two highly influential contributors to Catholic education and catechetical renewal were the priests Peter Yorke (1864–1926) and Thomas Shields (1862–1921). Their passion for Catholic education spanned the theoretical and the practical, and each developed creative textual resources with respect for the needs of the child.[45]

NCEA's history includes specialized leadership for Catholic education[46] within diverse educational arenas, including a distinguished religious education department. The founding director was the respected scholar Alfred McBride, O.Praem., for decades a prolific author and significant leader of and contributor to catechetical development.[47] NCEA's organizational direction today is widely reflected in concerted efforts on behalf of Catholic school education. A professional organization, NCEA "provides leadership, direction, and service to fulfill the evangelizing, catechizing, and teaching mission of the Church."[48]

Another path was forged by the Religious Education Association (REA),[49] which was founded in Chicago in 1903 by William Rainey Harper. Heavily influenced in its early years by the progressive vision of the distinguished Protestant scholar George Albert Coe (and others, such as John Dewey), REA priorities were different from traditional Catholic priorities. "Coe assumed that religion was neither given nor transmitted, but rather a fundamental aspect of personality which needed to unfold naturally."[50] Scholar Helen Archibald states, "For Coe, Christianity itself was clearly the inspiration for religious education, but religious education was a process by which Christianity was to be sifted and refined."[51]

Today the organization is known as the Religious Education Association: An Association of Professors, Practitioners, and Researchers in Religious Education (REA:APPRRE). It represents the coming together in 2003 of the REA with what was then known as the Association of Professors and Researchers in Religious Education.[52] REA:APPRRE includes skilled academicians and practitioners from among many religious bodies and is also international. Catholic scholars became much more engaged in organizational work and leadership after the Second Vatican Council.

The early 1900s hosted the catechetical witness of St. Pius X. Like others before him, he recognized the importance of attending to the needs of adults. His 1905 encyclical *Acerbo Nimis* (*On the Teaching of Christian Doctrine*) states, "Since it is a fact that in these days adults need instruction no less than the young, all pastors and those having the care of souls shall explain the Catechism to the people in a plain and simple style adapted to the intelligence of their hearers" (AN, 24). The encyclical also gave new life to the Confraternity of Christian Doctrine, calling for its placement in every parish, with "lay helpers" assisting the clergy (AN, 24). Marthaler notes, "It was clear that he had in mind an association of dedicated, lay catechists banded together for mutual support."[53]

In the United States the banding together of lay Catholics was already underway, with roots sown in a parish in New York City in 1902.[54] The CCD would be influenced by the persuasive character and leadership of Bishop Edwin O'Hara (1881–1956), a major force behind the founding of its national center in 1935 and a deliberate promoter of the needs of the Church in rural areas.[55] According to Marthaler, O'Hara's "vision was to integrate the Confraternity in the parish, making catechesis a community activity."[56] The confraternity was broadly focused on ministry and outreach. "Instruction was . . . a means to foster Catholic identity and inculcate Christian values."[57] The confraternity would experience "phenomenal growth . . . in the years before Vatican II."[58]

With the passage of time came organizational change, including for the ministry of catechesis.[59] Also, persons holding diocesan leadership positions for this ministry had ordinarily been clergy, but the ministry would eventually see many from the vocations of religious, married, and single life serving as diocesan leaders. One arm of related support that eventually emerged was the National Advisory Committee on Adult Religious Education.

Today the United States Conference of Catholic Bishops[60] provides leadership, direction, and support for the Church's catechetical life through its bishops' committee and office structure (for example, the Committees on Evangelization and Catechesis, Catholic Education, and Doctrine). Committees and offices impacting the broad sweep of catechesis include (but are not limited to) Evangelization and Catechesis; Catholic Education; Doctrine; Divine Worship; Cultural Diversity in the Church; Justice, Peace, and Human Development; Child and Youth Protection; Children and Migration; Migration and Refugee Services; Domestic Social Development; International Justice and Peace; Pro-Life Activities; Laity, Marriage, Family Life, and Youth; Clergy, Consecrated Life, and Vocations; and Ecumenical and Interreligious Affairs. Episcopal catechetical roots run deep in our history to include the visionary work of Bishop O'Hara[61] as well as many others who fervently lead and address contemporary catechetical needs of the Church.

Offering specialized witness to this ministry is the National Conference for Catechetical Leadership (NCCL).[62] NCCL's deep-rooted and sustained commitment to catechesis is noteworthy. The NCCL "grew out of the early Confraternity of Christian Doctrine (CCD) movement in this country, with roots going back to 1934."[63] Susanne Hofweber, O.P., was the first executive secretary when the organization became independent in 1982.[64]

Numerous constituencies benefit from NCCL's promotion of the Church's mission of evangelization and catechesis through collaboration with bishops, diocesan and parish catechetical leaders, and other groups. A diversified membership organization, NCCL serves a wide swath of constituencies. Its "global end" is clear: "Members of the NCCL will achieve competence as leaders in the ministries of evangelization and catechesis within the teaching mission of the multi-cultural Catholic Church in the United States."[65] The Federation for Catechesis with Hispanics in NCCL has a mission "to serve those who minister in catechesis with Hispanics,"[66] a critical life-giving dimension of the Church in the United States, especially for long-term catechetical development and faith witness. One particularly enriching aspect of the NCCL is its growing reliance on and nurturance of new generations of catechetical leaders, a clear and sustained commitment to the future of this ministry.

Other national organizations, such as the National Federation for Catholic Youth Ministry (NFCYM), also serve catechesis through dedicated constituencies. NFCYM "supports and strengthens those who accompany young people as they encounter and follow Jesus Christ."[67] For many years NFCYM has provided distinguished leadership for youth ministry. Its advocacy efforts benefit young people and those who commit to this essential ministry in significant ways as they witness to the call of the Gospel.

The National Association of Catholic Family Life Ministers (NACFLM)[68] is another example of organizational commitment. Ministerial organizations offer a place to specialize and serve, as members carry out their "daily belonging" to Christ and his Church through professional commitments rooted in faith and mutual trust. They bring a particularly enriching commitment in working toward a future "already present" as constituencies grow and new needs surface.

Jesus Christ, the Message

The mercy of the Father, offered through the sacraments, touches us in our most frail inner and outer selves as we humbly gather as one to "enter the mystery" and offer praise and thanks to God for the gift of his Son in the Eucharist. Hands of mercy reach as one to others yearning for God's care. Pope Francis reminds us that "the Eucharist, although it is the fullness of sacramental life, is not a prize for the perfect but a powerful medicine and nourishment for the weak" (EG, 47).[69] A contemporary resource, the *United States Catholic Catechism for Adults*, titles its first chapter in Part II "The Celebration of the Paschal Mystery of Christ."[70]

We cannot live as Christians without "paschal presence" enlivening the faith community. Even when we are at our worst, prayerful discernment in response to the sweet breath of the Spirit can lead us to return to what some might see as the anomaly of the Cross: in our failures, Christ welcomes us, always. This is fundamental to what we believe and how the Church expresses belonging to Christ. Discernment can lead us to sacramental celebration. Mercy and forgiveness go hand in hand in home and community. Again, the Holy Spirit abides.

Catechesis occupies an important place at the table of faith and discipleship. The principal table is that of Word and sacrifice, the table of the Lord around which we gather for Eucharist.

Liturgical historian and scholar Keith Pecklers, S.J., identifies the beginnings of the liturgical movement in Europe primarily with Benedictine monks and monasteries, most notably "the Benedictine monastery of Solesmes and its founder, Dom Prosper Guéranger (1805–1875)."[71] In the United States, over a span of decades the broadening context for catechesis would engage more explicit connections to liturgy, especially through the efforts of the influential monk Virgil Michel (1890–1938) of St. John's Abbey in Minnesota. But he was not alone.

Pecklers writes that Estelle Hackett, O.P. (1888–1948), and Jane Marie Murray, O.P. (1896–1987), met with him in 1929; the three of them agreed that "a new type of integrative text was needed for the teaching of religious education, based on the liturgical year."[72] They would pursue together the development of such resources for nearly a decade.[73] Pecklers also notes that "from the very beginning, leaders of the liturgical movement argued that liturgy, well-celebrated, was the best and most fundamental form of adult education which the Church could offer American Catholics."[74] Jay Dolan states that "a vigorous catechetical movement had gained a full head of steam by the 1930s; summer-vacation schools, discussion clubs, and a number of other programs became very popular."[75]

The early twentieth-century search for new and "life-centered"[76] methodological support was, in the end, insufficient. Something more was needed.[77] The scholar Luis Erdozain, S.J., addresses "a shift in perspective: emphasis was now to be transferred from method to content. The ground had been prepared for this . . . a century before, by the biblical-patristic studies of the School at Tübingen."[78]

Two principal figures whose work shaped the coming era were the Austrian Jesuits Josef Jungmann (1890–1975) and Johannes Hofinger. Each ardently promoted what catechesis was, leading toward what it was to become. At the halfway point of the twentieth century Jungmann would write that "what is lacking among the faithful, is a sense of unity, seeing it all as a whole, an understanding of the wonderful message of divine grace." He would add, "Both our teaching and our catechisms are too much in the nature of theological treatises."[79]

Jungmann proposed a powerful Christ-centered focus on the kerygma. His assertions on behalf of sharing the Good News would contribute significantly to shifting the catechetical landscape. He would write, "Christ is the pivotal point of all God's ways—those by which His mercy descends to His creation and those by which the creature mounts back to its Source. All dogmatic treatises converge about Christ. His person and work form the true core of the Christian message of salvation."[80] Hofinger says of his fellow Jesuit and teacher that he proposed "*a more dynamic presentation of the Christian message.*"[81]

Jungmann's classic book *The Good News Yesterday and Today* came upon the catechetical scene in the United States in abridged form in 1962.[82] First published in German in 1936, it "immediately caused a great sensation"[83] but would not be available for long. Hofinger indicates that "in 1936 . . . it was still dangerous to suggest that some of the developments within the church were errant."[84] Not long after its publication, the book would be withdrawn by the general of the Jesuits.[85]

The Good News provides a compelling sense of the heart of kerygmatic renewal, of faith proclaimed and handed on. Although the "core" content of catechesis was captured by emphasis on the kerygma, this was no mere set of words of an outline being readied for analysis. Jungmann's voice was clear: the kerygma was a reality to be experienced, truth given voice by heralds of faith whose witness would neither dissipate nor discourage. With pastoral care, Jungmann vigorously proposed a christocentric focus for catechesis, an invitation to proclaim and participate in the mystery and love of Christ. What, indeed, is the essence of the message, if not the Good News focused on Christ? Building a relationship with Christ was essential, not just for understanding but for the movement of life itself. This is no static activity, but cause for ongoing discernment.

Jesus Christ *is* the message we proclaim. Life-giving relationships are formed in him. Salvation is in Christ, in whom we believe and to whom we belong. Jungmann wrote with energy of the pursuit of "*a vital understanding* of the Christian message, bringing together 'the many' into a consistent, unified whole, that then *there may be joyous interest and enthusiastic response* in living faith."[86]

But how was such a dynamic initiative to be applied beyond familiar shores? Part of the answer would come from adaptation. Marthaler indicates: "Just as developmental psychology made evident the need to adapt to the age of the learner, missionaries and catechists in Africa and Asia found it necessary also to adapt the Christian message to the different linguistic and cultural patterns."[87] His observation is important for any student of catechesis and culture. Adaptation is not merely a matter of change but a function of catechetical discernment, and it is no easy exercise.

The International Study Weeks

The convergence of *kerygma, didache, leiturgia, koinonia,* and *diakonia* was then and remains now part of the fabric of an ever-developing catechesis. Numerous examples could be cited from both before and after the council. The Church was experiencing an explosion of research and resources, along with attention to catechesis from within mission lands. From 1959 to 1968 a series of six "study weeks," held at various locations around the world, probed and mined numerous aspects of catechesis, surrounding the council with a variety of catechetical perspectives as the future became the present.

Hofinger led the East Asian Pastoral Institute in Manila and was the driving force behind the study week concept. These gatherings yielded sustained international catechetical exploration.[88] Erdozain recounts three underlying "phases": kerygmatic, anthropological, and political. Locations for these international meetings included Nijmegen, Netherlands (1959), Eichstätt, Germany (1960), Bangkok, Thailand (1962), Katigondo, Uganda (1964), Manila, Philippines (1967), and Medellin, Colombia (1968). Michael Warren, scholar of catechesis and religious education, makes this important point about the study weeks: "They represent an evolving series of focuses, each building on the insights of those preceding."[89]

The Eichstätt gathering was a high point of kerygmatic renewal.[90] The conclusions of this gathering included reliance on the Bible and affirmation of liturgy: the Bible deserves "a very prominent place in catechetical teaching," and "latent in the liturgy [is] a colossal wealth of meaning and a tremendous instructive power."[91] Among the many principles put forth was this: "Catechesis embraces a four-fold presentation of the faith: through liturgy, Bible, systematic teaching aud [*sic*] the testimony of Christian living."[92] The linkage of the kerygmatic perspective and the "four sources" just noted is of historic significance. Mongoven stresses that "the Eichstätt Study Week . . . brought together the kerygmatic approach of the Jungmann school and the developmental catechesis and pedagogy of signs of the French."[93]

German, French, and Belgian initiatives inhabited a main floor of the renewal.[94] Nebreda writes, "The German concern was directed primarily to people who were at least nominally Christian. Faith was the point of departure. For the French, faith was the point of arrival. Their approach was primarily missionary, and hence helpful to the missions."[95]

A strong voice in affirming and promoting the four sources was that of the French Sulpician priest Joseph Colomb, S.S. (1902–1979). Other distinctive voices of the era were those of Pierre-André Liégé, O.P. (1921–1979), and Alfonso Nebreda (1926–2005). Both especially valued and promoted the *reality* of people's lives as a fundamental milieu for welcoming the Good News. Scholar Catherine Dooley indicates that they "recognized the psychological and sociological conditions that supported or deterred growth in faith, [and] saw the need to consider the influence of the environment on the individual."[96] Among his many significant contributions, Liégé provided foundational insights into "pre-evangelization."[97] Nebreda's 1965 book *Kerygma in Crisis?* offers many perspectives on the same topic; he vigorously promotes adult movement toward "living faith."[98]

The kerygma lay at the core of the entire Christian life lived through the Church. As Hofinger points out, "This phase accomplished much more than answering the question, 'What is to be taught in genuine catechesis?'"[99] The catechist's own formation in faith was as "herald of Christ."[100] Combining "liturgy, Bible, systematic teaching aud [*sic*] the testimony of Christian living,"[101] the kerygmatic approach went to the heart of what we believe and how we are to be formed as disciples in witness to God's love given in Christ.

Before the council, major developments were already underway, drawn from educational theories and their application to catechesis (e.g., the importance of attention to the experience of the learner), forming a type of template. Growing emphasis on "the person" coming to faith was a given. Hofinger states that "just as the kerygmatic renewal found its authentic formulation in the Eichstätt Program of 1960, the anthropological approach found its pertinent expression in the Asian Catechetical Study Week of 1967 held in Manila."[102] In between were the Bangkok and Katigondo gatherings.

Bangkok affirmed the fourfold emphasis reported above (liturgy, etc.) and addressed "the basic aims of modern catechetics," a discussion considered important "for the sake of a better understanding in the missions." In Bangkok, there was also significant discussion of the three stages of the kerygmatic approach to the missions, identified as "pre-evangelization, evangelization, and catechesis proper."[103] The first two relate to a precatechumenal mode and the third to a catechumenal one. One of the informative related notes from an account of this meeting states, "The guiding principle of pre-evangelization is anthropocentrical because we must start with the individual as he or she is."[104]

The gathering at Katigondo displayed a kerygmatic sense, attention to cultural and other factors regarding the African scene, and a growing anthropological focus.[105]

Erdozain proposes that the anthropological can be seen "more as the unexpected fruit of the seed sown by the kerygmatic renewal."[106] He adds, "The kerygmatic movement, by insisting on the importance of content, permitted of a deeper understanding of the Word of God which is never to be found in its pure state but centred in the heart of man."[107]

With study weeks occurring before and after the council, catechetical movement in several directions was underway and ongoing.[108] Hofinger promoted Jungmann's perspectives while offering his own in addressing the kerygma and shaping its catechetical implications. He would popularize the renewal in the United States.[109] Scholar Matthew Halbach points out that Hofinger, in a later work, "describes the need to understand catechesis as the means by which the *kerygma* is proclaimed. Thus, he refers to catechesis as an 'evangelizing catechesis.'"[110]

The "four sources" did not represent a call for faith formation by segmentation; such a move would provide no clear answer for fulfilling the demands of catechesis. Dooley observes that "the integration of these sources freed the catechetical endeavor from its isolation. Catechesis was no longer limited to instruction and to the classroom. Instead, it coalesced with the biblical and liturgical renewal into one organic movement that was reflective of the catechesis in the early Church."[111]

The Belgian center Lumen Vitae (International Institute of Pastoral Catechetics) became a major world center for thoughtful and shared conversation, especially in print. According to Marthaler, we see from the work of George Delcuve (1908–1976) and others the "approach to catechesis called 'pedagogy of signs.' Ideally every catechetical program weaves Bible, doctrine, liturgy, and Christian witness together in such a way as to present the Christian message as an organic whole."[112] Mongoven points out that for Joseph Colomb, the term "human experience" rather than "witness" was used for the fourth source.[113] Depending upon one's perspective—and yes, experience—"human experience" would come to popularize or de-popularize entire periods for catechesis in the United States.

In 1966, less than a year after the promulgation of *Gaudium et Spes* (*Pastoral Constitution on the Church in the Modern World*) at the Second Vatican Council, the Belgian scholar Marcel van Caster, S.J., addressed the topic "Signs of the Times and Christian Tasks."[114] The signs of the times would become a dominant catechetical theme; we recall from *Gaudium et Spes* that "at all times the Church carries the responsibility of reading the signs of the times and of interpreting them in the light of the Gospel, if it is to carry out its task" (GS, 4).

This responsibility reminds all who serve and promote an evangelizing catechesis that people's lives are in our hands. Indeed, belonging and believing do come together, often through the clarifying path of sound catechetical formation. This path is not some idyllic byway removed from the realities of people and societies: the study week held in Latin America (Medellin, Colombia) confronted the reality of economic, demographic, social, and cultural challenge and change.[115] This gathering's "General Conclusions" stated that "a catechesis open to the action of God demands that catechists walk to the same rhythms and at the same pace as the catechized, sharing as much as possible their lives."[116] Walking together, we see collaboration, evangelization, and community as vital elements of the collective faith-driven effort of the way of catechesis and immersion in Christ.

Distinctive Witness

During the twentieth century, support for catechetical renewal came from many quarters, including determined women of faith and fortitude. Many women have devoted lives of service and exemplary leadership in national, diocesan, and parish catechetical settings. For example, Dr. Carol Dorr Clement tells part of the story of Miriam Marks (1896–1961), who worked with Bishop O'Hara in the Diocese of Great Falls, Montana, before going on to serve as executive secretary of the Confraternity of Christian Doctrine for a quarter-century.[117]

The majority of catechists in this country today are women, who form a distinctive witness to faith and the Church's catechetical foundation. The list of those who helped to shape catechetical renewal is populated by giants of catechesis who gave their lives to adults and families in service of the Word. Many of these women, known by name, represent numerous unnamed disciples, especially from within religious, parish, and school communities. I include only a few examples.

M. Rosalia Walsh, M.H.S.H. (1896–1982), provided extraordinary service on behalf of catechists and children in public schools, especially through an approach called "The Adaptive Way" that is geared toward more effective child engagement. Nolan summarizes: "The five steps of the lesson plan as explained by Sister Rosalia in *Teaching Religion the Adaptive Way* (1966) are: (1) Orientation; (2) Presentation; (3) Assimilation; (4) Organization; and (5) Recitation."[118]

Frequent reference has been made in this book to Mary Charles Bryce (1916–2002), whose research and teaching helped to shape the developing field. Among the many contributions of Anne Marie Mongoven is *The Prophetic Spirit of Catechesis*, a popular text with many insights into the nature of catechesis, including "The Process of Symbolic Catechesis."[119] Jane Marie Murray (1896–1987) and Maria Harris (1932–2005) invigorated not only catechetical conversation but theoretical development. The latter's visionary *Fashion Me a People: Curriculum in the Church* applies insightful understandings of "curriculum" to essential aspects of the Christian community.[120]

Johannes Hofinger's work benefited from the sharp eye of Mary Perkins Ryan (1912–1993).[121] A prolific writer, Ryan would write in 1962, "Clearly, the central work of all forms of catechesis must be to help persons to receive and respond to God's own self-revelation and self-giving, above all in the liturgy."[122] She worked tirelessly in addressing fundamental dimensions of liturgy, catechesis, and adult formation.

During my years of catechetical service at William H. Sadlier, Inc., I was privileged to interact with and learn from Maria de la Cruz Aymes,

H.H.S. (1919–2009). Her lifetime of service to the Church included an appointment to the International Council for Catechesis in Rome. This catechetical legend advanced kerygmatic renewal for children through the *On Our Way* series of graded texts published by Sadlier and later revised in light of the council. An initial and valued partner in her work was Johannes Hofinger; later came Francis J. Buckley, S.J. (1928–2013).[123] A 1968 third-grade text identifies to parents a three-step catechetical approach: *"experience," "message"* ("scripture" and "doctrinal summary"), and *"response."*[124] My interactions with Sr. Maria (and Fr. Buckley) were as a "hungry student." Her death in 2009 and his in 2013 left a personal cathechetical void.[125]

One of the pillars supporting my foundation for this ministry was shaped by interaction with women leaders. If memory serves correctly, there were only a few male parish catechetical leaders in the region where I served in the Diocese of Albany in the early 1970s. My previous positions had been in the air force and it was a change for me to be in the minority. I thank God for that growth opportunity. Diocesan staff members Mary Reed Newland (1915–1989) and Eileen Flanagan, C.N.D. (d. 1997), took me under their wings. The Franciscan Missionaries of St. Joseph who staffed various posts at the parish where I served helped to form me in hospitality, spirituality, and aspects of leadership through their nurturing witness of "undiminished faith" (PC, 25).

Warmed by the Council

My introduction to the Second Vatican Council and the catechetical warming that resulted from it came via the ecclesial experience of community. Faith was afire. Communal enthusiasm was contagious. Experiencing the Church as sacrament was both humbling and demanding: How might I participate in this mystery? How might we see ourselves and come to Christ through the scriptures? What did it mean to be called to holiness and faithful discipleship individually and as a community?

The Catholic Church to which I joyfully affirmed loyalty sharpened my vision. I began to probe more deeply the many Eastern Churches (see OE) and the Latin Church. Those moments offered a profound sense of a people formed in faith in common yet distinctive witness to the Gospel. Over time, Catholics would grow in understanding, appreciating, and living the Church as People of God, Body of Christ, and Temple of the Holy Spirit.[126]

In addition, ecumenical dialogue moved from polite conversation to mutually challenging and sometimes fragile and painful discussion. But at least people were talking—and witnessing. I recall the hope that relations with the Jewish community would in my own lifetime overcome centuries of sadness, tragedy, and discord. The Council's groundbreaking declaration *Nostra Aetate* (*Declaration on the Relation of the Church to Non-Christian Religions*) spoke of "a common spiritual heritage" between Christians and Jews in the interest of "further[ing] mutual understanding and appreciation" (NA, 4).

I also began to explore the meaning of religious freedom (see DH, 2).Whether or not they were viewed by most catechists as connected to *Dignitatis Humanae* (*Declaration on Religious Liberty*), such phrases as "freedom from" and "freedom for" became for some serving in this ministry supports for promoting the Christian moral life and responsibility as well as understanding and cultivating discipleship.

Enlivened by the movement of the Holy Spirit in the life of the Church, the council provided more than a legacy. It yielded greater awareness of the complex world in which we live and challenged prior assumptions of preferential "first-world" approaches to humanity, suffering, and the Gospel. *Dei Verbum* (*Dogmatic Constitution on Divine Revelation*) would affirm at its outset the desire for "the whole world to hear the summons to salvation, so that through hearing it may believe, through belief it may hope, through hope it may come to love" (DV, 1).[127] Little more than a dozen years after the council, *Sharing the Light of Faith* (SLF), "the first document of its kind to attempt to guide catechesis for the United States,"[128] would promote discipleship-movement toward justice, mercy, and peace in society.[129] Projects and programs exemplified these priorities as heightened attention to conversion of heart and spiritual formation, along with renewed appreciation for the dignity of the human person, took hold. Life was/is on the line; Christ was/is still waiting (cf. LG, chap.

V, "The Call to Holiness"). This motivation has staying power as we look ahead.

The passage of time is gift to us, enabling exploration of the Second Vatican Council as an event that affirmed the transcendence and immanence of God. The *aggiornamento* that is descriptive of the renewal generated within and by the Second Vatican Council and the embrace of earlier Church sources represented by *ressourcement* together serve a deeper purpose: the renewal of our identity in Christ through the Church. This continues today as part of the wave of New Evangelization.

My proposal is that the reigniting of catechetical witness continues *because* the council was an extended catechetical moment. The council, "which Pope Paul VI considered the great catechism of modern times" (CCC, 10), broadened pathways for a more firmly and deeply rooted catechesis on behalf of the Gospel, sparked from within the life of the Church. It is a matter of urgency that the fire of faith continue to warm all the faithful.

We listen today for echoes of the council with ears and hearts receptive to ongoing conversion to Jesus Christ, echoes that remind us of our own disposition of faith as we engage others on behalf of the Gospel. The other person is not "just" another but God's own creation discerning his or her own next steps and relationships. Fortunate is that believer who benefits from naturally offered parish support along the way. We do well to remember that "the incarnation of the only Son of God is the original inculturation of God's word. The mystery of the incarnation is also the model of all evangelization by the Church" (NDC, 21A).

Energetic Renewal

There was much catechetical territory to cover during the post-conciliar years. Approaches linked to both theological and educational perspectives helped to set the stage for what is frequently identified within the Church in the United States as "religious education."[130]

The glue of the Spirit has held for decades, with the impact of the council assured by its own widely recorded history and a rich preserve of new, proven outcomes for ecclesial life and ministry. One such outcome had to do with the reassertion of catechetical scholarship concurrent with faithful communal witness. Supporting this journey of discovery were theological perspectives whose foundation is Christ and whose mystery is paschal. There was much to be studied, probed, examined, and explained. An intensified interest in spirituality[131] only sweetened the catechetical enterprise.

The Second Vatican Council had already identified the role of all the baptized in the active promotion of the faith. *Lumen Gentium* notes the essential role of "the domestic Church," stating that "parents, by word and example, are the first heralds of the faith with regard to their children" (LG, 11). However, neither parents nor children are alone within the Christian community: "All the faithful . . . are called by the Lord to that perfection of sanctity by which the Father himself is perfect. The holy People of God shares also in Christ's prophetic office" (LG, 11–12).

Scriptural, liturgical, and catechetical renewal, well underway before the council, found lasting affirmation in the experience and impact of the council. Among the many extraordinary statements of *Dei Verbum* is this one: "Access to sacred Scripture ought to be open wide to the Christian faithful" (DV, 22). Despite longstanding advances in the advocacy of biblical study,[132] the council precipitated a new curiosity about and an explosion of interest in the Word of God.

Many adults eagerly welcomed the opportunity for faith formation, for probing teachings and practices of faith. Their experience of daily life, their "story," was real and sometimes painful; it offered a ready connection to the Gospel and the challenge of living witness.[133] Much of this seems to be recognized and reflected in the holy witness of Pope Francis.

Gravissimum Educationis, the council's *Declaration on Christian Education*, had declared that "all Christians—that is, all those who having been reborn in water and the Holy Spirit are called and in fact are children of God—have a right to a Christian education" (GE, 2). Succeeding documents would use such terms as "chief form,"[134] "summit,"[135] and "center" in referring to the place of adult catechesis in the catechetical sphere. John Paul II would identify adult catechesis as "the principal form of catechesis" (CT, 43).[136]

In the United States, adult formation programs and approaches became a usual expectation. Although the catechetical leader's plate remained full, major support came with the 1999 publication of *Our Hearts Were Burning Within Us: A Pastoral Plan for Adult Faith Formation in the United States*.[137] This brief but detailed plan is an important resource for parishes large and small. Growing and in some places gradual awareness of the benefits of family faith formation led to the development of an array of pertinent approaches. Sometimes the term "adult" would be used as a synonym for "parent," thereby unintentionally limiting attention to the needs of young adults, single adults, couples with no children, and older adults.

A wealth of catechetical documents fueled discussion and enlivened faith. Activating catechetical plans rich in biblical, liturgical, ecclesial, and natural signs (see SLF, 42–46)—reflective of contemporary approaches for understanding the learning-teaching experience—placed broader demands on catechetical leaders, school principals, catechists, teachers, and the catechized in their care.

As we have already seen, review of the catechetical enterprise had been underway for some time. Many people, including scholars and practitioners, became part of the conversation at various times and in various ways. A few examples follow; many more could be identified.[138]

The influential leadership of Gerard Sloyan continues to leave its mark on this ministry. Such works as *Shaping the Christian Message* (1958) and *Modern Catechetics* (1960),[139] for both of which he served as editor, informed and shaped new voices in catechesis and religious education. At a historic 1963 conference, while chair of the department of religious education of the Catholic University of America, Sloyan addressed "Catechetical Crossroads" and assessed "the new catechetical frontier." His insights regarding Jesus Christ, the Bible, and the Eucharist swell with conviction. This architect of catechetical renewal identified the vital importance of a sustained commitment, including preparation, study, and formation. He would urge, "Do all in your power to get solid training at a graduate level for some persons who can assume a leadership role in this central work of the church." He concludes this must-read address with the profound assertion that "Christian formation is mostly doing."[140]

In his book *Catechesis of Revelation,* Gabriel Moran writes, "The cate-chist is to serve the Word and through service and experience point to this Word in his teaching."[141] Moran's many works have received a wide reader-ship. Mongoven seems to summarize when she states that "he emphasized the need for a christocentric, biblical, doctrinal, liturgical catechesis."[142] Moran's *Education toward Adulthood*[143] helped to shape, undergird, and inform efforts on behalf of the religious education of adults.

The respected scholar Catherine Dooley exemplified catechetical integration across the boundary of two centuries, bridging theology, scrip-ture, doctrinal teaching, liturgy, and pedagogy. She was a "go-to" expert, especially for matters relating to mystagogical catechesis and liturgical-cat-echetical formation. She could grip people's attention as she taught and clarified issues while identifying key insights from ecclesial documenta-tion. Her life gave definition to the term "herald," even after some distance in time from the peak decades of kerygmatic renewal. By guiding numer-ous catechists in understanding liturgical catechesis, she helped to prepare them not just intellectually but spiritually for this ministry.

The approach called "shared Christian praxis,"[144] put forward by the distinguished scholar Thomas Groome, has garnered significant national and international attention. Groome's *Christian Religious Education* and *Sharing Faith: A Comprehensive Approach to Religious Education and Pas-toral Ministry*[145] provide in-depth explanation and development of the foundations of his approach. A beginning sense for the reader of the term *praxis* is "reflective action";[146] "critical reflection"[147] plays an essential role in implementing this approach, which has been used for groups ranging from children to adults.

Some practitioners and scholars understood *curriculum* as more than what "the course of study" might predictably imply.[148] Over time, specialized approaches for adult faith formation, family faith formation, intergenerational catechesis, and "whole community catechesis" also became part of the expansive catechetical environment.

A heightened sense of pastoral integration of many elements that contributed to sound catechetical approaches had been emerging for years, inluding human development.[149] Catechetical renewal during the last part of the twentieth century witnessed a surge in methodological approaches that seemed to form a center point for religious education. Developmentally appropriate and systematic ways of presenting catechetical lessons and promoting catechetical understanding, especially with regard to children and young people, sprang up and secured a prominent place. These processes and patterns often incorporated methodologies derived from educational practices of the time.

Existing catechetical priorities for children and teens in parish programs and in Catholic schools were joined by recognition of the importance of comprehensive youth ministry approaches and their accompanying outreach to young people. A multitude of contemporary needs reinforces all of these priorities for ministry today. Supportive catechetical resources for children and young people in parish catechetical programs, Catholic schools, and youth ministry programs demand careful development. Both the Bible and the *Catechism of the Catholic Church* form part of the rich preserve of resources that guide such an effort, which includes developmentally appropriate methodological approaches.

Overall, the "catechetical bar" was set with high expectations for people of all ages and situations. In the years following the council, expectations and challenges were, to put it mildly, massive. The weary leader was often expected to serve catechetical, theological, educational, spiritual, and even counseling functions.

Some observers might propose that one outcome of these process-driven developments was a type of content-process dualism that yielded a less integrated reliance on "holy scripture, tradition, liturgy, and on the teaching authority and life of the Church" (CD, 14) for catechesis, thereby impacting doctrinal understanding and active discipleship. Other observers might propose that the impact of efforts to promote Catholic teaching and active discipleship in living the Christian life would have been markedly weakened without implementation of advanced methodological approaches rooted in the social sciences.

Perhaps it is wise to look back to October 11, 1962, the day the council got underway. In his opening address, St. John XXIII spoke of the importance of "sacred doctrine." He used such terms as *treasure, patrimony,* and *doctrinal penetration.* The Holy Father also stated that "the substance of the ancient doctrine of the Deposit of Faith is one thing, and the way in which it is presented is another."[150]

Doctrine offers substantial ways of participating in the living heritage that helps to shape the tradition we share and the people we are. Such doctrinal exposition requires attentive study. Creedal statements are invitatory, opening us to a wider world of reflection, tradition, and Christian life. Insight gained from knowing the catechetical environment within which one catechizes is essential. For example, *Disciples Called to Witness: The New Evangelization* provides clear guidance; it states, "Catechetical methodologies are based on the proclamation of the faith from Sacred Scripture and Tradition and their application to human experience, or they are based on human experience examined in light of the Gospel and teachings of the Church."[151]

Our bishops preach and teach with hope. We recall that the council called on the bishops to "ensure that catechists are adequately prepared for their task, being well-instructed in the doctrine of the Church and possessing both a practical and theoretical knowledge of the laws of psychology and of educational method" (CD, 14).

So often we find connections to our doctrinal heritage through "windows of the soul," enabling possibilities for a robust evangelizing catechesis in real time.[152] Both inductive and deductive processes can guide our movement toward doctrinal understanding. "The deductive method, however, has full value only when the inductive process is completed" (NDC, 29; cf. GCD, 72).

Our era benefits from greater understanding of the nature of the human person, greater appreciation of the impact of multiple intelligences for catechesis, enhanced awareness and understanding of doctrinal teaching, and a widening appreciation of cultural diversity. We also benefit from the treatment of Catholic social teaching as an essential dimension of the Church's doctrinal foundations. "Life experience" is a healthy part of catechetical discourse and should never be portrayed as a mere stop along the way of catechesis. Nor should setting a prayerful environment be so treated.

"Yet I live, no longer I, but Christ lives in me" (Gal 2:20). The Gospel is for all, and ministerial witness applies to all. People, including children, approach Christ as they are; Christ welcomes them as they are. We can do no less. Existential realities can be doorways to sustained faith formation. Of particular urgency is the pursuit of justice for persons who have suffered racial or ethnic discrimination. Within the Church, genuine witness yields genuine welcome. Belonging and believing serve together to advance understanding and form relationships for living the Christian faith. We do not lose hope! "In Jesus Christ, Lord and Teacher, the Church finds transcendent grace, permanent inspiration and the convincing model for all communication of the faith" (GDC, 137). No one culture is *the* culture of opportunity in matters of faith.

Documents Helping to Guide Ministry

Our living and faithful witness serves as a type of ongoing welcoming agent for the council as we appeal to accounts of the council, to its documents, and to the catechetical experience derived from it. We look ahead, inspired by the dynamic and spirited deliberations of people of faith on whose shoulders we stand. The conciliar moment becomes our own, not through rose-colored glasses but through lenses seeking deeper understanding.

Council documents and other resources of the Church give shape to and support the Church's ongoing catechetical efforts.[153] One could argue that every council document has essential catechetical implications that guide the steady development of diocesan and parish catechetical leaders. The council's four constitutions (*On the Sacred Liturgy, On the Church, On Divine Revelation,* and *On the Church in the Modern World*) provide theologically rich and persuasive foundations for believing, teaching, and living the Christian proposal, not just individually but collectively.

For example, *Sacrosanctum Concilium* (*Constitution on the Sacred Liturgy*), the first promulgated constitution, continues to help set the tone for probing the understanding of worship and the dynamic experience of faith and birth into discipleship. Its oft-quoted statement, "The liturgy is the summit toward which the activity of the Church is directed; it is also the fount from which all her power flows" (SCo, 10), informs and shapes the Christian life before, during, and after the liturgical experience; this is distinctive for the gathering of the baptized. Nearly three decades after the council, the *Catechism of the Catholic Church* would cite that just-quoted statement and then affirm that the liturgy "is therefore the privileged place for catechizing the People of God" (CCC, 1074). After the council, liturgy entered more deliberately into existing catechetical settings and catechesis identified more deliberately its sharing in the journey to the altar. However, this is not a mutually exclusive relation, for liturgy and catechesis lead to merciful discipleship.

We are wise to view catechesis through a catechumenal lens. The conciliar document *Christus Dominus* (*Decree on the Pastoral Office of Bishops in the Church*) set a lasting tone that has impacted the way in which catechesis is understood for all. It prescribes, for example, that "they should take steps to reestablish or to modernize the adult catechumenate" (CD, 14). The convergence of people, practices, and pedagogy offers a dynamic blend of catechumenal influence for catechesis through the *Rite of Christian Initiation of Adults*. Marthaler points out: "The catechumenate changed the catechetical model from school to apprenticeship and shifted the emphasis from instruction to experience."[154] It remains an opportunity for enacting the Church's catechetical mission and reinvigorating communal foundations as people come to Christ. The RCIA is a recurring host for the commingling of liturgy and catechesis.

Applying a catechumenal mentality[155] includes inviting the entire parish to confirm its role as catechist. This is more than a theoretical wish; it is a natural expression of communal responsibility, motivating the baptized toward lived faith and mutual care. The belonging arms of the Church are wide. "God's love for us is fundamental for our lives" (DCE, 2), Pope emeritus Benedict XVI reminds us in his first encyclical.

I would suggest that *Gaudium et Spes* helps to guide the Church forward with particular urgency. It was promulgated on the day before the council closed (the Feast of the Immaculate Conception, December 8, 1965). When Pope Francis declared the Jubilee Year of Mercy on December 8, 2015, it was the fiftieth anniversary of the close of the council. The weakened human condition demands merciful attention, especially in light of present-day challenges of survival and displacement. Communal witness to faith is confronted by sectarianism, secularism, consumerism, and unrestrained individualism. Stories of martyrs, told to me as a child in safety, are not limited to centuries past; accounts of Christians and others dying at the hands of terrorists abound. Struggles within the Church reaffirm the need for repentance, sustained healing, and renewed witness to the Word of God. This necessarily includes self-examination of one's own life of faith within the Christian community. A look in the mirror may confirm for us that the mercy giver is first a mercy seeker.

The document *Christus Dominus* called for the development of "a directory for the catechetical instruction of the Christian people" (CD, 44). Enhanced efforts for developing "a living, explicit and active faith, enlightened by doctrine" (CD, 14) would begin to shape even more directly the ministry of catechesis. The *General Catechetical Directory* and the *Rite of Christian Initiation of Adults*,[156] issued within a year of each other (1971, 1972), became groundbreaking, seminal texts for an emerging catechesis formed in light of the council. Relying on pastoral theology as a foundation, the GCD[157] identifies several aspects of the Church's ministry of the Word, including evangelization and catechetical, liturgical, and theological forms. These are neat distinctions, but the GCD realistically states that "in the concrete reality of the pastoral ministry, they are closely bound together" (GCD, 17).

Near the end of the 1970s, John Paul II addressed "the Original Pedagogy of the Faith" in his landmark apostolic exhortation *Catechesi Tradendae (On Catechesis in Our Time)*. After identifying some elements that contribute to pedagogy, he wrote, "Pedagogy of faith is not a question of transmitting human knowledge, even of the highest kind; it is a question of communicating God's Revelation in its entirety" (CT, 58). I am reminded of the synod on catechesis regarding children and youth held just two years before the Church received *Catechesi Tradendae*. From that synod we would hear that "pedagogy of faith therefore has this specific characteristic: an encounter with the person of Christ, a conversion of the heart, the experience of the Spirit in the ecclesial community."[158]

In 1985, about six years after *Catechesi Tradendae*, a proposal was made for a catechism for the entire Church. The setting was the synod that focused on the twentieth anniversary of the closing of the Second Vatican Council. The *Catechism of the Catholic Church* would become the first officially declared worldwide catechism since the sixteenth-century *Roman Catechism*. Catechesis continues to benefit from established and growing reliance on this important resource. As a significant reference sourcebook, it serves the pedagogy of faith with its systematic presentation of the profession of faith, liturgy and sacraments, living the Christian moral life, and prayer.

Published a few months after its 1997 approval by the Holy Father, the *General Directory for Catechesis* came after more than three decades of post-conciliar history.[159] When the GDC was published, the *Catechism* was already in use worldwide, making a dramatic impact on people, products,[160] and catechetical perspectives. It identifies the *Catechism* as "the doctrinal point of reference for all catechesis" (GDC, 93). While acknowledging the "generous dedication, worthy initiatives and . . . positive results for the education and growth in the faith of children, young people and adults" since the end of the council, the GDC also asserts the reality of "crises, doctrinal inadequacies, influences from the evolution of global culture and ecclesial questions derived from outside the field of catechesis which have often impoverished its quality" (GDC, 2). Among its many topical areas, the GDC addresses the connection between evangelization and catechesis, promotes the inspiring place of the baptismal catechumenate for catechesis, describes contributing elements to the pedagogy of the faith, and promotes six tasks of catechesis.[161] The term *six tasks* is part of the woodwork of catechesis; mere mention of the term evokes the breadth of this ministry.

Daniel Mulhall writes that the *National Directory for Catechesis*, which replaced *Sharing the Light of Faith* in 2005, "covers most of the themes presented in SLF, but addresses them from the perspective of evangelization and in greater depth."[162] With its established linkage to evangelization, the NDC provides an underlying, unifying framework in support of "proclaiming Christ, preaching Christ, bearing witness to Christ, teaching Christ, and celebrating Christ's sacraments" (NDC, 17C; EN, 17).

A Deepening Relationship

Among all of the initiatives put forth for specifying and engaging the ministry of catechesis since the Second Vatican Council, the relationship between evangelization and catechesis has continued to deepen. Catechesis, which serves both initiatory and ongoing functions of faith formation, lives within "the context of the Church's mission of evangelization" and is "an essential moment of that mission" (GDC, 59).

The Church "exists in order to evangelize" (EN, 14). So wrote Pope Paul VI in *Evangelii Nuntiandi* (*On Evangelization in the Modern World*), his apostolic exhortation that followed the Second Vatican Council by ten years and the synod on evangelization by one year. Emphasis on the relationship between evangelization and catechesis became an even stronger part of catechetical conversation. Identifying catechetics as "a means of evangelization" (EN, 44), the Holy Father connected systematic instruction and Christian living, promoted methodological adaptation,[163] noted the importance of the catechumenate, and addressed ensuring due attention to children (cf. EN, 44).

The New Evangelization demands engagement of catechists and catechetical leaders with both the active faithful and with those who are considering a return to the faith they once called their own. This cross-generational effort can be made without abandoning evangelization initiatives directed to those who have not experienced any initial proclamation of the Good News (see RMi, 33) and those of no religious tradition who yearn for the lasting peace of a relationship with Christ. New Evangelization is not only about the person "alongside of me,"[164] but also about me: "The New Evangelization calls all Catholics first to be evangelized and then in turn to evangelize."[165] Catechesis is an essential aspect of that process, a linchpin between generations, within families, and across cultures. A distinctive contributor to this dynamic was the renowned theologian Virgilio Elizondo (1935–2016), who was widely esteemed for his leadership in Hispanic theology. He possessed an innately pastoral sense of the growing Latino community, keen and gracious awareness of diverse cultures, and sharp pastoral insights for evangelization, catechesis, and spirituality.

Perhaps ongoing linkages to the New Evangelization will yield broader and more creative approaches for adult faith formation in this digital age. Greater attention is needed for an evangelizing catechesis that engages both young adults and older adults. The *United States Catholic Catechism for Adults* is a widely available resource for use as part of a comprehensive plan.

The Second Vatican Council yielded a spurt of interest in new ways of participating in the life of the Church—ways to live, not just to work or to serve. *Sustained collaboration* is a password among persons engaged in diocesan and parish catechetical ministry, within networks of Catholic schools, and across other Catholic institutions.

Pastors bear "the primary responsibility" (NDC, 54B1) for a parish's catechetical effort. "Priests . . . owe it to everybody to share with them the truth of the Gospel in which they rejoice in the Lord" (PO, 4). They are identified by the NDC as "absolutely essential contributors to an effective catechetical program" (NDC, 54B2). In fact, a postconciliar document identifies the priest as "the *catechist of catechists.*"[166] Such a catechetical call is both opportunity and gift. In addition, the catechetical service of deacons offers enriching and distinctive perspectives as "the deacon participates as an evangelizer and teacher in the Church's mission of heralding the word."[167]

An encouraging outcome in the United States of the Second Vatican Council was the growth in the number of listings in the Catholic press for positions in catechetical ministry. Many consecrated persons and married and single lay faithful secured viable leadership positions that enabled them to participate in new ways in the Church's catechetical mission and foster catechetical growth. Today, collaborative trust continues to reinforce service on behalf of the Church's catechetical ministry. This is no insignificant responsibility. The lay faithful, with a baptismal call lived and deepened over a lifetime, have much to continue to offer the Church. This witness emerges from seasoned, new, and younger catechetical leaders.

Catechist formation remains an essential priority. This formation includes authentic witness to faith and a pedagogical sense rooted in the faith we profess; it goes beyond acquiring necessary teaching skills. It must include discernment, spiritual formation, and prayer with other catechists. Wrapped in mercy, catechist formation is not just a periodic encounter but also a defining opportunity for forming relationships in Christ. Ongoing witness to life in Christ—in service to the Gospel through the witness of the Church—demands no less. What is true of renewal in faith for all applies of course to those serving the ministry of catechesis: "The New Evangelization invites people to experience God's love and mercy through the sacraments, especially through the Eucharist and Penance and Reconciliation."[168]

Our Yes to an Evangelizing Catechesis for All

Where is the way of catechesis leading us?

We remember from chapter 3 that Jesus tells Martha, "I am the resurrection and the life" (Jn 11:25). Jesus Christ invites us into his own life. He accompanies us along the way of an evangelizing catechesis: a way of belonging, of believing, of discerning, and of living, dying, and rising.

The mission to go out and "make disciples" (Mt 28:19) that Christ offers us does not cease when we grow weary. Christ is with us in this effort in an everlasting accompaniment of mercy. "Christ teaches us how to evangelize, how to invite people into communion with him, and how to create a culture of witness: namely, through love."[169] He reminds each of us, "Be merciful, just as [also] your Father is merciful" (Lk 6:36).

One significant disposition for building a vibrant catechesis has to do with the formation of an informed attitude of faith regarding cultural diversity within the Church and in society. The Second Vatican Council continues to speak to people of all cultures and backgrounds as people come together in communities of living faith.

Distinctive gifts represented by a lively multicultural blend impact catechesis and catechetical options in parish life. Multicultural catechetical witness, deliberately and joyfully applied, is especially important. Belonging, believing, and discernment are key characteristics of this blessed reality.

Catechesis provides the opportunity to raise up the faithful and heroic Christian witness of people of a diversity of backgrounds. Consider, for example, the distinguished witness of St. Kateri Tekakwitha (1656–1680), Ven. Pierre Toussaint (1766–1853), St. Katharine Drexel, S.B.S. (1858–1955), Bl. Carlos Manuel Rodríguez Santiago (1918–1963), and Sr. Thea Bowman, F.S.P.A. (1937–1990).

Signs of hope strengthen our resolve. For example, in reporting on and writing about "parishes with Hispanic ministry,"[170] the scholar Hosffman Ospino indicates that "nearly four out of five parishes offer programs of faith formation for Hispanic adults."[171] Looking to the future, Ospino points to the importance of "adult faith formation initiatives as Hispanic families pass on the faith to the largest sector—more than half—of the Catholic population in the United States in our day."[172]

In a section on ethnic diversity, the *National Directory for Catechesis* notes that "since persons can only achieve their full humanity by means of culture, the Catholic Church in the United States embraces the rich cultural pluralism of all the faithful, encourages the distinctive identity of each cultural group, and urges mutual enrichment. At the same time, the Catholic Church promotes a unity of faith within the multicultural diversity of the people" (NDC, 11C1). For people with disabilities, catechesis is essential to the experience of faith. "Persons with disabilities, especially children, are particularly beloved of the Lord and are integral members of the Christian community" (NDC, 49). The NDC also addresses the importance of catechesis for persons "in special situations." Catechetical outreach to groups of people in such situations is an important faith witness, and careful adaptation can help ensure their benefiting from "a sound and adequate catechesis" (NDC, 50).

When numbers are low or logistics difficult, it is wise to develop strategies for effective small-group catechesis. It remains important to explore just solutions that reflect consideration of *all* catechetical priorities when facing parish and diocesan challenges. Remember, "the communication of the faith in catechesis is an event of grace, realized in the encounter of the word of God with the experience of the person. It is expressed in sensible signs and is ultimately open to mystery" (GDC, 150).

Consistent efforts to affirm Catholic identity draw strong support from the implementation of the RCIA, prayerful study of scripture, regular in-depth consultation with the *Catechism*, and careful application of the six tasks of catechesis. Contemporary catechetical processes and programs demonstrate this important awareness.

Today's catechetical leaders are expected to develop programs in service to families, the elderly, young adults (single and married), adolescents, children, the newly married, and other groups. They reach out to distant horizons well beyond familiar and comfortable boundaries so that the Gospel can be offered to all. Some markers along the way of catechesis, New Evangelization, and doctrinal foundations in this twenty-first century include

- enhanced reliance on sacred scripture and heightened understanding of sacred tradition;

- Christian living shaped by worship and prayer;

- inspired episcopal and pastoral leadership;

- comprehensive formation for lay ecclesial ministry;

- increased significance of inculturation for forming community;

- engaging the experience of initial and ongoing conversion;

- mining even more the baptismal catechumenate and its implications for all of catechesis;

- promoting the Catholic social tradition and the pursuit of justice and peace;

- forming disciples of accompaniment for a lifetime of merciful, faithful witness; and

- joyfully embracing all of the faithful as vital to this ministry.

Harvesting what has been produced from roots planted by other generations, we approach the way ahead with strong catechetical foundations. This is our reality as our living and dying lead us to offer and take comfort in the hope of resurrection.

As we look to future decades, sacred tradition and sacred scripture continue to resound through unmuted voices. The Word of God sustains, directs, and envelops us in God's care while simultaneously calling us to risk Gospel living marked by faithful and prophetic witness. We may walk to Emmaus, but we run back to Jerusalem.

Catechetical leaders and catechists cannot wait to share what they witness. The Church, "on earth, the seed and the beginning of . . . [the] kingdom" (LG, 5; cf. CCC, 541), is watered by our expressed discipleship through relationships marked by joy and struggle. Although the terrain may shift beneath us, one thing remains: the love of God for each person. And we offer that love to others.

No longer clearly separated, collaborative threads of diversity weave together heritage and history while finding meaning and lively expression of faith across cultures and generations. In helping to form communities with an incarnational awareness, catechetical leaders and catechists share with other disciples mysteries so powerful that words fall short of explaining why they do what they do. And yes, complex interactions with parishioners are vital to the parish's response to the Gospel as a community of faith.

The six tasks of catechesis are reflected in "real time," a testament to those who have stayed the course and to those who enter the way of catechesis not without some trepidation. Such discomfort is a blessing worthy of the faithful servant, secure in a foundation built on Christ, Master Catechist and cornerstone of faith (cf. Acts 4:11 and Eph 2:20). In such an ecclesial setting, love knows no end. "Since God has first loved us (cf. 1 Jn 4:10), love is now no longer a mere 'command'; it is the response to the gift of love with which God draws near to us" (DCE, 1).

The person immersed in this ministry—seeking no thanks but offering thanks to the Father for the privilege of serving—is reminded that "among the laity who become evangelizers, catechists have a place of honor" (RMi, 73). As we look ahead, we actively seek to continue "to mature as a person, a believer and as an apostle" (GDC, 238).

One realistic faith-filled example comes to us from Mary, mother of Jesus and Mother of the Church. By her fiat, she shows what risk and discipleship are about, regardless of the era in which people live. Any rebirth of interest in ongoing discipleship need not stray far from her. She "is acknowledged and honored as being truly the Mother of God and of the redeemer" (LG, 53). It goes without saying that teaching about "Mary, Star of Evangelization" (NDC, 74; see EN, 82), remains an important priority for catechesis. Here we find new opportunities for creative engagement of the six tasks of catechesis.

We are called to the prophetic discomfort of risk-taking discipleship, following in the footsteps of the faithful over the centuries who offered their lives in witness to faith and service to the Church, oftentimes unsure of what they were undertaking. The commitment implied here is modeled by the women who find the emptiness of the tomb of the Risen One a reason for belief. "Fearful yet overjoyed" (Mt 28:8), they run to tell others of their experience.

Similarly, one can invoke the account of Peter's response to Jesus' question, "Who do you say that I am?" in exploring the commitment of the faithful disciple (Mk 8:29). Peter demonstrates firm commitment in his confession of faith: "You are the Messiah" (Mk 8:29). Although Peter's deep sense of commitment might be deemed questionable in light of his forthcoming denial of the Lord, he subsequently demonstrates faithful adherence to the living Word in proclaiming, "God raised this Jesus; of this we are all witnesses" (Acts 2:32). Peter, one who weeps bitterly along the way of discipleship, is not one who "gives up" (cf. Mt 26:75, Lk 22:62).

In the parish catechetical leader, this witness is born of high but not impossible expectations, with such a role limited to "only fully initiated, practicing Catholics who fully adhere to the Church's teaching in faith and morals and who are models of Christian virtue and courageous witnesses to the Catholic faith" (NDC, 54B5). Human, spiritual, intellectual, and pastoral formation put ministerial flesh on one's willingness to serve as a lay ecclesial minister.[173] The catechetical leader must know the message of faith and be aware of the social context from within which he or she catechizes. Collaboration is essential. This is especially important in an age as diverse as ours. Such a person commits his or her life to Christ and, in so doing, loses that life in him.

With confidence in what he or she proclaims, the leader invites others to life in Christ risen and to the experience of self-examination. We belong, together. We believe, together. This is part of the New Evangelization, that recognition that each of us is called to a renewal of self and a recommitment to the Church of the ages. "The faithful become agents of evangelization through living witness and commitment to the Gospel."[174]

When the Spirit seizes us forthrightly, there is no turning back, only toward, never far from that first echo. And this turning involves joyful embrace of the Cross—a difficult lesson for many to consider, let alone understand, in contemporary life. Constants for us are "the light of faith and meditation on the Word of God" (AA, 4).

We respond with integrity, with trust, and by the decisions of our lives to the call of the Spirit. May our recommitment to an evangelizing catechesis be an energetic "Yes!" embedded in our heritage of faith. Our roots run deep in the love of Christ, the One who first loved us. Driven by mission, we serve as co-workers in the vineyard of the Lord.[175]

The mystery of the Incarnation is gift beyond measure; "the Word became flesh" (Jn 1:14).What saving love! Jesus Christ, the One with whom union is possible through this astonishing gift of the Father, was "tested in every way, yet without sin" (cf. Heb 4:15). He is the One whom death cannot hold and the One whom we seek, together, in faith as his disciples. He offers us the way of life and the way to live in the Spirit as the Church, through which we come to participate in the life of the Risen One.

Driven by mission, we journey on, pilgrims all, for Jesus Christ is the way of catechesis.

Reflection Questions

1. Consider the faith you profess and live. What is Jesus calling you to explore at this point in your life?
2. What is your earliest memory of hearing about the Second Vatican Council? What questions did you have?
3. What questions about the Second Vatican Council do you have now?
4. How might your discernment regarding challenges you are facing today strengthen your catechetical perspective?
5. Who is a witness of faith for you? What person might you want to thank for his or her care for you?
6. What might your parish consider doing to strengthen even more its commitment to catechesis for all? How might you help?
7. What makes you proud to belong to the Church?
8. What gives you pause about our catechetical history? What issue, person, or event might now lead you to further study?
9. What lessons do you take from our history? Will you share them with others? How might the Holy Spirit be leading you?
10. Whom might you accompany this week in witness to the mercy of the Father? What will move you to act?

APPENDIX
Selected Documents and Other Sources since the Second Vatican Council

Many documents and other sources have helped to guide and shape catechesis since the council. Space permits discussion of only a few of them in this work. A partial list includes the following ("US" refers to entries from the United States). Since this is a blended list, please consult each entry for its origin.

1971 *General Catechetical Directory*

1971 *Justice in the World*, Synod of Bishops

1972 *Rite of Christian Initiation of Adults* (Provisional Text, English, 1974)

1972 *To Teach as Jesus Did: A Pastoral Message on Catholic Education* (US)

1973 *Basic Teachings for Catholic Religious Education* (US)

1973 *Behold Your Mother: Woman of Faith* (US)

1974 *Marialis Cultis* (Apostolic Exhortation *For the Right Ordering and Devotion to the Blessed Virgin Mary*, Paul VI)

1975 *Evangelii Nuntiandi* (Apostolic Exhortation *On Evangelization in the Modern World*, Paul VI)

1976 *A Vision of Youth Ministry* (US)

1977 *Message to the People of God*, Synod of Bishops

1978 *Pastoral Statement of U.S. Catholic Bishops on Persons with Disabilities* (US)

1979 *Sharing the Light of Faith: National Catechetical Directory for Catholics of the United States* (US)

1979 *Redemptor Hominis* (Encyclical Letter *The Redeemer of Man*, John Paul II)

1979 *Catechesi Tradendae* (Apostolic Exhortation *On Catechesis in Our Time*, John Paul II)

1979 *Brothers and Sisters to Us: U.S. Catholic Bishops' Pastoral Letter on Racism in Our Day* (US)

1980 *Dives in Misericordia* (Encyclical Letter *Rich in Mercy*, John Paul II)

1981 *Familiaris Consortio* (Apostolic Exhortation *Regarding the Role of the Christian Family in the Modern World* [*On the Family*], John Paul II)

1983 *Code of Canon Law*

1983 *The Challenge of Peace: God's Promise and Our Response* (US)

1984 *"What We Have Seen and Heard": A Pastoral Letter on Evangelization from the Black Bishops of the United States* (US)

1984 *Reconciliatio et Paenitentia* (Apostolic Exhortation *On Reconciliation and Penance in the Mission of the Church Today* [*Reconciliation and Penance*], *Reconciliation and Penance*, John Paul II)

1985 *Notes on the Correct Way to Present the Jews and Judaism in Preaching and Catechesis in the Roman Catholic Church*

1986 *Economic Justice for All* (US)

1986 *The Challenge of Adolescent Catechesis: Maturing in Faith* (US)

1987 *Sollicitudo Rei Socialis* (Encyclical Letter *On Social Concern*, John Paul II)

1987 *Redemptoris Mater* (Encyclical Letter *Mother of the Redeemer*, John Paul II)

1987 *National Pastoral Plan for Hispanic Ministry* (US)

1988 *Rite of Christian Initiation of Adults* (final edition)

1988 *The Religious Dimension of Education in a Catholic School*

1988 *God's Mercy Endures Forever: Guidelines on the Presentation of Jews and Judaism in Catholic Preaching* (US)

1988   *Christifideles Laici* (Apostolic Exhortation *On the Vocation and the Mission of the Lay Faithful in the Church and in the World,* John Paul II)

1988   *Here I Am, Send Me: A Conference Response to the Evangelization of African Americans and "The National Black Catholic Pastoral Plan"* (US)

1988   *A Family Perspective in Church and Society* (US)

1990   *Guidelines for Doctrinally Sound Catechetical Materials* (US)

1990   *Adult Catechesis in the Christian Community*

1990   *Redemptoris Missio* (Encyclical Letter *On the Permanent Validity of the Church's Missionary Mandate* [*On the Mission of the Redeemer*], John Paul II)

1991   *Centesimus Annus* (Encyclical Letter *On the Hundredth Anniversary of Rerum Novarum,* John Paul II)

1991   *Plenty Good Room: The Spirit and Truth of African American Catholic Worship* (US)

1992   *Catechism of the Catholic Church* [Spanish, 1993; English, 1994]

1992   *Go and Make Disciples: A National Plan and Strategy for Catholic Evangelization in the United States* (Tenth Anniversary Edition, 2002) (US)

1993   *Guide for Catechists*

1993   *Veritatis Splendor* (Encyclical Letter *Regarding Certain Fundamental Questions of the Church's Moral Teaching* [*The Splendor of Truth*], John Paul II)

1993   *Directory for the Application of Principles and Norms on Ecumenism*

1994   *Tertio Millennio Adveniente* (Apostolic Letter *On Preparation for the Jubilee of the Year 2000* [*On the Coming of the Third Millennium*], John Paul II)

1994   *Principles for Inculturation of the Catechism of the Catholic Church* (US)

1994   *Communities of Salt and Light: Reflections on the Social Mission of the Parish* (US)

1995   *Evangelium Vitae* (Encyclical Letter *On the Value and Inviolability of Human Life* [*The Gospel of Life*], John Paul II)

1995 *Ut Unum Sint* (Encyclical Letter *On Commitment to Ecumenism,* John Paul II)

1995 *Guidelines for the Celebration of the Sacraments with Persons with Disabilities* (US)

1996 *Sons and Daughters of the Light: A Pastoral Plan for Ministry with Young Adults* (US)

1996 *Who Are My Sisters and Brothers? Reflections on Understanding and Welcoming Immigrants and Refugees* (US)

1996 *Keep Your Hand on the Plow: The African American Presence in the Catholic Church* (US)

1996 *The Hispanic Presence in the New Evangelization in the United States* (US)

1997 *General Directory for Catechesis*

1997 *Renewing the Vision: A Framework for Catholic Youth Ministry* (US)

1998 *Fides et Ratio* (Encyclical Letter *On the Relationship between Faith and Reason,* John Paul II)

1998 *Welcome and Justice for Persons with Disabilities: A Framework of Access and Inclusion* (US)

1998 *Sharing Catholic Social Teaching* (US)

1999 *Our Hearts Were Burning within Us: A Pastoral Plan for Adult Faith Formation in the United States* (US)

1999 *Eastern Catholics in the United States of America* (US)

1999 *Ecclesia in America* (Apostolic Exhortation *On the Encounter with the Living Jesus Christ: The Way to Conversion, Communion, and Solidarity in America* [*The Church in America*], John Paul II)

2000 *Dominus Iesus* (*On the Unicity and Salvific Universality of Jesus Christ and the Church*)

2000 *Welcoming the Stranger among Us: Unity in Diversity* (US)

2001 *Love Thy Neighbor as Thyself: U.S. Catholic Bishops Speak against Racism* (US)

2001 *Asian and Pacific Presence: Harmony in Faith* (US)

2002 *Encuentro and Mission: A Renewed Pastoral Framework for Hispanic Ministry* (US)

2002 *Native American Catholics at the Millennium* (US)

2003 *Ecclesia de Eucharistia* (Encyclical Letter *On the Eucharist in Its Relationship to the Church*, John Paul II)

2003 *Opening Doors of Welcome and Justice to Parishioners with Disabilities* (US)

2004 *Compendium of the Social Doctrine of the Church*

2004 *25th Anniversary, U.S. Bishops' Pastoral Letter on Racism (A Research Report)* (US)

2005 *National Directory for Catechesis* (US)

2005 *Co-Workers in the Vineyard of the Lord* (US)

2005 *Deus Caritas Est* (Encyclical Letter *On Christian Love* [*God Is Love*], Benedict XVI)

2005 *Compendium, Catechism of the Catholic Church*

2006 *United States Catholic Catechism for Adults* (US)

2007 *Spe Salvi* (Encyclical Letter *On Christian Hope*, Benedict XVI)

2007 *Sacramentum Caritatis* (Apostolic Exhortation *On the Eucharist as the Source and Summit of the Church's Life and Mission* [*Sacrament of Charity*], Benedict XVI)

2008 *Catechetical Formation in Chaste Living: Guidelines for Curriculum Design and Publication* (US)

2008 *Doctrinal Elements of a Curriculum Framework for the Development of Catechetical Materials for Young People of High School Age* (US)

2009 *Caritas in Veritate* (Encyclical Letter *On Integral Human Development in Charity and Truth* [*Charity in Truth*], Benedict XVI)

2009 *Marriage: Love and Life in the Divine Plan* (US)

2010 *Verbum Domini* (Apostolic Exhortation *On the Word of God in the Life and Mission of the Church*, Benedict XVI)

2012 *Disciples Called to Witness: The New Evangelization* (US)

2013 *Lumen Fidei* (Encyclical Letter *The Light of Faith*, Francis)

2013 *Evangelii Gaudium* (Apostolic Exhortation *On the Proclamation of the Gospel in Today's World* [*The Joy of the Gospel*], Francis)

2013 *Reconciled through Christ: On Reconciliation and Greater Collaboration between Hispanic American Catholics and African American Catholics* (US)

2014   *Hispanic Ministry in Catholic Parishes: A Summary Report of Findings from the National Study of Catholic Parishes with Hispanic Ministry* (US)

2015   *Misericordiae Vultus* (Bull of Indiction of the Extraordinary Jubilee of Mercy *The Face of Mercy*, Francis)

2015   *Laudato Si'* (Encyclical Letter *On Care for Our Common Home*, Francis)

2015   *The Gifts and the Calling of God Are Irrevocable (Rom 11:29)* (A Reflection on Theological Questions Pertaining to Catholic-Jewish Relations on the Occasion of the 50th Anniversary of *Nostra Aetate* No.4)

2016   *Amoris Laetitia* (Apostolic Exhortation *On Love in the Family*, Francis)

NOTES

For explanations of and citations for the document abbreviations used in the text and in the notes, see pages xiii–xvi.

1. Our Journey on the Way of Catechesis

1. See, for example, these web pages: http://www.usccb.org/beliefs-and-teachings/how-we-teach/catechesis/catechetical-sunday/catechetical-sunday-about.cfm; and http://www.usccb.org/beliefs-and-teachings/how-we-teach/catechesis.

2. The five senses listed here are from the marginal notes to "A Wycliffite Adaptation of the Catechism, with Latin Rubrics, Put Forth under the Name of Archbishop Thoresby, from the Lambeth ms., no. 408; and Additions [*Within Brackets*] from York Minster ms., XVI, L. 12," in Thomas Frederick Simmons and Henry Edward Nolloth, "Introduction, Notes, Glossary, and Index," in *The Lay Folks' Catechism, or the English and Latin Version of Archbishop Thoresby's Instruction for the People; Together with a Wycliffite Adaptation of the Same, and the Corresponding Canons of the Council of Lambeth*, 19 (London: Kegan, Paul, Trench, Trübner and Co., 1901). The original Thoresby work in Latin dates from 1357. However, see the following article by Anne Hudson, which includes discussion of the work in English and attribution regarding the Lambeth ms., no. 408: "A New Look at the *Lay Folks' Catechism*," *Viator: Medieval and Renaissance Studies* 16 (1985): 243–258.

3. See this complete section for treatment of inculturation.

4. See, for example, IM, 4.

5. The interested reader may wish to pursue other treatments by the author related to this theme. See Gerard F. Baumbach, "Eucharistic Myst-agogy" (Washington, DC: United States Conference of Catholic Bishops, 2011), 1–9, http://www.usccb.org/beliefs-and-teachings/how-we-teach/catechesis/catechetical-sunday/eucharist/upload/catsun-2011-doc-baum bach-mystagogy.pdf; or "*Mistagogía eucarística*" (USCCB, 2011), 1–10, http://www.usccb.org/beliefs-and-teachings/how-we-teach/catechesis/catechetical-sunday/eucharist/spanish/upload/catsun-2011-doc-sp-baum bach-mystagogy.pdf; and "The Pedagogy of Faith," *Church Life: A Journal for the New Evangelization* 2, no. 2 (September 2013): 37–48, accessed March 9, 2016, http://liturgy.nd.edu/assets/112681/baumbach_pedago gyoffaith_vol2issue2.pdf; republished August 1, 2016, http://churchlife. nd.edu/2016/08/01/the-pedagogy-of-faith.

6. Gerard F. Baumbach, "Jubilee: Turning Time for Conversion and Reconciliation," *NCCL Catechetical Update* no. 20 (2000): 8; entire article, 8–11.

7. In broad terms, "the field" is represented by a variety of terms for a variety of reasons and preferences. These terms include faith formation, religious education, Christian education, catechetics, and catechesis. Cat-echesis forms the principal focus of the present work.

Many scholars have contributed to the historical study of religious education, Christian education, and catechesis. An incomplete list of the work of some of these scholars includes Guy de Bretagne, "The History of the Catechesis," *Lumen Vitae* 5 (1950): 363–370; Mary C. Boys, *Educating in Faith: Maps and Visions* (Lima, OH: Academic Renewal Press, 1989); Mary Charles Bryce, O.S.B., "Evolution of Catechesis from the Catholic Reformation to the Present," in John H. Westerhoff III and O. C. Edwards Jr., eds., *A Faithful Church: Issues in the History of Catechesis* (Wilton, CT: Morehouse-Barlow, 1981), 204–235; Harold W. Burgess, *Models of Religious Education: Theory and Practice in Historical and Contemporary Perspective* (Nappanee, IN: Evangel Publishing House, 2001) (see especially chapter 2, "The Historic Prototype of Religious Education: A Backdrop to Twen-tieth-Century Models"); James P. Campbell, *Finding God: Our Response to God's Gifts* (Chicago: Loyola Press, 2005); Joseph B. Collins, *CCD Methods in Modern Catechetics* (Milwaukee: Bruce, 1966); Catherine Dooley, O.P., and Mary Collins, O.S.B., eds., *The Echo Within: Emerging Issues in Religious Education* (Allen, TX: Thomas More, 1997); John L. Elias, *A History of Christian Education* (Malabar, FL: Krieger, 2002); Maureen Gallagher, *The Art of Catechesis* (New York/Mahwah, NJ: Paulist Press, 1998); Milton McC. Gatch, "The Medieval Church: Basic Christian Education from the Decline of Catechesis to the Rise of the Catechisms," in Westerhoff and Edwards, *A Faithful Church*, 79–108; Thomas H. Groome, *Christian Religious Education: Sharing Our Story and Vision* (San Francisco: Harper and Row, 1980), *Sharing Faith: A Comprehensive Approach to Religious Education and Pastoral Ministry* (New York: HarperCollins, 1991), and *Will There Be Faith?* (New York: HarperCollins, 2011); Robert J. Hater, *Catholic Evangelization: The Heart of Ministry* (Orlando: Harcourt Religion, 2002); Johannes Hofinger, S.J., *The Art of Teaching Christian Doctrine: The Good News and Its Proclamation* (Notre Dame, IN: University of Notre Dame Press, 1957); Josef Andreas Jungmann, S.J., *The Good News Yesterday and Today*, trans. and ed. William A. Huesman, S.J., from Jungmann's *The Good News and Our Proclamation of the Faith* (New York: W. H. Sadlier, 1962), and *Handing on the Faith* (New York: Herder and Herder, 1959); Berard L. Marthaler, O.F.M. Conv., *The Creed*, rev. ed. (Mystic, CT: Twenty-Third Publications, 1993), "Catechesis: 'A Semantic Evolution'?" *Liturgical Ministry* 18 (Winter 2009): 1–10; Anne Marie Mongoven, O.P., *The Prophetic Spirit of Catechesis* (New York: Paulist Press, 2000); Gabriel Moran, *Education toward Adulthood: Religion and Life-long Learning* (New York: Paulist Press, 1979); Lucinda A. Nolan, "Events of Grace: Seven Moments in the History of Catechesis," *Catechetical Leader* 20, no. 2 (March/April 2009): 8–9, 18–19; James E. Reed and Ronnie Prevost, *A History of Christian Education* (Nashville, TN: Broadman and Holman, 1993); Gerard S. Sloyan, "Religious Education: From Early Christianity to Medieval Times," in Gerard S. Sloyan, ed., *Shaping the Christian Message* (New York: Macmillan, 1958), 3–37, and reprinted in Michael Warren, ed., *Sourcebook for Modern Catechetics* (Winona, MN: Saint Mary's Press, 1983), 1:110–139; and Westerhoff and Edwards, *A Faithful Church*.

8. For an informative overview of these developments in the nineteenth century, see Bryce, "Evolution of Catechesis," 223–226.

9. Catechesis since the Second Vatican Council is addressed in chapter 8. Parts of this and two succeeding paragraphs are from or adapted from Gerard F. Baumbach, "Catechesis since the Second Vatican Council: An Incomplete Reflection (Part Two)," *Catechetical Leader* 23, no. 6 (November 2012): 15–20.

10. Also see LG, 10, on "the common priesthood of the faithful and the ministerial or hierarchical priesthood."

11. "Lay ecclesial ministry flows from an explicit faith commitment and is animated by the love of God and neighbor. It also entails an explicit relationship of mutual accountability to and collaboration with the Church hierarchy." United States Conference of Catholic Bishops, *Co-Workers in the Vineyard of the Lord* (Washington, DC: USCCB, 2005), 25.

12. For example, a sense of "belonging" may often be experienced within a precatechumenal expression of initial faith; "believing" is particularly relevant to the time of the catechumenate (and is more expansive than the term may at first appear since it implies an essential activity within the community of belonging); "discernment and reflection" describe an essential activity of the purifying time of illumination; and "living, dying, and rising" relate well to coming to grips with the lifetime challenge of lived faith during mystagogical participation and beyond. The characteristics are not, of course, mutually exclusive or mutually limiting when applied to catechesis. In practice, overlap occurs, but the general framework is a useful starting point for catechetical reflection.

13. Congregation for the Evangelization of Peoples, *Guide for Catechists* (Washington, DC: USCCB, 1993), 8.

2. Rooting the Journey: Some Old Testament Foundations

1. Before this statement, he cited the guiding role of *Nostra Aetate* (*Declaration on the Relation of the Church to Non-Christian Religions*) from the Second Vatican Council.

2. After briefly addressing Hinduism and Buddhism, *Nostra Aetate* (2) addresses other religions and notes that "the Catholic Church rejects nothing

of what is true and holy in these religions." Later in the same paragraph we read, "Yet she [the Catholic Church] proclaims and is in duty bound to proclaim without fail, Christ who is the way, the truth and the life (Jn 1:6 [*sic*])"; citation: Jn 14:6. It is important to read *Nostra Aetate* in its entirety. A benefit of the present era is that serious discussion has surfaced among a number of religious bodies, enabling frank exchange of ideas and discussion of doctrinal teaching and religious history, with a concurrent development of relationships among representatives of different religious traditions.

3. See, for example, Anthony Cirelli, "New U.S. Catholic-Buddhist 'Dialogue of Fraternity' Begins Today in Rome," USCCB blog, June 22, 2015, http://usccbmedia.blogspot.com/2015/06/new-us-catholic-bud dhist-dialogue-of.html.

4. A homily of St. Bernard of Clairvaux (d. 1153) includes the following regarding awaiting Mary's reply to the angel Gabriel: "For it the whole world is waiting, bowed down at your feet. And rightly so, because on your answer depends the comfort of the afflicted, the redemption of captives, the deliverance of the damned; the salvation of all the sons of Adam, your whole race": "Homily Four: Praise of the Mother Touches the Son," in *Homilies in Praise of the Blessed Virgin Mary by Bernard of Clairvaux*, trans. Marie-Bernard Saïd (Kalamazoo, MI: Cistercian Publications, 1979), Hom. 4, 8, 53.

5. For scripture references, see Gn 12:1 and Gn 17:5; 12:3 (LXX); cf. Gal 3:8.

6. On the covenant God makes with Abraham, see Gn 15. For the Sinai covenant, linked to the great event of exodus and newfound freedom for the Israelites, see Ex 19ff.

7. For more on the term *Shema*, see NABRE, Deuteronomy 6:4 note (Washington, DC: Confraternity of Christian Doctrine, 2010, in edition published by World Catholic Press, Catholic Book Publishing Corp., NJ).

8. Lawrence Boadt, "Catechesis in the Old Testament," *Catechetical Leader* 16, no. 6 (November 2005): 5, 22. See GE, 3, which states in part, "The role of parents in education is of such importance that it is almost impossible to provide an adequate substitute."

9. Ibid., 22.

10. Reed and Prevost, *A History*, 50.

11. Ibid., 56.

12. See NABRE, Psalm 119 note, for a brief discussion of the term *instruction* as it applies to this psalm. One of the uses is "way."

13. NABRE, introduction to Proverbs, 663. (Page numbers refer to the edition published by World Catholic Press.)

14. Boadt notes that "the most common teaching technique of ancient sages was the use of proverbs" ("Catechesis," 23).

15. NABRE, introduction to Proverbs, 663. See especially the second full paragraph.

16. Isaiah prophesied during the last half of the eighth century BC in Judah, the kingdom in the south. The kingdom of Israel in the north fell to the Assyrians around 722 BC. Judah would fall to the Babylonians in 587 BC. Chapters 1 to 39 are identified as First Isaiah. Chapters 40 to 55 represent Second Isaiah and are from the period when the Babylonian exile (587–539 BC) was drawing to a close. Chapters 56 to 66, identified as Third Isaiah, are the work of others from the time after the exile. For much of this information and other details, see NABRE, introduction to Isaiah, 783–784.

17. The interested reader should pursue securing access to the cassette audiotape of the United States Holocaust Memorial Museum entitled *Witnesses to the Holocaust* (Washington, DC: United States Holocaust Memorial Council, 1996).

18. See John Paul II, "The Roots of Anti-Judaism in the Christian Environment" (excerpt of discourse, Rome Synagogue, April 13 ,1986), *Tertium Millennium* no. 5 (November 1997), http://www.vatican.va/jubilee_2000/magazine/documents/ju_mag_01111997_p-42x_en.html.

19. Cf. USCCB Bishops' Committee on the Liturgy, *God's Mercy Endures Forever: Guidelines on the Presentation of Jews and Judaism in Catholic Preaching* (Washington, DC: USCCB, 1988), 31.

20. Vatican Commission for Religious Relations with the Jews, "Conclusion," in "Notes on the Correct Way to Present the Jews and Judaism in Preaching and Catechesis in the Roman Catholic Church" in *Origins* 15, no. 7 (July 1985): 107, par. 27. It is important to read, study, and discuss these notes in their entirety.

21. Vatican Commission for Religious Relations with the Jews, "Relations between the Old and New Testaments," in "Notes on the Correct Way

to Present the Jews and Judaism in Preaching and Catechesis in the Roman Catholic Church" in *Origins* 15, no. 7 (July 1985): 104–105, par. 10–11. See the first footnote, which is about use of the term "old," which "does not mean 'out of date' or 'outworn.'" Paragraph 11 ends with a reference to the Commission's "Guidelines and Suggestions for Implementing the Conciliar Declaration 'Nostra Aetate' (n. 4)," December 1, 1974.

22. See Commission for Religious Relations with the Jews, *The Gifts and the Calling of God Are Irrevocable (Rom 11:29)* (A Reflection on Theological Questions Pertaining to Catholic-Jewish Relations on the Occasion of the 50th Anniversary of *Nostra Aetate* No.4) (December 15, 2015) at http://www.vatican.va/roman_curia/pontifical_councils/chrstuni/relations-jews-docs/rc_pc_chrstuni_doc_20151210_ebraismo-nostra-aetate_en.html.

3. Identifying the Way: Jesus Christ, Teacher and Catechist

1. Quoting DV, 21.
2. This paragraph and a portion of the succeeding one are adapted from Gerard F. Baumbach, *Faith in a Self-Revealing God*, Catechism for US (Cincinnati: St. Anthony Messenger Press, 2006).
3. United States Conference of Catholic Bishops, *United States Catholic Catechism for Adults* (Washington, DC: USCCB, 2006), 27.
4. Ibid., 25.
5. For example, see Ephesians 1:7–10.
6. Campbell, *Finding God*, 3.
7. Ibid., 4.
8. Reed and Prevost, *A History*, 62.
9. See Boadt, "Catechesis," 23.
10. Quoting AG, 10; cf. AG, 22a, and also quoting CT, 53; cf. EN, 20.
11. Also see, for example, LG, 31; AA, 10; and CCC, 783ff.
12. Portions of this paragraph are from Baumbach, "Eucharistic Mystagogy," 2.
13. Eric Franklin points out that "the passage is actually a composite one, taken from the LXX [Septuagint] version of Isa 61:1–2 into which is

fitted a clause, 'to let the oppressed go free,' from Isa 58:6." Eric Franklin, "59. Luke," in John Barton and John Muddiman, eds., *The Oxford Bible Commentary* (New York: Oxford University Press, 2001), 932. See also Robert J. Karris, O.F.M., "The Gospel According to Luke," in Raymond E. Brown, S.S., Joseph A. Fitzmyer, S.J., and Roland E. Murphy, O.Carm., eds., *The New Jerome Biblical Commentary* (Englewood Cliffs, NJ: Prentice-Hall, 1990), 2:689–690.

14. Karris addresses "God's Promises Fulfilled in Jesus for All (4:16–30)" in his "The Gospel According to Luke," in Brown et al., *The New Jerome Biblical Commentary*, 2:689–690.

15. Judith Dunlap, "Article 7. Divine Pedagogy and Methodologies," Evangelizing Catechesis (Washington, DC: National Conference for Catechetical Leadership, 2001), 2.

16. For example, Pilate: cf. Mk 15:2, Mt 27:11, Lk 23:3, Jn 19:10.

17. See Mk 12–13 for the context of this interaction. Also cf. Mt 22:34–40 and Lk 10:25–28. Cf. Dt 6:4–5; also cf. Lv 19:18 for the command to love one's neighbor as oneself.

18. Quoting DV, 2.

19. Dunlap, "Divine Pedagogy," 2.

20. See Heb 11 for repeated and informative use of the phrase "by faith."

21. Quoting CT, 7, 5. GDC, 98, states, "Jesus Christ not only transmits the word of God: he *is* the Word of God. Catechesis is therefore completely tied to him."

22. G. Emmett Carter, *The Modern Challenge to Religious Education*, ed. William J. Reedy (New York: William H. Sadlier, 1961), 23–24.

23. Carroll Stuhlmueller, "The Gospel According to Luke," in Raymond E. Brown, Joseph A. Fitzmyer, and Roland E. Murphy, eds., *The Jerome Biblical Commentary* (Englewood Cliffs, NJ: Prentice-Hall, 1978), 148–149. Also see Karris, "The Gospel According to Luke," in Brown et al., *The New Jerome Biblical Commentary*, 2:707.

24. This is a significant choice. Scripture scholar Kenneth E. Bailey observes: "First century Jewish custom dictated that if a Jewish boy lost the family inheritance among the Gentiles and dared to return home, the community would break a large pot in front of him and cry out 'so-and-so

is cut off from his people.'" *The Cross and the Prodigal,* 2nd ed. (Downers Grove, IL: InterVarsity Press, 2005), 52.

25. For discussion of the son's motive, see DM, part IV, "The Parable of the Prodigal Son," 5. Also see, for example, Franklin, "59. Luke," 947; and Bailey, *The Cross and the Prodigal,* 59ff.

26. Franklin indicates that "it is generally agreed that the father's act of running to meet his son and the manner of his embrace would be regarded as demeaning for a Near-Eastern parent." "59. Luke," 947. Also see Bailey, *The Cross and the Prodigal,* 67, for detailed discussion of this point.

27. For informative commentary on the older brother, see Franklin, "59. Luke," 947–948.

28. For a fresh look at the inviting challenge of the parables, see Matthew Halbach, "What Parables Can Teach the Synod Fathers and the Church Today," *Catechetical Leader* 26, no. 2 (March 2015): 9–12.

29. See NABRE, introduction to John, 1182, for brief comment on the signs in chapter 6.

30. The Emmaus reflection here is adapted from Baumbach, *Experiencing Mystagogy: The Sacred Pause of Easter* (New York/Mahwah, NJ: Paulist Press, 1996). Used by permission.

31. Portions of this paragraph are from or adapted from Baumbach, "The Pedagogy of Faith."

4. Marking the Way: New Testament and the Emerging Church

1. See Brendan Byrne, S.J., "The Letter to the Philippians," in Brown et al., *The New Jerome Biblical Commentary,* 2:794–795. Also see RMa, 18.

2. The next sentence reads: "This is perhaps the deepest *'kenosis' of faith* in human history" (RMa, 18).

3. Parts of this paragraph are adapted from Baumbach, "Eucharistic Mystagogy," 2–3.

4. Ambrose, "*The Mysteries* 9:53," in *Saint Ambrose: Theological and Dogmatic Works,* trans. Roy J. Deferrari, The Fathers of the Church (Washington, DC: Catholic University of America Press, 1963), 25–26.

5. Cyril of Jerusalem, "Mystagogical Lectures," 2:8, trans. Anthony A. Stephenson, in *The Works of Saint Cyril of Jerusalem*, trans. Leo P. McCauley and Anthony A. Stephenson (Washington, DC: Catholic University of America Press, 1970), 2:167; cf. Rom 6:4, RCIA, 244.

6. "The word *Church* is based on both the Greek word *ekklesia* and the Hebrew word *qahal*, which mean the gathering of the community." USCCB, *United States Catholic Catechism for Adults*, 122. See Mt 18:17 for the other use of the term.

7. See Gerard F. Baumbach, *The Church: People, Body, Temple*, Catechism for US (Cincinnati: St. Anthony Messenger Press, 2007).

8. The late scholar of catechesis Joseph B. Collins notes that Peter's sermon on Pentecost "might well be called the first catechetical lesson in the history of the Church." *CCD Methods in Modern Catechetics*, 3.

9. Aidan Kavanagh, *The Shape of Baptism: The Rite of Christian Initiation* (New York: Pueblo, 1978), 17.

10. John McKenzie, S.J., "'Proclamation' and 'Teaching' in the Primitive Church," *The Living Light* 1, no. 2 (Fall 1964): 118–119. McKenzie links "the content of the proclamation" (120) to such passages from the Acts of the Apostles as 2:14–40 (Peter's classic address after the coming of the Holy Spirit on Pentecost), 3:12–26 (Peter's address after the cure of a crippled beggar), and 10:28–43 (Peter's address to the Gentile Cornelius and those gathered together with him). See 120–122.

11. Quoting CT, 19.

12. In a related footnote (GDC, 62n6), the GDC states, "In the present directory it is supposed that those to whom *kerygmatic catechesis* or *pre-catechesis* is addressed will be interested in the Gospel. In situations where they have no such interest then primary proclamation is called for" (italics in the original).

13. See NDC, 17A; also see Committee on Evangelization and Catechesis, *Disciples Called to Witness: The New Evangelization* (Washington, DC: United States Conference of Catholic Bishops, 2012), http://www.usccb.org/beliefs-and-teachings/how-we-teach/new-evangelization/upload/Disciples-Called-To-Witness-The-New-Evangelization.pdf.

14. McKenzie, "'Proclamation' and 'Teaching,'" 127.

15. "The gathering [in Acts] is possibly the same as that recalled by Paul in Gal 2:1–10" NABRE, 1234.

16. See NABRE, Acts 15:13–35 note, 1235. For commentary on the account in Acts, including the comments of James that begin in 15:13, see Richard J. Dillon, "Acts of the Apostles," in Brown et al., *The New Jerome Biblical Commentary*, 2:751–752.

17. See Antoine Bakh, ed., *The One Church and the Communion of Churches* (Anaheim, CA: The Eastern Catholic Pastoral Association of Southern California [ECPA], 2002), 6.

18. For an informative look at the link between Romans 6 and the emergence of Easter baptismal practice, see Maxwell E. Johnson, *Images of Baptism* (Chicago: Liturgy Training Publications, 2001), 4–5. Johnson writes, "Easter baptism, viewed through the lens of Romans 6, although already at least an emerging *preference* in the West (Tertullian and Hippolytus), probably becomes, for a variety of reasons, the universal Christian *ideal* for baptism and its interpretation only in the late fourth century" (4) (italics in the original). In a note after "reasons," he references his *The Rites of Christian Initiation: Their Evolution and Interpretation* (Collegeville, MN: Liturgical Press, 1999), 106–112, for further discussion. In his *The Rites of Christian Initiation,* rev. ed. (Collegeville, MN: Liturgical Press, 2007), see 134ff. Also see Pierre-Marie Gy, "Sacraments and Liturgy in Latin Christianity," in Bernard McGinn and John Meyendorff, eds., with Jean Leclercq, *Christian Spirituality: Origins to the Twelfth Century* (New York: Crossroad, 1985), 368.

19. See Johnson, *The Rites of Christian Initiation* (2007), 333, who cites S. Anita Stauffer for her historical identification of how baptism has been practiced: *"submersion,"* . . . *"immersion,"* . . . *"affusion,"* . . . and *"aspersion"*; each includes a brief explanation. *On Baptismal Fonts: Ancient and Modern,* Alcuin/GROW Liturgical Study 29–30 (Bramcote/Nottingham, UK: Grove Books, 1994), 9–10.

20. GDC, 78n1: "As has been stated in chapter 1 of this part in 'The transmission of Revelation by the Church, the work of the Holy Spirit' and in part II, chapter 1 in 'The ecclesial nature of the Gospel message.' Cf. EN 60 which speaks of the ecclesial nature of any evangelizing activity."

21. This paragraph is adapted from Baumbach, "The Pedagogy of Faith."

22. Actually, for all of life (i.e., eternal life) since "lifetime," commonly understood, implies for many *this* life.

23. Mary Charles Bryce, "Catechesis," in Iris V. Cully and Kendig Brubaker Cully, eds., *Harper's Encyclopedia of Religious Education* (New York: Harper and Row, 1990), 98.

24. The tasks are listed without their intervening commentary from the GDC.

25. Bryce, "Catechesis," 99.

26. Collins, *CCD Methods in Modern Catechetics*, 5. Italics in original.

27. Stuhlmueller comments on the phrase "the certainty of the words" this way: "The Greek can also mean 'that you may be more solidly and certainly grounded in the mysteries of salvation.'" "The Gospel According to Luke," in Brown et al., *The Jerome Biblical Commentary*, 119. Also see Karris, "The Gospel According to Luke," in Brown et al., *The New Jerome Biblical Commentary*, 2:678–679.

28. My reflection is for Acts 10:36–48. See Carter, *The Modern Challenge to Religious Education*, 45.

29. The authorship of 1 Peter is a matter of discussion among scripture scholars. For informative commentary on this question, see NABRE, introduction to 1 Peter, 1380–1381.

30. Carolyn Osiek, R.S.C.J., "Who Did What in the Church in the New Testament?" in Richard W. Miller II, ed., *Lay Ministry in the Catholic Church* (Liguori, MO: Catholic Community Foundation of Kansas City, 2005), 7. The interested reader will benefit from this informative chapter by a distinguished scholar and from others in this work.

31. Parts of this and the succeeding two paragraphs are from or adapted from Baumbach, "The Pedagogy of Faith."

32. "Ignatius to the Smyrnaeans," 8, in *The Epistles of St. Clement of Rome and St. Ignatius of Antioch,* trans. James A. Kleist, S.J. (Westminster, MD: Newman Bookshop, 1946), 93. See the accompanying note.

33. Kevin L. Hughes, *Church History: Faith Handed On* (Chicago: Loyola Press, 2002), 13–14.

34. See ibid., 14ff., for Hughes's assessment of the persecution and the ways in which Romans dealt with "these troublesome dissidents" (14).

35. Tertullian, "*Apology* 50:13," in Tertullian and Minucius Felix, *Tertullian Apologetical Works and Minucius Felix Octavius*, trans. Rudolph Arbesman, O.S.A., Emily Joseph Daly, C.S.J., and Edwin A. Quain, S.J. (New York: Fathers of the Church, 1950), 125.

36. Descriptive titles vary among scholars: for example, *Doctrine of the Twelve Apostles* (Aelred Cody, O.S.B., "The *Didache*: An English Translation," in Clayton N. Jefford, ed., *The "Didache" in Context: Essays on Its Text, History and Transmission* [Supplements to Novum Testamentum] [Leiden; New York; Köln: E. J. Brill, 1995]); *Training of the Twelve Apostles* (Aaron Milavec, *The Didache* [Collegeville, MN: Liturgical Press, 2003]); and *The Teaching of the Twelve Apostles* (Clayton N. Jefford, *Didache: The Teaching of the Twelve Apostles* [Salem, OR: Polebridge Press, 2013]). See the variety of sources in this section for detailed and informative insight into the nature of the *Didache*.

37. Richard E. McCarron, "Liturgy, Christian Living, and Catechesis: Insights from the *Didache*," *The Living Light* 39, no. 1 (Fall 2002): 6–7, quoting Paul Bradshaw, "Ancient Church Orders: A Continuing Enigma," in Bradshaw's *The Search for the Origins of Christian Worship*, 2nd ed. (New York: Oxford, 2002), 73. McCarron identifies the practice of connecting a work's "contents to the apostles or Christ himself as a way to bolster the authority and prestige of the work" (7). He refers the reader to Bradshaw, *Search for the Origins*, 81.

38. Bradshaw, *Search for the Origins*, 78. The *Didache* has been examined by many scholars, including Paul Bradshaw, Aelred Cody, James A. Kleist, Clayton Jefford, Maxwell Johnson, Richard McCarron, Aaron Milavec, and Gerard S. Sloyan. I am grateful for their insights.

39. McCarron, "Liturgy, Christian Living, and Catechesis," 8.

40. Ibid., 7.

41. Bradshaw, *Search for the Origins*, 77.

42. Kavanagh, *Shape of Baptism*, 37. See 70, n3, for additional information.

43. Gerard S. Sloyan, "Religious Education: From Early Christianity," 4.

44. McCarron, "Liturgy, Christian Living, and Catechesis," 7.

45. Cody, "The *Didache*: An English Translation," 5.

46. James A. Kleist, trans., *The Didache* (New York: Newman Press, 1948), 154nn3–4. In notes, Kleist identifies familiar scripture verses: Mt 22:37, 39; Dt 6:5; and Lv 19:18 in note 3 and Mt 7:12 for the Golden Rule in note 4.

47. Sloyan, "Religious Education: From Early Christianity," 4–5.

48. McCarron, "Liturgy, Christian Living, and Catechesis," 15n11.

49. Cody, "The *Didache*: An English Translation," 9; cf. Kleist, *The Didache*, 19.

50. Ibid., 10.

51. Johnson, *The Rites of Christian Initiation* (2007), 43–44.

52. Cody, "The *Didache*: An English Translation," 12.

53. Cody's translation of chapter 15 begins, "Select, then, for yourselves bishops and deacons." Kleist uses the term "elect" in his translation, stating "it was the privilege of 'the people' to elect candidates for these offices" (164n90). Kurt Niederwimmer states that "the injunction to choose officers is, at any rate, addressed to the entire (individual) congregation." Linda Maloney, trans., and Harold W. Attridge, ed., *The Didache: A Commentary on the Didache*, Hermeneia Commentary (Minneapolis: Augsburg Fortress, 1998), 200.

54. Cody, "The *Didache*: An English Translation," 13.

55. Ibid.

56. Marthaler, *The Creed*, 3.

57. Italics in the original.

58. The Apostles' Creed is used in the *Catechism of the Catholic Church* for presenting the elements of faith along with the accompanying reliance on the Nicene Creed (see CCC, 196).

59. GDC, 78, reinforces the importance of cultural gifts when it states that "the profession of faith received by the Church (*traditio*), which germinates and grows during the catechetical process, is given back (*redditio*), enriched by the values of different cultures. The catechumenate is thus transformed into a center of deepening catholicity and a ferment of ecclesial renewal" (italics in the original). The footnote (5) states in part: "Cf. CT28, RCIA 25 and 183–187. The *traditio-redditio symboli* (the

handing over and giving back of the Creed) is an important element of the baptismal catechumenate" (italics in the original).

60. Cyril of Jerusalem, "Catechesis 5:12," trans. Leo P. McCauley, in *The Works of Saint Cyril of Jerusalem*, trans. Leo P. McCauley and Anthony A. Stephenson (Washington, DC: Catholic University of America Press, 1969), 1:146.

61. Ibid.

62. Italics in the original.

63. USCCB Secretariat of Divine Worship, "Exploring the Biblical Allusions in the Order of Mass: Nicene Creed," *Committee on Divine Worship Newsletter* 47 (October 2011): 39.

5. Framing the Way: The Church and the Catechumenate

1. My remarks in this chapter are informed in part by my earlier work, *Experiencing Mystagogy* (Mahwah, NJ: Paulist Press, 1996). Used by permission.

2. See Christopher M. Bellitto, *Church History 101: A Concise Overview* (Liguori, MO: Liguori, 2008), 17. Bellitto notes that "apologists (often also called *Church Fathers*, but including others, among them women) followed several strategies to help establish Christian identity because, like the gospel writers, they were addressing a variety of audiences" (italics in the original).

3. Johannes Quasten, *Patrology*, vol 1: *The Beginnings of Patristic Literature* (Westminster, MD: Christian Classics, 1992 [first published 1950]), 186.

4. *St. Irenaeus: Proof of the Apostolic Preaching*, trans. Joseph P. Smith, S.J. (New York: Paulist Press, 1952), 3, 49. See the associated notes (20–22) on p. 135 for this selection.

5. Ibid., 20. See the associated reference information at note 47.

6. Ibid.

7. In addition to relying on my own work, my remarks in this chapter are informed by the work of Michel Dujarier (e.g., *A History of the*

Catechumenate, trans. Edward J. Haasl [New York: William H. Sadlier, 1979]), Maxwell E. Johnson (e.g., *The Rites of Christian Initiation*), and Paul Turner (e.g., *The Hallelujah Highway: A History of the Catechumenate* [Chicago: Liturgy Training Publications, 2000]), all scholars of Christian initiation. Dujarier's work in exploring catechumenal practice was a significant help in the implementation of the RCIA decades ago. Johnson's detailed analyses provide much food for thought in examining and assessing initiation practices historically, theologically, liturgically, and catechetically. For many years, Turner has offered expert commentary on the rites and practice of Christian initiation with pastoral care and interpretive skill. The reader should consult directly the works of Dujarier, Johnson, and Turner for further study. I am indebted to these scholars for their historical analyses and critical review of the ancient catechumenate.

8. Michel Dujarier, "A Survey History of the Catechumenate," in W. J. Reedy, ed., *Becoming a Catholic Christian* (New York: William H. Sadlier, 1981), 27 (italics in the original). Elsewhere Dujarier notes that "at the end of the first century, the catechumenate did not yet exist as a settled institution, but the catechumenal reality was lived." *A History of the Catechumenate,* 26. Also see Alois Stenzel, "Temporal and Supra-temporal in the History of the Catechumenate and Baptism," trans. E. Quinn, in Johannes Wagner, ed., *Adult Baptism and the Catechumenate* [Concilium 22] (New York: Paulist Press, 1967), 33.

Deacon William J. Reedy, named above, was instrumental in the restoration of the catechumenate in the United States and also served the ministry of catechesis for many years. He introduced me to the many dimensions of Christian initiation and to its significance in the life of the Church. His audio presentation, "A Brief History of the Catechumenate," was part of Sadlier's *Adult Initiation Ministries Institute (AIMI) Kit.* See William J. Reedy, ed., *AIMI Leader's Guide, Training Program for Parish Ministries in RCIA* [*Rite of Christian Initiation of Adults*] (New York: William H. Sadlier, 1984).

9. Cf. William J. Reedy, "A Brief History of the Catechumenate," audiotape side 1A, *Adult Initiation Ministries Institute (AIMI) Kit* program component; packaged with Reedy, *AIMI Leader's Guide.*

10. "The First Apology of Justin, the Martyr," ed. and trans. Edward Rochie Hardy, in Cyril C. Richardson, trans. and ed., *Early Christian Fathers* (New York: Macmillan, 1970), chap. 61, p. 282.

11. Dujarier, *A History of the Catechumenate*, 38–39. Also see "The First Apology of Justin, the Martyr," chap. 61, p. 282.

12. Collins, *CCD Methods in Modern Catechetics*, 6.

13. Dujarier, "A Survey History of the Catechumenate," 27. See this chapter for identification of both of these requirements and related aspects. Also see Dujarier's *A History of the Catechumenate* for further elucidation. Acts 16:30–33 deals specifically with confirming one's faith.

14. Dujarier, "A Survey History of the Catechumenate," 27.

15. Today this term is frequently used in relation to persons who are already baptized and who are seeking to be received into the Catholic Church. See RCIA, part 2, chapter 5.

16. Dujarier, "A Survey History of the Catechumenate," 28.

17. J. B. Xavier, "The Catechumenate in the Early Church," in D. S. Amalorpavadass, *Adult Catechumenate and Church Renewal* (Bangalore, India: National Biblical, Catechetical, and Liturgical Centre, 1973), 18.

18. Ibid., 19.

19. See Joseph Martos, *Doors to the Sacred: A Historical Introduction to Sacraments in the Catholic Church* (Garden City, NY: Image Books, 1982) for a discussion of Baptism with pertinent scriptural references. Martos notes that "baptism was therefore like Jewish circumcision in that it stripped off the ways of the flesh and initiated a convert into the ways of the spirit (Col 2:11–13; Eph 2:1–6)": p. 166.

20. See CCC, 1216, for a brief treatment of the "enlightenment" understanding of baptism.

21. See especially Maxwell E. Johnson's *Images of Baptism* with regard to John 3 and Romans 6 and the preface to Johnson's *The Rites of Christian Initiation* (2007).

22. Tertullian, "*Apology* 18:4," in *Tertullian Apologetical Works*, 54. See Johannes Quasten, *Patrology*, vol. 2: *The Ante-Nicene Literature after Irenaeus* (Westminster, MD: Christian Classics, 1992 [first published 1950]), 256, for reference to Tertullian's audience (and pages 255–264 for treatment of the *Apology*).

23. *Origen: Contra Celsum*, trans. Henry Chadwick (Cambridge: The First Syndics of the Cambridge University Press, 1965), III:51, 163. See Dujarier, *A History of the Catechumenate*, 62–63, for his development of this topic, which is helpful here. Paul Turner points out that, for Origen, "the period of preparation for baptism included doctrinal and moral formation": *The Hallelujah Highway*, 33. See his complete treatment at 31–35.

24. *Origen: Contra Celsum*, III:59, 168; see Dujarier, *A History of the Catechumenate*, 63, for his interpretation of this topic. His treatment of Origen includes discussion of the development of stages for the catechumenate (pp. 56ff.).

25. For informative insights within a broader Church history context, see Francine Cardman, "Who Did What in the Church in the First Millennium?" in Miller, *Lay Ministry in the Catholic Church*, 13–31.

26. GDC, 102, states in part, "Jesus, in announcing the Kingdom, proclaims the justice of God: he proclaims God's judgment and our responsibility. . . . The call to conversion and belief in the Gospel of the Kingdom—a Kingdom of justice, love and peace, and in whose light we shall be judged—is fundamental for catechesis."

27. See Turner, *The Hallelujah Highway*, 24, for his comments on Clement and the period of "catechumenal instruction."

28. Clement of Alexandria, *Stromateis, Books One to Three*, trans. John Ferguson (Washington, DC: Catholic University of America Press, 1991), 2:18, 95–96, 220–221. In the related footnote, Ferguson includes the observation that "the text in paragraph (2) [of 96] is uncertain." Regarding Clement's mention of the three-year time frame (from agriculture), Maxwell E. Johnson indicates that this is probably a metaphorical usage having to do with "the necessity of Christian maturity and virtue" and not a measure of actual time (*The Rites of Christian Initiation* [2007], 65–66).

29. Matthew Bunson, *Our Sunday Visitor's Encyclopedia of Catholic History* (Huntington, IN: Our Sunday Visitor, 1995), 173.

30. Leonel L. Mitchell, "The Ancient Church: The Development of Catechesis in the Third and Fourth Centuries: From Hippolytus to Augustine," in Westerhoff and Edwards, *A Faithful Church*, 53.

31. These *Catechism* paragraphs give a treatment of the senses of scripture. The living Word of God never ceases to be our guide and our hope.

32. Marthaler, "Catechesis: 'A Semantic Evolution'?" 2.

33. "We all hold this common gathering on Sunday," in "The First Apology of Justin, the Martyr," 287. See also CCC, 1345.

34. Eusebius, *The History of the Church from Christ to Constantine*, trans. G. A. Williamson (New York: New York University Press, 1965), 275–276.

35. See chapter 67 in "The First Apology of Justin, the Martyr," 287–288.

36. Catherine Dooley, "Liturgical Catechesis: Mystagogy, Marriage or Misnomer?" *Worship* 66, no. 5 (September 1992): 390.

37. *The Old English Version of Bede's Ecclesiastical History of the English People Part I, 1*, ed. and trans. Thomas Miller (London: Oxford University Press, 1898; unaltered reprint, 1997), book I, chap. VII, 35.

38. Ibid., 37.

39. Ibid., 39.

40. Hippolytus of Rome, *The Treatise on the Apostolic Tradition of St. Hippolytus of Rome*, ed. Gregory Dix, reissued with corrections, preface, and bibliography by Henry Chadwick. First published 1937; second revised edition 1968; reissued with additional corrections 1992 (London: Alban Press; Ridgefield, CT: Morehouse Publishing). Critical assessment of the *Apostolic Tradition* by Maxwell E. Johnson provides important information for contextualizing and placing this work historically, including issues of authorship and dating. See the extended treatment in his *The Rites of Christian Initiation* (2007), 96–112. Paul Turner points out that "the work seems to have been compiled from several sources over the span of a century": *The Hallelujah Highway*, 37.

For the question of attribution to Hippolytus, see Johnson, *The Rites of Christian Initiation* (2007), 96ff., and E. C. Whitaker, *Documents of the Baptismal Liturgy*, 3rd ed., rev. Maxwell E. Johnson (Collegeville, MN: Liturgical Press, 2003), 4. Also see Turner, *The Hallelujah Highway*, 36ff., and William Harmless, *Augustine and the Catechumenate* (Collegeville, MN: Liturgical Press, 1995), 40ff. For discussion of the dating of the *Apostolic Tradition*, see Johnson, *The Rites of Christian Initiation* (2007), 96ff. A source of great value to the researcher is the volume by Paul Bradshaw, Maxwell E. Johnson, and L. Edward Phillips, *The Apostolic Tradition: A Commentary*, Hermeneia Commentary (Minneapolis: Augsburg Fortress, 2002). See also John F. Baldovin, S.J., "Hippolytus and the Apostolic Tradition: Recent Research and Commentary," *Theological Studies* 64, no. 3 (September 2003): 520–542.

41. Johnson, *The Rites of Christian Initiation* (2007), 97; see also Hippolytus, *Treatise on the Apostolic Tradition*, chap. 16, 23.

42. Hippolytus, *Treatise on the Apostolic Tradition*, chap. 17, 28 (Greek interspersed in the the original is omitted here).

43. Ibid., chap. 17–19, 28–30.

44. Turner, *The Hallelujah Highway*, 42.

45. Hippolytus, *Treatise on the Apostolic Tradition*, chap. 19, 30 (italics in the original; Greek interspersed in original is omitted here).

46. Johnson, *The Rites of Christian Initiation* (2007), 117. For discussion regarding length of catechumenal preparation, see 64ff. See especially his remarks regarding the *Canons of Hippolytus*, which offers a time frame of forty days. Also see his "Christian Initiation," in Susan Ashbrook Harvey and David G. Hunter, eds., *The Oxford Handbook of Early Christian Studies* (New York: Oxford University Press, 2008), 699, and Turner, *The Hallelujah Highway*, 38.

47. "National Statutes for the Catechumenate," in *RCIA*, appendix III, 6.

48. Hippolytus, *Treatise on the Apostolic Tradition*, chap. 17, 28 (Greek interspersed in original is omitted here).

49. Dujarier, *A History of the Catechumenate*, 46; he quotes Tertullian's *On Baptism*. Dujarier references here his own work, *Le Parrainage des adultes aux trois premiers siècles de l'Eglise, Parole et mission* 4 (1962): 231–232. See also Dujarier, *A History of the Catechumenate*, 52, where he cites the verification of sponsors for enabling movement toward Baptism in Rome. Also see Michel Dujarier, *The Rites of Christian Initiation*, trans. and ed. Kevin Hart (New York: William H. Sadlier, 1979), 94–95.

50. Tertullian, *Tertullian's Homily on Baptism*, trans. Ernest Evans (London: SPCK, 1964), chap. 20, 41. Maxwell E. Johnson points out that

Tertullian's *On Baptism* is "the earliest treatise on baptism written in the history of the church (ca. 198–200)": *The Rites of Christian Initiation* (2007), 84. Separately, Paul Turner writes that "*Baptism* is the first treatise to make an explicit reference to sponsors, but only in the case of little children (18): Dissuading the baptism of the young, Tertullian cautions that their sponsors may die before completing their responsibility": *The Hallelujah Highway*, 29. Also see Quasten, *Patrology*, 2:278–281.

51. Dujarier, *A History of the Catechumenate*, 48, 52.

52. Mitchell, "The Ancient Church," 51 (italics in the original). He continues: "In Greek they are called *photizomenoi* (those being enlightened)."

53. See Hippolytus, *Treatise on the Apostolic Tradition*, chap. 20–21, 30–38. Also see Turner, *The Hallelujah Highway*, 40.

54. Hippolytus, *Treatise on the Apostolic Tradition*, chap. 21, 36–37. I have changed "Dost thou believe . . ." to "Do you believe . . ." See Johnson, *The Rites of Christian Initiation* (2007), 100, on Baptism by "submersion or immersion," and see also the proposed ritual text on 104.

55. Hippolytus, *Treatise on the Apostolic Tradition*, chap. 22, 38–39 (Greek interspersed in the original is omitted here). For more recent analysis of these and other aspects of the *Apostolic Tradition*, see Bradshaw et al., *The Apostolic Tradition*, 2002.

56. See also CCC, 1288, which quotes Paul VI (*Divinae consortium naturae*, 659) regarding Confirmation's origin, the imposition of hands, and Pentecost, and CCC, 1289, which addresses the addition of anointing with oil.

57. For presentation of the diversity of sources pertinent to the study of rites of Christian initiation, see Whitaker, *Documents of the Baptismal Liturgy*.

58. See Johnson, *The Rites of Christian Initiation* (2007), 111. Also see Hippolytus, *Treatise on the Apostolic Tradition*, chap. 23, 40–43.

59. Hippolytus, *Treatise on the Apostolic Tradition*, chap. 23, 42. Greek interspersed in the original is omitted here.

60. For brief historical reference to the term *faithful*, see Edward Yarnold, *The Awe-Inspiring Rites of Limitation: The Origin of RCIA*, 2nd ed. (Collegeville, MN: The Liturgical Press, 1994), 100n1. Dujarier observes that "the community's concern for neophytes [newly baptized] was clearly manifested

by the homilies and the communal catechesis": *The Rites of Christian Initiation*, 210.

61. Hippolytus, *Treatise on the Apostolic Tradition*, chap. 23, 42; slightly modified.

62. Christopher M. Bellitto, *The General Councils* (New York/Mahwah, NJ: Paulist Press, 2002), 18. This recommended work is an important reference for both its historical presentation and the author's insights regarding Church councils.

63. "Basil defended Trinitarian doctrine, just as Athanasius before him": Bradley Holt, *Thirsty for God: A Brief History of Christian Spirituality* (Minneapolis: Augsburg Fortress, 1993), 40. Basil the Great is identified with two other Fathers of the Church, Gregory of Nazianzus and Gregory of Nyssa, as the Cappadocians, a term taken from a geographic area of what is today Turkey (40–41).

64. Quoting Council of Nicaea I (AD 325), from Denzinger-Schonmetzer, *Enchiridion Symbolorum, definitionum et declarationum de rebus fidei et morum* (1965), 130, 126. Italics in the original.

65. Hughes, *Church History: Faith Handed On*, 32.

66. Ibid., 32.

67. Bellitto, *The General Councils*, 25. He states, "Chalcedon tried to summarize all the confusion, explanation, and counter-explanation of the 125 years since Nicaea I."

68. Ibid., 26.

69. Thomas Bokenkotter, *A Concise History of the Catholic Church*, rev. ed. (New York: Doubleday, 1990), 57, quoting *Codex Theodosianus*, XVI, i, 2.

70. Dujarier, *A History of the Catechumenate*, 79.

71. Augustine of Hippo, *Instructing Beginners in Faith*, trans. Raymond Canning and ed. Boniface Ramsey (Hyde Park, NY: New City Press, 2006), chap. 5:9, 74.

72. Ibid., 74–75.

73. See ibid., 75.

74. Josef Andreas Jungmann makes this point in his *Handing on the Faith*, 3. See also Craig Alan Satterlee, *Ambrose of Milan's Method of Mystagogical Preaching* (Collegeville, MN: Liturgical Press, 2002), 2.

75. Jungmann, *Handing on the Faith*, 3.

76. St. John Chrysostom, *Baptismal Instructions*, trans. Paul W. Harkins (New York: Newman Press, 1963), 1:18, 30.

77. Anthony A. Stephenson, "General Introduction," in *The Works of Saint Cyril of Jerusalem*, vol. 1. Stephenson refers to these candidates as "the higher class of catechumens." These candidates were *photizomenoi*, or "those to be enlightened," since they were soon to experience the sacraments of initiation (1). For other terms used (e.g., *elect*, *competentes*), also see Mitchell, "The Ancient Church," 51; Johnson, *The Rites of Christian Initiation*, 121 and 201. Also see Dujarier's brief discussion of the enrollment of names in *The Rites of Christian Initiation*, 96, and his "A Survey History of the Catechumenate" (29), where he indicates that "the examination of the candidates and the ceremony of inscribing their names that opened the season of Lent were, in fact, revivals of the entrance rite into the catechumenate." *Neophotistos*, or "newly enlightened," was another term used for the newly baptized (Dujarier, *The Rites of Christian Initiation*, 208). For use of "newly illumined" (by Cyril of Jerusalem) and "newly-illuminated" (by John Chrysostom), see Hugh M. Riley, *Christian Initiation: A Comparative Study of the Interpretation of the Baptismal Liturgy in the Mystagogical Writings of Cyril of Jerusalem, John Chrysostom, Theodore of Mopsuestia, and Ambrose of Milan* (Washington, DC: Catholic University of America Press, 1974), 11 and 351, respectively.

78. Turner, *The Hallelujah Highway*, 50.

79. Ibid., 54.

80. See Dujarier, *A History of the Catechumenate*, 99–100, for discussion of the limited time frame for final preparation. See also Johnson's informative excursus on "Baptismal Preparation and the Origins of Lent," in *The Rites of Christian Initiation* (2007), 201ff.; and Reedy, "A Brief History of the Catechumenate," audiotape side 1A.

81. Dujarier, *A History of the Catechumenate*, 100.

82. Ibid., 101–102. See 117n50 for reference to Dujarier's articles on the Creed. Johnson indicates in his treatment of Ambrose of Milan that "the Lord's Prayer was delivered only *after* initiation itself" (italics in the original). See Johnson, *The Rites of Christian Initiation*, 170.

83. See the charts in Harmless, *Augustine and the Catechumenate,* for what was treated by Cyril and other Fathers of the era. Also see Leo P. McCauley, "Foreword to the Catecheses," in *The Works of Saint Cyril of Jerusalem,* 1:89.

84. Cyril of Jerusalem, "The Procatechesis," 9, in Edward Yarnold, *Cyril of Jerusalem* (Routledge: London/New York, 2000) in Whitaker, *Documents of the Baptismal Liturgy,* 28. Also see Jungmann, *Handing on the Faith,* 4–5.

85. Cyril of Jerusalem, "Procatechesis," 16, trans. Anthony A. Stephenson, in *The Works of Saint Cyril of Jerusalem,* 1:83.

86. Dujarier, *A History of the Catechumenate,* 97, quoting John Chrysostom, with source given as "*II e Cat. Ad Illum.* PG 49, 221; c. 231 (Antioch, Lent, 387), LC 5, 185."

87. Walter J. Burghardt, "Catechetics in the Early Church: Program and Psychology," *The Living Light* 1, no. 3 (Fall 1964): 100.

88. Ibid., 101. Of the liturgy, Burghardt writes that "in the concrete, this meant the rites of initiation: Baptism, chrism, and the Eucharist" (106). Burghardt provides pertinent examples from several Church Fathers throughout the article. For the psychology section, his focus is on Augustine and *De catechizandis rudibus.*

89. Ibid., 104.

90. Ibid., 106.

91. Ibid., 110.

92. Yarnold, *The Awe-Inspiring Rites,* 12; also see chapter 2.

93. Egeria, *Diary of a Pilgrimage,* trans. George E. Gingras (New York: Newman Press; Paulist Press, 1970), chap. 46, 123. See note 467 for comment on Egeria and the term *catechesis.* See note 468 for comment on *traditio symboli* and *redditio symboli.* Also see Dujarier, *A History of the Catechumenate,* 100–101, for much of the same selection used here (from a different translation); "The Lenten Retreat" is the section of Dujarier's book in which this excerpt of Egeria appears.

94. Dujarier, *A History of the Catechumenate,* 97ff.

95. Turner, *The Hallelujah Highway,* 50. Cyril's Lenten catecheses date from the mid-fourth century, while the mystagogical catecheses are from thirty to forty years later (50). Scholars present differing views on the

attribution of the mystagogical catecheses to Cyril, with some proposing attribution to John of Jerusalem, Cyril's successor. For example, Turner (*The Hallelujah Highway*, 50) is inclined to attribute them to John, while Yarnold (*The Awe-Inspiring Rites*, 69) argues for attribution to Cyril. The present work attributes authorship of the mystagogical catecheses to Cyril.

96. Cyril of Jerusalem, "Mystagogical Lectures," 2:4, 2:164. See note 13 at "dipped" for brief discussion of the minister of the sacrament. Yarnold uses "submerged yourselves" (*The Awe-Inspiring Rites*, 78). He notes that "Ambrose compares the font with a tomb (S 3.1); Theodore compares it with a womb (BH 3.10)" (78). See Yarnold's *The Awe-Inspiring Rites* for an informative comparison of initiation practices, including ritual elements of the various liturgical celebrations, among Cyril of Jerusalem, Ambrose of Milan, John Chrysostom, and Theodore of Mopsuestia. Yarnold's work remains an important source for the sacramental and liturgical context for catechesis in the life of the Church.

97. Burkhard Neunheuser, *Baptism and Confirmation*, trans. John Jay Hughes (Montreal: Palm, 1964), 131–132.

98. Riley, *Christian Initiation*, 2. Yarnold, *The Awe-Inspiring Rites*, 167, points out that both John Chrysostom and Theodore treat Baptism prior to the sacramental celebration, whereas Ambrose and Cyril do not. The four of them treat Eucharist after the celebration of the sacrament. See St. John Chrysostom, *Baptismal Instructions*, 53; "The Mystagogical Lectures," 1:1, in *The Works of Saint Cyril of Jerusalem*, vol. 2; and Ambrose, *The Sacraments* 1:1, *Theological and Dogmatic Works*, 269ff.

99. Riley, *Christian Initiation*, 220–221.

100. Ibid., 221.

101. Adapted from Baumbach, *Experiencing Mystagogy*, 4. Used by permission.

102. See the related notes, NABRE, 1290.

103. Riley, *Christian Initiation*, 141.

104. See Riley, *Christian Initiation*, for his comprehensive treatment of these Fathers on Baptism with regard to "Conformity to Christ in Death and Resurrection" (222ff.) and "New Birth" (298ff.).

105. "Mystagogical Lectures," 3:1, in *The Works of Saint Cyril of Jerusalem*, 2:168. Footnotes indicate that the first two phrases refer to Gal 3:27, and the last part of the sentence says to confer Rom 8:29.

106. Limited parts of the commentary on mystagogy in this chapter are adapted from Baumbach, "Eucharistic Mystagogy," 1–9.

107. Cyril of Jerusalem, "Sermon 2:1," in Yarnold, *The Awe-Inspiring Rites*, 76. For dating of the mystagogical catecheses, see Turner, *The Hallelujah Highway*, 50.

108. "The Mystagogical Lectures," in *The Works of Saint Cyril of Jerusalem*, vol. 2.

109. Cyril of Jerusalem, "Sermon 3," "The Anointing at Baptism," 1, in Yarnold, *The Awe-Inspiring Rites*, 81. See note 7 regarding "sign."

110. "Second Lecture on the Mysteries," 8, in *The Works of Saint Cyril of Jerusalem*, 2:167.

111. Ambrose, *The Mysteries*, in *Theological and Dogmatic Works*. Both sets appear in this volume. *The Mysteries*, while covering themes in common with *The Sacraments*, is shorter and less inclusive. Satterlee states that "*De mysteriis* is a version of *De sacramentis* polished and edited for publication (doubtless by Ambrose himself), which maintains only the literary appearance of a sermon and omits certain details, perhaps out of respect for the *disciplina arcani*" (italics in the original). *Ambrose of Milan's Method*, 13; also see 155–156.

112. Ambrose, *The Sacraments* 2:7, in *Theological and Dogmatic Works*, 286. Note after "buried together with Christ": "Cf. Rom 6:4; Col 2:12." See also Yarnold, *The Awe-Inspiring Rites*, 118.

113. Ambrose, "Sermons on the Sacraments," 3:5–6, in Yarnold, *The Awe-Inspiring Rites*, 122–123. See the accompanying footnotes. The Yarnold source is used here for clarity.

114. Ambrose, *The Mysteries* 1:3, in *Theological and Dogmatic Works*, 6.

115. Ambrose, "Sermons on the Sacraments," 1:2–3, in Yarnold, *The Awe-Inspiring Rites*, 100–101. Also see Ambrose, *The Mysteries* 1:3–4, in *Theological and Dogmatic Works*, 6. For informative commentary, see Satterlee, *Ambrose of Milan's Method*, 157–158.

116. This note gives some details regarding John Chrysostom and his contemporary, Theodore of Mopsuestia. Perhaps the greatest preacher of

his time was John Chrysostom (ca. 344–407). His mystagogical writings can be gleaned from three sets of sermons he delivered in Antioch in the late fourth century, together identified as *Baptismal Instructions*. "As an orator and exegete he was without peer. . . . His homilies, which often lack a structural unity, always have an interior, a spiritual unity. There is never a digression, never a detail, which swerves from the end he constantly sets for himself: the confirmation of his hearers' faith and the correction of their lives" (Harkins in John Chrysostom, *Baptismal Instructions*, 5).

Blessed with vigorous moral persuasiveness, Chrysostom identifies the powerful witness of Paul when he urges his hearers, "Imitate him, I beg you, and you will be able to be called newly baptized not only for two, three, ten, or twenty days, but you will be able to deserve this greeting after ten, twenty, or thirty years have passed and, to tell the truth, through your whole life" (John Chrysostom, *Baptismal Instructions*, 88–89). Such an exhortation remains timely for twenty-first-century Christians.

For the homilies of Theodore of Mopsuestia (ca. 350–428), we refer to his "Baptismal Homilies" in Yarnold, *The Awe-Inspiring Rites*. See Johannes Quasten, who states that Theodore's "mystagogical catecheses . . . [were given] to the neophytes in the course of the week following baptism": *Patrology*, vol. 3: *The Golden Age of Greek Patristic Literature from the Council of Nicaea to the Council of Chalcedon* (Westminster, MD: Newman Press, 1963), 408–409. In addition, Theodore offered ten homilies on the Creed prior to the catechumens' baptism, but they are not part of his mystagogical catecheses.

One of Theodore's key points has to do with the baptized Christian as risen with Christ: "When I am baptized and put my head under the water, I wish to receive the death and burial of Christ our Lord, and I solemnly profess my faith in his resurrection; when I come up out of the water, this is a sign that I believe I am already risen": "Baptismal Homily 3:5," in Yarnold, *The Awe-Inspiring Rites*, 183.

117. Yarnold, *The Awe-Inspiring Rites*, x.

118. Mark Francis, C.S.V., "Liturgical Participation of God's People," in *With One Voice* (Washington, DC: Federation of Diocesan Liturgical Commissions [FDLC], 2010), 75.

119. The tasks are listed without their intervening commentary from the GDC directory.

120. Augustine, "Sermon 272," in Maurice Wiles and Mark Santer, eds., *Documents in Early Christian Thought* (Cambridge: Cambridge University Press, 1975), 199.

121. Harmless, *Augustine and the Catechumenate*, 336.

122. Ibid.

123. Augustine, *Instructing Beginners in Faith*. Another translation often referenced is *St. Augustine: The First Catechetical Instruction*, trans. Joseph P. Christopher (New York/Mahwah, NJ: Newman Press [Paulist Press]), 1946. Also of interest is Augustine's *De doctrina christiana*. See the summary by Elias in his *A History of Christian Education*, 42.

124. Sloyan, "Religious Education: From Early Christianity," 18.

125. See Canning's introduction to *Instructing Beginners in the Faith*, 11–16.

126. See, for example, Burghardt, "Catechetics in the Early Church," 117–118, and Sloyan, "Religious Education: From Early Christianity," 18, where he identifies Augustine as "an apostle of divine love."

127. Augustine, *Instructing Beginners in Faith*, chap. 4:7, 67; note after "force": "See Rom 5:8."

128. Ibid., chap. 4:7, 67–68.

129. Ibid., chap. 4:8, 70. Note after "first loved them": "See 1 Jn 4:10, 19."

130. Ibid., chap. 2:4, 57–59.

131. Christopher points out that "according to Augustine, those who present themselves for instruction fall into three classes: the well-educated (cf. ch. 8 n. 86); the half-educated, who come from second-rate schools of rhetoric (*quidam de scholis usitatissimis*); and the illiterate, *idiotae*" (italics in the original). *St. Augustine: The First Catechetical Instruction*, 111n95.

132. Augustine, *Instructing Beginners in Faith*, chap. 3:5 (p. 63) and chap. 6:10 (p. 76).

133. See ibid., chap. 18:29ff. (p. 124ff.).

134. Ibid., chap. 24:44, 153.

135. Ibid., chap. 26:50, 163. See the footnote after "Church" for brief discussion of admission to the catechumenate.

136. Turner, *The Hallelujah Highway*, 62.

137. Mongoven, *The Prophetic Spirit of Catechesis*, 37. Mongoven cites *St. Augustine: The First Catechetical Instruction*, trans. Christopher, for this reference to Augustine.

138. Collins, *CCD Methods in Modern Catechetics,* 8.

139. See John Paul II, Apostolic Letter *Augustinum Hipponensem* (*On the Occasion of the 16th Centenary of the Conversion of St. Augustine*), August 28, 1986, where he cites his Discourse to the Professors and students of the "Augustinianum" (May 8, 1982): AAS 74 (1982), 800; cf. *L'Osservatore Romano*, English edition, June 14, 1982, http://w2.vati can.va/content/john-paul-ii/en/apost_letters/1986/documents/hf_jp-ii_ apl_26081986_augustinum-hipponensem.html.

140. See also this sentence in Baumbach, "Eucharistic Mystagogy," 3, where it is part of the first of four points on the topic.

141. Satterlee, *Ambrose of Milan's Method*, 4.

142. Augustine, *The Augustine Catechism: The Enchiridion on Faith, Hope, and Love,* trans. Bruce Harbert (Hyde Park, NY: New City Press, 1999), 39.

6. Spanning the Way: Catechesis through the Middle Ages

1. The insights of the following scholars are of particular benefit for considering the Middle Ages; I recommend their work for further study: Danièle Alexandre-Bidon and Didier Lett, *Children in the Middle Ages,* trans. Jody Gladding (Notre Dame, IN: University of Notre Dame Press, 1999); Aubert Clark, "Medieval Catechetics and the First Catechisms," *The Living Light* 1, no. 4 (Winter 1965): 92–107; Milton McC. Gatch, "The Medieval Church: Basic Christian Education," 79–108; and Gerard S. Sloyan, "Religious Education: From Early Christianity to Medieval Times," in Sloyan, *Shaping the Christian Message* (1958), 3–37.

2. Jungmann, *Handing on the Faith*, 11. See especially 1–19.

3. Aubert Clark states that "the Middle Ages were by no means uniform; the differences between 800 A.D. and 1300 A.D. are greater than the

similarities, and analagous [*sic*] contrasts can be made century by century."
"Medieval Catechetics and the First Catechisms," 92.

4. See Nathan D. Mitchell, "Dissolution of the Rite of Christian Ini-
tiation," in *Made, Not Born*, by Murphy Center for Liturgical Research
(Notre Dame, IN: University of Notre Dame Press, 1976), 50–82; and
Jungmann, *Handing on the Faith*, 7.

5. Jungmann, *Handing on the Faith*, 7.

6. Collins, *CCD Methods in Modern Catechetics*, 11.

7. Charles W. Gusmer, "How Do Liturgists View Initiation?" *Christian Initiation Resources* 1, no. 1 (1980): 15. Gusmer references the work
of such scholars as J. D. C. Fisher and Nathan Mitchell (among others)
when he addresses the "continuum" matter. See also Thomas A. Marsh,
Gift of Community (Wilmington, DE: Michael Glazier, 1984), 130ff., and
Mitchell, "Dissolution of the Rite of Christian Initiation."

8. Marthaler, "Catechesis: 'A Semantic Evolution'?" 3. Lest we imagine, however, a "catechumenal switch" being quickly shut off, Michel
Dujarier presents pertinent historical information in pointing out that
"there were, in fact, many mission areas, especially from the sixth to the
ninth century, where adult baptism was still more common than infant
baptism" ("A Survey History of the Catechumenate," 30). He also identifies
Lenten scrutinies of the sixth century as an example of ritual practice that
involved infants and mothers (30).

9. *The Oxford Dictionary of the Christian Church* indicates that "by
a tradition at least as old as the 3rd cent., and virtually universal until the
Reformation, children born to Christian parents have been baptized in
infancy." F. L. Cross and E. A. Livingstone, eds., *The Oxford Dictionary of
the Christian Church*, 2nd ed. (New York: Oxford University Press, 1983),
s.v. "Infant Baptism."

10. The work of Joachim Jeremias is often cited regarding the practice
of infant Baptism in the early Church. See his *Infant Baptism in the First
Four Centuries*, trans. David Cairns (Eugene, OR: Wipf and Stock, 1960),
and *The Origins of Infant Baptism*, trans. Dorothea M. Barton (Eugene, OR:
Wipf and Stock, 1962). These works "bookend" the challenge to Jeremias's
position put forward by Kurt Aland in his *Did the Early Church Baptize
Infants?* trans. G. R. Beasley-Murray (Philadelphia: Westminster, 1963).

11. Also see Rom 5:12–21 and CCC, 389ff. See CCC, 404, for use of the term *sin* with regard to the "state" of original sin. See CCC, 1250, on the necessity of the Baptism of children.

12. See CCC, 1261.The *Catechism* paragraph gives teaching on children who die without having been baptized. For informative historical review, see International Theological Commission, *The Hope of Salvation for Infants Who Die without Being Baptised* (Vatican City: Libreria Editrice Vaticana, 2007), especially 8–25, http://www.vatican.va/roman_curia/congregations/cfaith/cti_documents/rc_con_cfaith_doc_20070419_un-baptised-infants_en.html.

13. Jungmann, *The Good News Yesterday and Today*, 26.

14. Gerard Sloyan notes that "the catechumenate became the training ground for reduced numbers of converts; primarily it became an institution for parents and godparents, in their children's interest. In other words, the instructional situation went from pre-baptismal to post-baptismal." "Religious Education: From Early Christianity," 21, citing H. Leclercq, "Catéchèse—Catéchisme—Catéchumène," in *Dictionnaire d'archéologie chrétienne et de liturgie* (Paris: Letouzey et Ané, 1925), 2:2566f.

15. Joseph Martos, *Doors to the Sacred: A Historical Introduction to Sacraments in the Catholic Church* (Garden City, NY: Image Books, 1982), 176–177.

16. Ibid., 177.

17. Alexandre-Bidon and Lett, *Children in the Middle Ages*, 26. For discussion of the role of godparent see Janet L. Nelson, "Parents, Children, and the Church in the Earlier Middle Ages" (presidential address), in *The Church and Childhood*, ed. Diana Wood (Oxford: Blackwell Publishers, 1994), 100ff.

18. Alexandre-Bidon and Lett, *Children in the Middle Ages*, 61.

19. De Bretagne, "The History of the Catechesis," 366.

20. Alexandre-Bidon and Lett, *Children in the Middle Ages*, 62.

21. Ibid., 53.

22. Ibid., 54.

23. Shulamith Shahar, *Childhood in the Middle Ages*, trans. Chaya Galai (New York: Routledge, 1992), 2.

24. Bellitto, *Church History 101*, 64.

25. Collins, *CCD Methods in Modern Catechetics*, 10.

26. Elias, *A History of Christian Education*, 45.

27. Clark, "Medieval Catechetics and the First Catechisms," 94, citing Henri Marrou, *A History of Education in Antiquity* (New York: Sheed and Ward, 1956), 344.

28. Alexandre-Bidon and Lett, *Children in the Middle Ages*, 40–41.

29. Reed and Prevost, *A History*, 153.

30. Ibid., 154.

31. Elias, *A History of Christian Education*, 49.

32. Alexandre-Bidon and Lett, *Children in the Middle Ages*, 46–47. Cf. Sloyan, "Religious Education: From Early Christianity," 27, with regard to the same point for episcopal schools.

33. Alexandre-Bidon and Lett, *Children in the Middle Ages*, 46; cf. 40. However, see Clark, "Medieval Catechetics and the First Catechisms," 98, who addresses the limited preparatory formation and resources for the priest.

34. Alexandre-Bidon and Lett, *Children in the Middle Ages*, 45.

35. Ibid., 40–41.

36. On the development of the medieval family, see David Herlihy, "The Making of the Medieval Family: Symmetry, Structure, and Sentiment," in *Medieval Families: Perspectives on Marriage, Household, and Children*, ed. Carol Neel (Toronto: University of Toronto Press, 2004), 192–213.

37. Medieval scholar Shulamith Shahar indicates that "the outlook of some churchmen on childhood, and on the place of parental obligations within the duties of the Christian believer, did not unequivocally stress the welfare of the child." See Shahar, *Childhood in the Middle Ages*, 2.

38. See such diverse sources as Alexandre-Bidon and Lett, *Children in the Middle Ages*; Steven A. Epstein, "The Medieval Family: A Place of Refuge and Sorrow," in Neel, *Medieval Families*, 405–428; John Doran, "Oblation or Obligation? A Canonical Ambiguity," in Wood, *The Church and Childhood*, 127–141; Nelson, "Parents, Children, and the Church," 81–114; Joel T. Rosenthal, "Introduction," in Joel T. Rosenthal, ed., *Essays on Medieval Childhood: Responses to Recent Debates* (Donington, Lincolnshire, UK: Shaun Tyas, 2007), 1–11; Louis Haas and Joel T. Rosenthal,

"Historiographical Reflections and the Revolt of the Medievalists," in Rosenthal, *Essays on Medieval Childhood*, 12–26; Shahar, *Childhood in the Middle Ages*; and Linda E. Mitchell, *Family Life in the Middle Ages* (Westport, CT: Greenwood Press, 2007).

39. Alexandre-Bidon and Lett, *Children in the Middle Ages*, 2. The reader interested in pursuing the topic of the Middle Ages and children is advised to review Alexandre-Bidon and Lett's informative work in its entirety.

40. Ibid., 138. The interested reader should consult the work of the distinguished medieval scholar Janet L. Nelson, who gives compelling witness to the era in her paper on "Parents, Children, and the Church in the Earlier Middle Ages." Her informative paper offers frank and insightful discussion of the early medieval parent-Church relationship. She also discusses the significant place of godparents in this piece. Also see Shahar, *Childhood in the Middle Ages*, 2–3; and John Doran, "Oblation or Obligation?" 127–141.

41. Julia Ann Upton, "A Solution to the Infant Baptism Problem," *The Living Light* 16, no. 4 (Winter 1979): 487.

42. For example, see NDC, 48–50.

43. GDC, 275n24: "Cf. DCG (1971) 20, where it is shown how the other forms of catechesis are ordered (*ordinantur*) to adult catechesis" (italics in the original). In this work, DCG is identified as GCD (*General Catechetical Directory*).

44. Francis, "Homily on the Occasion of the Canonization of St. Junípero Serra" (National Shrine of the Immaculate Conception, Washington, DC, September 23, 2015), http://w2.vatican.va/content/francesco/en/homilies/2015/documents/papa-francesco_20150923_usa-omelia-washington-dc.html.

45. See NDC, chapter 4, "Divine and Human Methodology," and chapter 7, "Catechizing the People of God in Diverse Settings." For example, the latter treats catechesis for adults, the elderly, young adults, adolescents, infants and children, persons with disabilities, and persons in special situations and addresses ecumenical and interreligious considerations. Chapter 8 deals with "Those Who Catechize."

46. Campbell, *Finding God*, 23.

47. Ibid., 23. Also see Gatch, "The Medieval Church: Basic Christian Education," 90. Scholar Harold Burgess writes that what appears to have emerged were "milder processes such as token memorization of the creeds and commandments." Burgess, *Models of Religious Education*, 42. This is a critical assessment, for sure, but one to be received in light of changing dynamics of the times.

48. Gatch, "The Medieval Church: Basic Christian Education," 88, indicates that "the *Ave Maria* . . . became an increasingly common form of devotion from the twelfth century." Italics in the original.

49. Carter, *The Modern Challenge to Religious Education*, 56; Gatch, "The Medieval Church: Basic Christian Education," 88.

50. Nolan, "Events of Grace," 9. Jungmann notes the lack of "a regular ecclesiastical catechesis for children." *Handing on the Faith*, 11.

51. Gatch, "The Medieval Church: Basic Christian Education," 80.

52. Berard Marthaler, "The *Catechism of the Catholic Church* in U.S. Context," *The Living Light* 30, no. 1 (Fall 1993): 66; full article: 65–71.

53. Carter, *The Modern Challenge to Religious Education*, 58–59.

54. Clark, "Medieval Catechetics and the First Catechisms," 101–102, citing A. N. Fuerst, *The Systematic Teaching of Religion* (New York: Benziger, 1939), 43.

55. Clark, "Medieval Catechetics and the First Catechisms," 107; see Carter, *The Modern Challenge to Religious Education*, 59, and Marthaler, "Catechesis: 'A Semantic Evolution'?" 3.

56. See *Handbook on the Conformity Review Process* (Washington, DC: United States Conference of Catholic Bishops), http://www.usccb.org/about/evangelization-and-catechesis/subcommittee-on-catechism/upload/CR-Handbook-only-FINAL.pdf.

57. Carter, *The Modern Challenge to Religious Education*, 58.

58. Ibid., 58.

59. Collins, *CCD Methods in Modern Catechetics*, 10–11; italics in original.

60. Clark, "Medieval Catechetics and the First Catechisms," 100–101.

61. See, for example, Reed and Prevost, *A History*, 121–122.

62. Elias, *A History of Christian Education*, 50.

63. Katharina M. Wilson, "Introduction," in *Medieval Women Writers*, ed. Katharina M. Wilson (Athens, GA: University of Georgia Press, 1984), vii.

64. Dhuoda, *Handbook for William: A Carolingian Woman's Counsel for Her Son / by Dhuoda,* trans. and ed. Carol Neel (Lincoln, NE, and London: University of Nebraska Press, 1991). For subsequent insights on women in the medieval period and on Dhuoda, see the afterword in the 1999 edition from the Catholic University of America Press, Washington, DC.

65. Dhuoda, *Handbook for William*, xxvii.

66. Ibid., ix.

67. Ibid., selections from 8, 18, 60; italics in original are from scripture (Acts 17:28). Entries are stacked in this form for ease of reading.

68. See ibid., xi.

69. Sloyan, "Religious Education: From Early Christianity," 23–26. Sloyan gives the title as *Disputatio puerorum per interrogationes et responsiones* (23). For scholarly study of the *Disputatio,* including discussion of authorship, dating, and provenance, see Liam Ethan Felsen, "*Disputatio Puerorum:* Analysis and Critical Edition" (PhD diss., University of Oregon, 2003), ProQuest (305303844). Clark calls it "the first question-and-answer manual": "Medieval Catechetics and the First Catechisms," 101.

70. Sloyan, "Religious Education: From Early Christianity," 26.

71. Clark, "Medieval Catechetics and the First Catechisms," 101.

72. Felsen, "*Disputatio Puerorum,*" 2.

73. Evelyn Scherabon Firchow, trans. and ed., *The Old Norse Elucidarius* (original text and English translation) (Columbia, SC: Camden House, 1992), ix. The interested reader may also want to consult C. W. Marx, "An Abbreviated Middle English Prose Translation of the *Elucidarius,*" in Catherine Batt, ed., *Leeds Studies in English,* New Series 31 (2000): 1–53.

74. Firchow, *Old Norse Elucidarius,* 3ff.

75. Ibid., x. See also Marx, *Elucidarius,* 1–2, and Sloyan, "Religious Education: From Early Christianity," 28.

76. Firchow, *Old Norse Elucidarius,* x.

77. Sloyan, "Religious Education: From Early Christianity," 28.

78. Ibid., 28.

79. Ibid., 27.

80. See, for example, Johannes Hofinger, "Looking Backward and Forward: Journey of Catechesis," *The Living Light* 20, no. 4 (June 1984): 348–357. See especially 349–350.

81. Carter, *The Modern Challenge to Religious Education*, 59.

82. Holt, *Thirsty for God*, 57.

83. Bellitto, "Four Lateran Councils: 1123–1215," chap. 4 in *The General Councils*, 49–56.

84. Marthaler, "Catechesis: 'A Semantic Evolution'?" 4.

85. For the Fourth Lateran Council in relation to treatment of Jews (and related observations), see Bellitto, *The General Councils*, 55.

86. Gatch, "The Medieval Church: Basic Christian Education," 93.

87. Ibid.

88. Ibid., 98.

89. Martos, *Doors to the Sacred*, 261.

90. Jungmann, *The Good News Yesterday and Today*, 44.

91. Simmons and Nolloth, *Lay Folks' Catechism*, xviii. See chap. 1, n2.

92. Miss Lockhart, *The Life of St. Francis of Assisi from the "Legenda Santa Francisci" of St. Bonaventure*, 7th ed. (London: R. and T. Washbourne, 1915), 99–100.

93. Herlihy, "The Making of the Medieval Family," 203.

94. Ibid., 203–207.

95. Ibid., 206.

96. R. Morris, LL.D., ed. and trans., *Old English Homilies of the Twelfth Century* (London: N. Trübner, 1873; unaltered reprint, 1998), 14.

97. Harry Rothwell, ed., "*Canons* of the Fourth Lateran Council, 1215," in *English Historical Documents 1189–1327* (London: Eyre and Spottiswoode, 1975), 10, in *Readings in Medieval History*, 4th ed., ed. Patrick J. Geary (Toronto: University of Toronto Press, 2010), 436.

98. Regarding this term, see Reed and Prevost, *A History*, 140.

99. See "Boniface VIII," in J. N. D. Kelly, *The Oxford Dictionary of Popes* (Oxford: Oxford University Press, 1986), 208–210, for discussion of the disputes between Pope Boniface VIII and King Philip IV of France

in the 1290s and early 1300s. It was Boniface VIII who would proclaim 1300 a jubilee year. Catechists will recall celebrating a jubilee at the turn of the second millennium. Also see Bellitto, *The General Councils*, 61–63.

100. Reed and Prevost, *A History*, 169. See especially chapter 16, "Antecedents of the Reformation," and chapter 17, "Humanism and Christian Education."

101. Reed and Prevost state that "various factors contributed to the rise of universities in medieval Europe. Among these were Islamic influence, church schools, Scholasticism, and the guild system." *A History*, 140; see the chapter "Medieval Universities."

102. Bunson, *Our Sunday Visitor's Encyclopedia of Catholic History*, 759.

103. Marthaler, "Catechesis: 'A Semantic Evolution'?" 4.

104. Ibid. Marthaler cites in particular Hugh of St. Victor, *De quinque septenis seu septenariis opusculum*, Patrologia Latina 175: cc. 4–5–14. He also directs the reader to see Gerard S. Sloyan, *Shaping the Christian Message*, A Deus Book (Glen Rock, NJ: Paulist Press, 1963), 38–39.

105. Marthaler, "Catechesis: 'A Semantic Evolution'?" 4.

106. Anselm, "Proslogion," in *Anselm: Basic Writings*, ed. and trans. S. N. Deane (LaSalle, IL: Open Court, 1962), 47–80, quoted in Geary, *Readings in Medieval History*, 329.

107. Thomas Aquinas, *Catechetical Instructions of St. Thomas Aquinas*, trans. Joseph B. Collins (Fort Collins, CO: Roman Catholic Books, 1939 [date of Imprimatur]).

108. Sloyan, "Religious Education: From Early Christianity," 32. In this part Sloyan indicates his indebtedness to James E. Kraus, "The Catechetical Sermons of St. Thomas Aquinas" (diss., Athenaeum Angelicum, Rome, under Angelus Walz, O.P.).

109. Sloyan, "Religious Education: From Early Christianity," 32.

110. Aquinas, *Catechetical Instructions*, 88.

111. See Aquinas, *Catechetical Instructions*.

112. Rudolph G. Bandas, "Introduction," in Aquinas, *Catechetical Instructions*.

113. Mark Heath, "Thomistic Theology and Religious Education," in *Theologies of Religious Education*, ed. Randolph Crump Miller (Birmingham, AL: Religious Education Press, 1995), 50, 44.

114. See Simmons and Nolloth, "Introduction," in *Lay Folks' Catechism*, xiiff.; and Bokenkotter, *A Concise History of the Catholic Church*, 129ff. Bokenkotter (129) points out that seminary formation would come about as a result of the Council of Trent (mid-sixteenth century).

115. Gatch, "The Medieval Church: Basic Christian Education," 99, citing Decima Douie, *Archbishop Pecham* (Oxford: Clarendon Press, 1952), 134f.; G. R. Owst, *Preaching in Medieval England: An Introduction to Sermon Manuscripts of the Period c. 1350–1450,* Cambridge Studies in Medieval Life and Thought, ed. G. G. Coulton (Cambridge: Cambridge University Press, 1926), 282. Also see Marthaler, "Catechesis: 'A Semantic Evolution'?" 5.

116. Simmons and Nolloth, "Introduction," in *Lay Folks' Catechism*, xii.

117. Ibid. The note after "ebb" states, "See Gower (*Confesio Amantis*, Prologue); Hocleve's *Regement of Princes*, edited by Dr. Furnivall (Early Eng. Text Soc., Extra Series, LXXIL, 1897), 1408–1442."

118. Ibid., xv. Simmons and Nolloth indicate this point for both Thoresby and Pecham before him.

119. Hudson, "A New Look at the *Lay Folks' Catechism*," 244. See chap. 1, n2. In a *Lay Folks' Catechism* marginal note, we read, "With advice of his Convocation he requires all curates to teach and preach publicly in English": Simmons and Nolloth, *Lay Folks' Catechism*, 6. The summary-type marginal notes are additions that aid the reader in understanding the older English usage of the work.

120. Simmons and Nolloth, "Introduction," in *Lay Folks' Catechism*, xvi.

121. W. A. Pantin, *The English Church in the Fourteenth Century* (Notre Dame, IN: University of Notre Dame Press, 1963), 212.

122. Simmons and Nolloth, "Introduction," in *Lay Folks' Catechism*, xv. Marthaler identifies this work as the first to have the word *catechism* used for a book (66). "The *Catechism of the Catholic Church* in U.S. Context," 65–71.

123. Simmons and Nolloth, "Introduction," in *Lay Folks' Catechism*, xvii. However, they assess this particular use of verse as being "unpoetical . . . and almost devoid of rhymes" (xvii).

124. Pantin, *The English Church in the Fourteenth Century*, 212.

125. Hudson, "A New Look at the *Lay Folks' Catechism*," 244.

126. Pantin, *The English Church in the Fourteenth Century*, 212.

127. Simmons and Nolloth, *Lay Folks' Catechism*, 20, 22 (marginal note).

128. Ibid., 22 (marginal note). Although this is reported in relation to the mid-fourteenth century, I am reminded of Harold Burgess's statement with regard to the tenth and eleventh centuries that "much popular religious education seems to have been primarily rote memorization of the creed, the Our Father, the Hail Mary, and the Ten Commandments with some enrichment through the use of pictures and 'spiritual stories'": Burgess, *Models of Religious Education*, 43. Catechists today do well to rely on memorization as a helpful tool worthily applied through learning and teaching in support of understanding, lest the act of memorizing a statement or prayer be considered synonymous with grasping the depth of its intended meaning (and layers therein).

129. Brian Patrick McGuire, "Catechesis as Pastoral Theology: Jean Gerson's *Opus Tripartitum*," *The Living Light* 39, no. 1 (Fall 2002): 33.

130. Jungmann, *Handing on the Faith*, 18–19. In a note that accompanies the first of these points, Jungmann indicates that "catechesis within the family setting was still the general rule until the eighteenth century" (20). He invites the reader to confer J. Hofinger, *Geschichte des Katechismus in Österreich von Canisius bis zur Gegenwart. Mit besonderer Berücksichtigung der gleichzeitigen gesamtdeutschen Katechismusgeschichte* (Innsbruck, 1937), 21.

131. Campbell, *Finding God*, 26.

132. See, for example, Morris, *Old English Homilies of the Twelfth Century*, 14–30 (for homilies on the Creed and Lord's Prayer), and Richard Morris, ed. and trans., *Old English Homilies and Homiletic Treatises* (London: N. Trübner, 1868; repr. New York: Greenwood Press, 1969), 72–77 (for homily on the Creed).

7. Sustaining the Way: Fracture and Reform

1. Bellitto, *The General Councils*, 86–87.

2. Brian Patrick McGuire, "In Search of Jean Gerson: Chronology of His Life and Works," in *A Companion to Jean Gerson*, ed. Brian Patrick McGuire, vol. 3 of Brill's *Companions to the Christian Tradition* (Leiden, The Netherlands: Koninklijke Brill NV, 2006), 19. I am grateful for the work of Brian Patrick McGuire in making substantial commentary on Gerson accessible to an English-speaking audience.

3. See Clark, "Medieval Catechetics and the First Catechisms," 105–106, and McGuire, "Catechesis as Pastoral Theology," 36.

4. *Jean Gerson: Oeuvres Complètes*, vol. 7, part 1, ed. Palémon Glorieux (Paris: Desclée and Cie, 1966), and McGuire, "Catechesis as Pastoral Theology," 33–42.

5. Brian Patrick McGuire, *Jean Gerson and the Last Medieval Reformation* (University Park, PA: Pennsylvania State University Press, 2005), 180; see also Brian Patrick McGuire, *Jean Gerson: Early Works* (Mahwah, NJ: Paulist Press, 1998), 224.

6. See *Jean Gerson: Oeuvres Complètes*, vol. 7, part 1, entry 312: 193–206, entry 330: 396–400, and entry 332: 404–407; McGuire, *Jean Gerson and the Last Medieval Reformation*, 180; and McGuire, "Catechesis as Pastoral Theology," 37–40, which provides the names of the parts in English as "Mirror of the Soul," "Examination of Conscience," and "The Science of Dying Well," also known as "The Medicine of the Soul." See also Clark, "Medieval Catechetics and the First Catechisms," 105–106.

7. Roderick MacEachen, "The Catechism: Its Origin and Development," *Catholic University Bulletin* 27, no. 2 (February 1921): 11–16 (quotations are from 15), https://books.google.com/books?id=T3zOAAAAMAAJ&pg=RA1-PA15&dq=On+Leading+Little+Ones+to+Christ+gerson&hl=en&sa=X&ved=0ahUKEwjEypvN58X-KAhXK5yYKHTkmBgkQ6AEILDADv=onepage&q=On%20Leading%20Little%20Ones%20to%20Christ%20gerson&f=false.

8. Francis Oakley, "Gerson as Conciliarist," in McGuire, *A Companion to Jean Gerson*, 189–190. Oakley cites *De parvuli ad Christum trahendis* (1406), 9.669–86 (at 670–71), and adds, "Cf. the pertinent discussion in

[D. Catherine] Brown, *Pastor and Laity* [in *The Theology of Jean Gerson* (Cambridge, Eng., 1987)], 238–251."

9. McGuire, "Catechesis as Pastoral Theology," 33ff.; McGuire, *Jean Gerson and the Last Medieval Reformation,* 180; and McGuire, *Jean Gearson: Early Works,* 224.

10. See "Leo X" in Kelly, *Oxford Dictionary of Popes,* 256–258, for pertinent discussion and for the dispute with and ensuing excommunication of Martin Luther in 1521.

11. See Bellitto, *Church History 101,* 80–81, and Committee on Evangelization and Catechesis of the United States Conference of Catholic Bishops, Electives "Option B: History of the Catholic Church," in *Doctrinal Elements of a Curriculum Framework for the Development of Catechetical Materials for Young People of High School Age* (Washington, DC: USCCB, 2008), 36–37.

12. See Campbell, *Finding God,* 31.

13. Ibid., 32.

14. Bellitto, *Church History 101,* 80.

15. Cf. Ibid.

16. The Lutheran World Federation and the Catholic Church, *Joint Declaration on the Doctrine of Justification,* 13, October 31, 1999, http://www.vatican.va/roman_curia/pontifical_councils/chrstuni/documents/rc_pc_chrstuni_doc_31101999_cath-luth-joint-declaration_en.html.

17. Ibid., 25.

18. Hughes, *Church History: Faith Handed On,* 70.

19. Ibid.

20. The distinguished scholar J. N. D. Kelly observes that "the hesitations and delays in his [Pope Leo X's] dealings with the reformer are partly explained by his preoccupation with political and family manoeuvres, but even more by the complete failure of himself and the curia to appreciate the significance of the revolution taking place in the church": Kelly, *Oxford Dictionary of Popes,* 258.

21. Martin Luther, "A Brief Explanation of the Ten Commandments, the Creed, and the Lord's Prayer," in *Works of Martin Luther,* trans. Charles M. Jacobs (Philadelphia: Muhlenberg Press, 1943), 2:354; also see Jacobs's introduction (351–353). See also William P. Haugaard, "The Continental

Reformation of the Sixteenth Century," in Westerhoff and Edwards, *A Faithful Church*, 120–121.

22. Simmons and Nolloth, *Lay Folks' Catechism*, 22 (marginal note).

23. Reed and Prevost, *A History*, 190.

24. *The Large Catechism of Martin Luther*, trans. Robert H. Fischer (Philadelphia: Fortress Press, 1959), 1.

25. See *Dr. Martin Luther's Small Catechism*, in *A Short Explanation of Dr. Martin Luther's Small Catechism* (St. Louis, MO: Concordia, 1943), and *The Large Catechism of Martin Luther*.

26. Haugaard, "The Continental Reformation of the Sixteenth Century," 122.

27. *Dr. Martin Luther's Small Catechism*. See p. 25 for "Table of Duties." Explanatory material (biblically based) is an addition to the volume identified here.

28. *Dr. Martin Luther's Small Catechism*, e.g., 5, 9, 12.

29. *The Large Catechism of Martin Luther*, 1.

30. Ibid., 3, 5; cf. Haugaard, "The Continental Reformation of the Sixteenth Century," 123.

31. *The Large Catechism of Martin Luther*, 6; cf. Haugaard, "The Continental Reformation of the Sixteenth Century," 122–123.

32. *The Large Catechism of Martin Luther*, 80. See the translator's note for terms relating to the use of the phrase "chief parts."

33. Ibid., 6n1.

34. Ibid., 6.

35. Though not contextually catechetical in nature, the brief section "Gerson and Luther" in Yelena Mazour-Matusevich, "Gerson's Legacy," in McGuire, *A Companion to Jean Gerson*, 3:387–388, may be of interest to the reader. For more on Gerson and the young, see McGuire, "Catechesis as Pastoral Theology," 35ff., and Clark, "Medieval Catechetics and the First Catechisms," 105–106.

36. *The Large Catechism of Martin Luther*, 6. A note after "three parts" identifies the "Ten Commandments, Creed, Lord's Prayer. From 1525 on catechetical instruction in Wittenberg was expanded to include material on Baptism and the Lord's Supper."

37. Haugaard, "The Continental Reformation of the Sixteenth Century," 123.

38. See the appendix.

39. The late Bishop G. Emmett Carter, writing about a half-century ago, noted that "down to the eighteenth century, the strong orientation of society to Christianity was still effective in catechesis. The family, society, and the parish church continued to nourish the roots of faith in those human groups": *The Modern Challenge to Religious Education*, 79.

40. Marthaler, "Catechesis: 'A Semantic Evolution'?" 6.

41. Fredrica Harris Thompsett, "Godly Instruction in Reformation England: The Challenge of Religious Education in the Tudor Commonwealth," in Westerhoff and Edwards, *A Faithful Church*, 175.

42. Resource from the Bishops' Committee for Ecumenical and Interreligious Affairs (United States Conference of Catholic Bishops [USCCB]) and Ecumenical and Inter-Religious Relations in the Office of the Presiding Bishop of the Evangelical Lutheran Church in America (ELCA). *Declaration on the Way: Church, Ministry and Eucharist* (2015); preface, 9 (italics in the original). This declaration is accessible on these websites: http://www.usccb.org/beliefs-and-teachings/ecumenical-and-interreligious/ecumenical/lutheran/upload/Declaration_on_the_Way-for-Website.pdf and http://download.elca.org/ELCA%20Resource%20Repository/Declaration_on_the_Way.pdf?_ga=1.70448144.1279943563.1453223979.

43. See UR.

44. Bellitto, *The General Councils*, 102. I am grateful to this scholar for his insights regarding this and other councils. See his informative discussion of the Council of Trent and the matters which formed the major concerns of this council (101–111).

45. See "Decree on Justification" and "Canons on Justification" in John E. Clarkson, S.J., John H. Edwards, S.J., William J. Kelly, S.J., and John J. Welch, S.J., trans., *The Church Teaches* (St. Louis, MO: B. Herder, 1955), 229–246.

46. Bellitto, *The General Councils*, 107.

47. John A. McHugh, O.P., and Charles J. Callan, O.P., trans., Introduction in *Catechism of the Council of Trent* (New York: Joseph F. Wagner, 1934), xxiii.

48. Ibid.

49. Eugene Kevane, Introduction in Robert I. Bradley, S.J., and Eugene Kevane, trans., *The Roman Catechism* (Boston: Daughters of St. Paul, 1985), iii–vi. Also see McHugh and Callan, Introduction in *Catechism of the Council of Trent*, xxiii–xxv.

50. Joseph B. Collins, "The Beginnings of the CCD in Europe and Its Modern Revival," in *Sourcebook for Modern Catechetics*, ed. Michael Warren (reprinted from *American Ecclesiastical Review* 168 [1974]: 695–706 by permission of The Catholic University of America Press), 1:147.

51. Collins, *CCD Methods in Modern Catechetics*, 14, citing I. Schuster, *L'insegnamento catechistico nelle parroccie dalla storia di venti seculi* (Milan: Archivi Arcidiocesani, 1937), 11.

52. Carter, *The Modern Challenge to Religious Education*, 75.

53. Mongoven, *The Prophetic Spirit of Catechesis*, 39.

54. It is not uncommon to see the work's title presented as *Catechism of the Council of Trent for Parish Priests*. Kevane points out that bishops were directed "to place it in the hands of all the pastors and catechetical teachers of the Catholic Church": Introduction in *Roman Catechism*, vi.

55. Jungmann, *Handing on the Faith*, 24–25. See the related notes. He points out that "the principal form of instruction was intended first of all for adults" (24–25). He also references K. Schrems and mentions Sunday afternoon gatherings of children as well, at least in the Diocese of Regensburg in 1588 (25n55).

56. Ibid., 24–25. See the related notes.

57. McHugh and Callan, *Catechism of the Council of Trent*, xxv–xxvi.

58. But see Marthaler, who indicates that "an English translation, dating from 1829, over 250 years after Roman Catechism first appeared, was only published in the U.S. in 1905": "The *Catechism of the Catholic Church* in U.S. Context," 66.

59. One sees this term applied to the parts of the *Catechism of the Catholic Church* on the "Frequently Asked Questions about the

Catechism of the Catholic Church" web page in the Beliefs and Teachings section of the USCCB website, http://www.usccb.org/beliefs-and-teach-ings/what-we-believe/catechism/catechism-of-the-catholic-church/fre-quently-asked-questions-about-the-catechism-of-the-catholic-church.cfm.

60. For information on the use of the terms *major* and *minor* in rela-tion to catechisms, see ibid.: "A major catechism is a resource or a point of reference for the development of minor catechisms."

61. Bryce, "Evolution of Catechesis," 208–209. I am indebted in this chapter to Mary Charles Bryce for her informative research and histori-cal treatment of this era. With regard to the Bible, I am reminded of my upbringing as part of a devout Catholic family. A nicely decorated Bible was centrally placed on a table in my childhood home, to be opened to record important dates of sacramental celebrations in an artfully designed section. But this Bible was not to be consulted independently. Fortunately, we live today in an age of plentiful scriptural awareness.

62. John C. Cavadini, "The Use of Scripture in the Catechism of the Catholic Church," *Letter & Spirit* 2 (2006): 46 (italics in the original). This article should be read and studied for its depth, clarity, and ministe-rial application (43–54). See CCC, 422–424; these paragraphs are part of Cavadini's presentation on scriptural catechesis.

63. Bradley and Kevane, *Roman Catechism*, 8.

64. Campbell, *Finding God*, 58.

65. See, for example, Ignatius of Loyola, *The Spiritual Exercises of St. Ignatius*, trans. Anthony Mottola (New York: Doubleday, 1964; Image Books, 1989).

66. Robert W. Gleason, S.J., "Introduction to the Spiritual Exercises," in Ignatius, *Spiritual Exercises*, 29.

67. Holt, *Thirsty for God*, 77.

68. Paul Begheyn, "The Catechism (1555) of Peter Canisius, the Most Published Book by a Dutch Author in History," *Quaerendo* 36, no. 1–2: 51–84 (Leiden, The Netherlands: Koninklijke Brill NV, 2006).

69. The title as given here is from Begheyn, "The Catechism (1555) of Peter Canisius." The source consulted for the present work is *St. Peter Canisius, A Summe of Christian Doctrine [1592–96]*, ed. A. F. Allison and

D. M. Rogers, in *English Recusant Literature 1558–1640*, ed. D. M. Rogers (Menston, Yorkshire, UK: Scolar Press, 1971), 35.

70. Begheyn, "The Catechism (1555) of Peter Canisius," 55.

71. Ibid., 57.

72. Bryce, "Evolution of Catechesis," 209.

73. Begheyn, "The Catechism (1555) of Peter Canisius," 57; Bryce, "Evolution of Catechesis from the Catholic Reformation to the Present," 209–210.

74. Begheyn, "The Catechism (1555) of Peter Canisius," 54. Begheyn provides Canisius's own words from chapter 7 ("His Writings and Scholarly Works") of Canisius's "spiritual testament," *Das Testament des Petrus Canisius: Vermächtnis und Auftrag,* ed. Julius Oswald and Rita Haub (Frankfurt am Main: Provinzialskonferenz der Deutschen Assisstenz, 1997). See Begheyn, 53–54.

75. Slightly adapted for contemporary English from *St. Peter Canisius, A Summe of Christian Doctrine [1592–96],* contents pages. Cf. Mongoven, *The Prophetic Spirit of Catechesis*, 38, and Bryce, "Evolution of Catechesis," 210, for insights about this division.

76. Bryce, "Evolution of Catechesis," 210; Mongoven, *The Prophetic Spirit of Catechesis*, 38.

77. Begheyn, "The Catechism (1555) of Peter Canisius," 59.

78. Bryce, "Evolution of Catechesis," 210–211.

79. Ibid., 211.

80. Ibid.

81. Ibid., 214–215.

82. John Patrick Donnelly, S.J., in *Robert Bellarmine: Spiritual Writings,* trans. and ed. John Patrick Donnelly and Roland J. Teske, S.J. (New York: Paulist Press, 1989), 15.

83. Bryce, "Evolution of Catechesis," 215.

84. *St. Robert Bellarmine, A Shorte Catechisme, 1614,* in *English Recusant Literature 1558–1640,* selected and edited by D. M. Rogers, vol. 126 (Menston, Yorkshire, England: Scolar Press, 1973).

85. Ibid., 41 (italics in the original; quotation slightly adapted for contemporary English).

86. Ibid., 61.

87. Ibid., 65 (italics in the original; quotation slightly adapted for contemporary English).

88. Bryce, "Evolution of Catechesis," 215.

89. Ibid., 214.

90. Carter, *The Modern Challenge to Religious Education*, 75. Jungmann is less enthusiastic on this point, at least through the 1600s. He notes that "special catechesis especially for children" within the parish met with limited success in the 1500s and 1600s (*Handing on the Faith*, 25). His accompanying note provides reference information about the period (25n55).

91. I am grateful to Edward J. Power, and Joseph Collins for their insights on this and other approaches. Edward J. Power, "Highlights in the History of Religious Education: 1600–1750," *The Living Light* 2, no. 1 (Spring 1965): 106–121. For another source of Sulpician Method information, see Collins, *CCD Methods in Modern Catechetics*, 16–18. Both sources offer summary treatment of Olier and the Sulpician Method.

92. Collins, *CCD Methods in Modern Catechetics*, 16.

93. Power, "Highlights in the History of Religious Education," 108. Also see 107–112.

94. Ibid.

95. Collins, *CCD Methods in Modern Catechetics*, 17.

96. Carter, *The Modern Challenge to Religious Education*, 77.

97. Power, "Highlights in the History of Religious Education," 115.

98. Claude Fleury, *An Historical Catechism, Containing a Summary of the Sacred History and Christian Doctrine. . . . Newly Translated from the French*, vol. 1 ([London?], 1726; Eighteenth Century Collections Online, Gale Group, University of Notre Dame Libraries), http://find.galegroup.com.proxy.library.nd.edu/ecco/infomark.do?&source=gale&prodId=ECCO&userGroupName=nd_ref&tabID=T001&docId=CW118535590&type=multipage&contentSet=ECCOArticles&version=1.0&docLevel=FASCIMILE Gale Document Number: CW118535590.

99. Fleury, *An Historical Catechism*, e.g., v, xxxii.

100. Reed and Prevost, *A History*, 230.

101. *The Great Didactic of John Amos Comenius Now for the First Time Englished,* trans. M. W. Keatinge (London: Adam and Charles Black, 1896), 407–410.

102. Elias, *A History of Christian Education,* 128. See also Jungmann's comment on catechisms, theology, and the Enlightenment in his *The Good News Yesterday and Today,* 35–37.

103. Collins, *CCD Methods in Modern Catechetics,* 19. See also Jungmann's informative assessment of the Enlightenment vis-à-vis catechesis in his *Handing on the Faith,* 27ff.

104. "Appendix I: General Conclusions [of Eichstätt Week]," in *Teaching All Nations: A Symposium on Modern Catechetics,* ed. Johannes Hofinger, English version rev. and partly trans. Clifford Howell (W. Germany: Herder KG; New York: Herder and Herder, 1961), 388.

105. USCCB, *United States Catholic Catechism for Adults.*

106. I am reminded of a critique of English translations of the *Roman Catechism* rendered in the first half of the nineteenth century. After identifying one effort with "English [that] was flowing and readable," McHugh and Callan add that the work "was singularly devoid of accuracy." Of an 1839 attempt, they note that "while more faithful to the original, this new edition was so slavish, stilted and inelegant as to be at times almost unintelligible, and at all times most uninviting, as totally bereft of that charm of style so characteristic of the original": Introduction in *Catechism of the Council of Trent,* xxix.

107. See Carter, *The Modern Challenge to Religious Education,* 78–79, for a brief, informative summary of much of the second half of the second millennium.

108. Bryce, "Evolution of Catechesis," 212. Bryce identifies the following important two-volume source: Teresa Ledochowska, *Angela Merici and the Company of St. Ursula,* trans. Mary Teresa Neylan (Rome and Milan: Ancora, 1968). She specifies 2:107ff.

109. Ibid.

110. Francis Xavier, "To His Companions Living in Rome" (January 15, 1544), in *The Letters and Instructions of Francis Xavier,* trans. M. Joseph Costelloe, S.J. (St. Louis, MO: Institute of Jesuit Sources, 1992), 20:3, 63, 65.

111. Ibid., 20:2–4, 65–66. See also "Instruction for the Catechists of the Society of Jesus" (November 10, 1545?), 53:1–5, 131–133.

112. Francis Xavier, "To His Companions Living in Rome," 20:6, 67.

113. See ibid., 20:4, 66. Also see Paul Turner's observations regarding limited baptismal preparation time later in the century. *The Hallelujah Highway*, 126.

114. *The Letters and Instructions of Francis Xavier*, 20:6, 67.

115. Ibid., 20:8, 67–68 (italics in the original).

116. I am reminded of the influential book from the Murphy Center for Liturgical Research, *Made, Not Born*.

117. Augustine, *The Augustine Catechism*, 6, 36. See chap. 5, n142. See also Bryce, "Evolution of Catechesis," 205. The catechetical leader or principal may want to consult the book by Patricia Sullivan, R.S.M., and Timothy Brown, S.J., entitled *Setting Hearts on Fire: A Spirituality for Leaders* (New York: Alba House, 1997).

118. Teresa of Avila, *The Way of Perfection: A Study Edition*, ed. Kieran Kavanaugh, O.C.D., trans. Kieran Kavanaugh and Otilio Rodriguez, O.C.D. (Washington, DC: ICS Publications, 1980, 2000), 205.

119. John of the Cross, "The Living Flame of Love," in *John of the Cross: Selected Writings*, ed. Kieran Kavanaugh (New York/Mahwah, NJ: Paulist Press, 1987), 291.

120. See chapter 1 of the present work.

121. *The Letters and Instructions of Francis Xavier*, "Doctrina Christiana" ("The Short Catechism") (May, 1542), 14:1, 41. See the accompanying note about Xavier's use of these words.

8. Reigniting the Way: Catechesis Bridging a Millennium

1. This chapter includes selections from or adapted from Gerard F. Baumbach, "Catechesis since the Second Vatican Council: An Incomplete Reflection (Part One)," *Catechetical Leader* 23, no. 5 (September 2012): 15–22, and "Catechesis since the Second Vatican Council: An Incomplete Reflection (Part Two)," *Catechetical Leader* 23, no. 6 (November

2012): 15–20. The periodical *Catechetical Leader,* a service of the National Conference for Catechetical Leadership, includes many pieces of topical interest for evangelization and catechesis.

2. *Memories of My Altar Boy Days, 1961* (Milwaukee, WI: Franklin X. McCormick, 1960), 23 (italics in original).

3. *Recordare*, the Yearbook of St. Mary's High School (Manhasset, NY, 1963), 5.

4. See my other reflection about this experience in chapter 4.

5. I had not counted on the "living/dying/rising" that was about to take place in my life. Soon after our return to the United States my family experienced the roar of Hurricane Agnes up close and sustained illness of family members (an experience that may resonate with the reader). For personal details of the Hurricane Agnes event, see my *Experiencing Mystagogy*, 50–52.

6. Johannes Hofinger, "Preface," in *The Good News and Its Proclamation: Post-Vatican II Edition of "The Art of Teaching Christian Doctrine"* (Notre Dame, IN: University of Notre Dame Press, 1968), x.

7. Alfonso M. Nebreda, *Kerygma in Crisis?* (Chicago: Loyola University Press, 1965), 34 (italics in the original). On p. 33, Nebreda cites as reference for his Enlightenment section F. X. Arnold, especially *Grundsätzliches und Geschichtliches zur Theologie der Seelsorge*, 69–104; 105–54; J. Rabas, *Katechetisches Erbe der Aufklärung* (Freiburg, Germany: Herder, 1963).

8. Collins, *CCD Methods in Modern Catechetics*, 20.

9. Nebreda, *Kerygma in Crisis?* 35.

10. The 1847 catechism of Joseph Deharbe, S.J., positioned teaching on the sacraments after that on the commandments. This was consistent with a prior Enlightenment era posture that Nebreda describes as "the anthropocentric deviation of the Enlightenment" (Nebreda, *Kerygma in Crisis?* 35). Deharbe's catechism became very popular (Collins, *CCD Methods in Modern Catechetics*, 19–20) and would be made available in English in 1869 (Gerard S. Sloyan, "Developments in Religious Education since 1800," *The Living Light* 2, no. 4 [Winter, 1965–1966] 83). Nebreda (*Kerygma in Crisis?* 35) states that "the Deharbe catechism . . . did mark definite progress, combining theological accuracy with clarity of ideas and

definitions. As far as arrangement of content was concerned, however, it continued in error." Cf. Hofinger, *Art of Teaching Christian Doctrine*, 69.

11. See the entire section on the Church's important teaching on grace in *CCC*, 1996–2005.

12. Gerard S. Sloyan, "Developments in Religious Education since 1800," 82ff.

13. Mary Charles Bryce, *Pride of Place: The Role of the Bishops in the Development of Catechesis in the United States* (Washington, DC: Catholic University of America Press, 1984), 69–70. Bryce points out that "the first recorded call for a 'common catechism' in the U.S. Church—one envisioned as desirable for all dioceses—was registered by Ambrose Maréchal [Archbishop of Baltimore], early in 1827" (67). Bryce's treatment of the history of the *Baltimore Catechism* is informative, detailed, and balanced. I appreciate her perspectives.

14. Ibid., 69.

15. Ibid., 69ff.

16. See ibid., 69. She also notes that other catechisms would be written within a decade of the 1885 Baltimore edition (94).

17. Ibid., 69–70.

18. Ibid., 90ff.

19. Ibid., 93ff.

20. Jay P. Dolan, *The American Catholic Experience* (Notre Dame, IN: University of Notre Dame Press, 1992), 391.

21. See Bryce, *Pride of Place*, 92.

22. For example, *A Catechism of Christian Doctrine, Revised Edition of the Baltimore Catechism No. 1* (Paterson, NJ: CCD / St. Anthony Guild Press, 1941).

23. For example, Ellamay Horan (Study Lessons), *A Catechism of Christian Doctrine No. 1 with Study Lessons* (New York: W. H. Sadlier, 1936).

24. See the foreword in Rev. Francis J. Connell, C.Ss.R., S.T.D., *The New Confraternity Edition Revised Baltimore Catechism* (New York: Benziger Brothers, 1949), 2.

25. Bennet Kelley, C.P., *Saint Joseph Baltimore Catechism, Official Revised Edition No. 2* (New York: Catholic Book Publishing, 1962), 3.

26. In today's terms, a brief review of the six tasks of catechesis confirms the breadth of the catechetical landscape. See GDC, 85–87, and NDC, 20.

27. The reader may want to consult Bellitto, *The General Councils*, for informative discussion of this council and its aftermath. See chapter 9.

28. Bryce, *Pride of Place*, 78–79. She states that "next to the debates and discussions on the matter of papal infallibility, the catechism question occupied more of the council's time than any other single issue" (p. 78).

29. Ibid., 79.

30. Ibid., 84.

31. Pontifical Council for Justice and Peace, *Compendium of the Social Doctrine of the Church* (Washington, DC: USCCB Publishing, 2004), 87; cf. CCC, 2421.

32. The observations presented here represent a few examples of the thinking of the era; many scholars, approaches, and issues could be cited, but space does not allow.

33. See the important work of Mary Charles Bryce in Part IV of her "Evolution of Catechesis," 204–235.

34. Bryce, *Pride of Place*, 96.

35. Lucinda A. Nolan, "Rosalia Walsh," in *Christian Educators of the 20th Century* online database (La Mirada, CA: Talbot School of Theology, Biola University), http://www.talbot.edu/ce20/educators/catholic/rosalia_walsh.

36. Hofinger, "Looking Backward and Forward," 349.

37. See Hofinger, "Looking Backward and Forward," and Berard L. Marthaler, "The Modern Catechetical Movement in Roman Catholicism: Issues and Personalities," *Religious Education* 73, no. 5–S (September–October 1978): S78ff.

38. See the section "On the Track of a Better Method" in Hofinger, *The Good News and Its Proclamation*, 3ff.

39. Marthaler, "The Modern Catechetical Movement," S78. Herbart's influential work *The Science of Education* is divided into three main parts: "The Aim of Education Generally," "Many-Sidedness of Interest" (which includes treatment of instruction), and "Moral Strength of Character." See the list of contents in Daniel M. Robinson, ed., *Significant Contributions to*

the History of Psychology 1750–1920 (Washington, DC: University Publications of America, 1977) from Johann Friedrich Herbart, *The Science of Education: Its General Principles Deduced from Its Aim, and the Aesthetic Revelation of the World,* trans. Henri M. Felkin and Emmie Felkin (Boston: D. C. Heath, 1902).

40. Nolan, "Events of Grace," 19; Mongoven, *The Prophetic Spirit of Catechesis,* 44; Marthaler, "The Modern Catechetical Movement," S78. Also see Reed and Prevost, *A History,* 250, and Heath, "Thomistic Theology and Religious Education," 53.

41. Nolan, "Events of Grace," 19.

42. Ibid.

43. Hofinger, *Art of Teaching Christian Doctrine,* 1.

44. NCEA website: http://www.ncea.org.

45. Mary Charles Bryce, "Four Decades of Roman Catholic Innovators," *Religious Education* 73, no. 5–S (September–October 1978): S37–S45; entire article, S36–S57.

46. For discussion of understandings of this term and others (including terminological distinctions), see the important work of Mary C. Boys, *Educating in Faith.*

47. Thomas P. Walters, "Alfred McBride," in *Christian Educators of the 20th Century,* http://www.talbot.edu/ce20/educators/catholic/alfred_mcbride/.

48. NCEA website, accessed September 6, 2016, http://www.ncea.org.

49. REA:APPRRE website: http://www.religiouseducation.net.

50. John H. Westerhoff III, prologue to George Albert Coe, "Religious Education as a Part of General Education," in John H. Westerhoff III, ed., *Who Are We? The Quest for a Religious Education* (Birmingham, AL: Religious Education Press, 1978), 14. Coe's address is from Religious Education Association, *Proceedings First Convention,* 1903, 44–52.

51. Helen A. Archibald, "George Albert Coe: The Years from 1920 to 1951," *Religious Education* 73, no. 5–S (September–October 1978): S28; entire article, S25–S35.

52. See www.religiouseducation.net, especially for the organization's historical development.

53. Berard L. Marthaler, "The Rise and Decline of the CCD," *Chicago Studies* 29, no. 1 (April 1990): 3; entire article, 3–15. See also AN, xxv. Pius X would direct that "in each and every parish the society known as the Confraternity of Christian Doctrine is to be canonically established" (AN, p. 24).

54. Marthaler, "The Rise and Decline of the CCD," 4–5.

55. Lucinda A. Nolan, "Edwin V. O'Hara," in *Christian Educators of the 20th Century*, http://www.talbot.edu/ce20/educators/catholic/edwin_ohara/; see also Marthaler, "The Rise and Decline of the CCD," 6–7.

56. Marthaler, "The Rise and Decline of the CCD," 7; cf. Nolan, "Edwin V. O'Hara."

57. Marthaler, "The Rise and Decline of the CCD," 8.

58. Ibid.

59. Ibid., 11. Marthaler states that "in January 1975, the United States Catholic Conference was reorganized, and with the reorganization the National Center of Religious Education—CCD—was abolished, the victim of its own success."

60. USCCB website: http://www.usccb.org.

61. Nolan, "Edwin V. O'Hara."

62. NCCL website: https://www.nccl.org.

63. NCCL website: accessed September 6, 2016, http://nccl.org.

64. At that time, the organization was known as the National Conference of Diocesan Directors of Religious Education, or NCDD.

65. NCCL website, accessed September 6, 2016, https://www.nccl.org/about.

66. Federation for Catechesis with Hispanics website, accessed September 6, 2016, http://fchcatechesis.org/about-us.

67. National Federation for Catholic Youth Ministry website, accessed September 6, 2016, https://www.nfcym.org/about/mission.htm.

68. NACFLM website: http://nacflm.org.

69. See the accompanying note in which Pope Francis cites St. Ambrose and St. Cyril of Alexandria. The interested reader may want to read the 1910 decree *Quam Singulari* (*Decree on First Communion*) (QS) approved by Pope Pius X and which addressed matters regarding children and First Holy Communion. Pius X, Decree *Quam Singulari* (*Decree on*

First Communion), in *Catechetical Documents of Pope Pius X,* trans. and ed. Joseph B. Collins (Paterson, NJ: St. Anthony Guild Press, 1946).

70. *United States Catholic Catechism for Adults,* 165.

71. Keith F. Pecklers, *The Unread Vision: The Liturgical Movement in the United States of America: 1926–1955* (Collegeville, MN: Liturgical Press, 1998), 1. See the accompanying footnote for other influential voices. Cf. Dolan, *The American Catholic Experience,* 388ff.

72. Pecklers, *The Unread Vision,* 172.

73. Angela Laesch, "Jane Marie Murray," in *Christian Educators of the 20th Century,* http://www.talbot.edu/ce20/educators/catholic/jane_murray.

74. Pecklers, *The Unread Vision,* 190.

75. Dolan, *The American Catholic Experience,* 391.

76. Hofinger, "Looking Backward and Forward," 350. The article appeared in *The Living Light* a few months after Hofinger's death in 1984. See especially Hofinger's assessment of this phase.

77. Ibid., 351.

78. Luis Erdozain, "The Evolution of Catechetics: A Survey of Six International Study Weeks on Catechetics," trans. from French by Peter Jones, *Lumen Vitae* 25, no. 1 (1970): 11; entire article, 7–31. The article was subsequently reprinted in Warren, *Sourcebook for Modern Catechetics,* vol. 1.

79. Joseph A. Jungmann, "Theology and Kerugmatic Teaching," *Lumen Vitae* 5, no. 2 (June 1950): 258–259; entire article, 258–263. See Erdozain's citation of this article in his discussion of "The Failure of Methodology" in Erdozain, "The Evolution of Catechetics," 10–11.

80. Jungmann, *The Good News Yesterday and Today,* 9–10.

81. Johannes Hofinger, "The Place of the Good News in Modern Catechetics, an Appraisal," in Jungmann, *The Good News Yesterday and Today,* 172.

82. Jungmann, *The Good News Yesterday and Today.* Jungmann would serve as a *peritus* (expert) in the area of liturgy during the Second Vatican Council.

83. Johannes Hofinger, "J. A. Jungmann (1889–1975): In Memoriam," *The Living Light* 13, no. 3 (Fall 1976): 354; entire article: 350–359.

Also see Daniel M. Ruff, "From *Kerygma* to Catechesis: Josef A. Jungmann's *Good News Yesterday and Today*," *The Living Light* 39, no. 1 (Fall 2002): 62–73.

84. Hofinger, "J. A. Jungmann (1889–1975)," 355.

85. Ibid., 355–356; Ruff, "From *Kerygma* to Catechesis," 64.

86. Jungmann, *The Good News Yesterday and Today*, 6 (italics in the original).

87. Marthaler, "The Modern Catechetical Movement," S83.

88. See Hofinger, *Teaching All Nations*.

89. Michael Warren, "Introductory Overview," in *Sourcebook for Modern Catechetics*, 1:26. For a detailed review of study weeks within a single source, see this volume. However, Warren does not include an article about the Nijmegen meeting in this work; he holds that "it did not have the direct catechetical focus of the later study weeks" (24).

90. Nebreda, *Kerygma in Crisis?* 38. The record of the Eichstätt documentation is in Hofinger, *Teaching All Nations*.

91. Hofinger, "General Conclusions," in *Teaching All Nations*, 388.

92. Ibid., 398.

93. Mongoven, *The Prophetic Spirit of Catechesis*, 53.

94. Marthaler, "The Modern Catechetical Movement," S81ff.

95. Nebreda, *Kerygma in Crisis?* 40.

96. Catherine Dooley, "Evangelization and Catechesis: Partners in the New Millennium," in Dooley and Collins, *The Echo Within*, 149.

97. For an informative review of the era and key contributors, see Matthew W. Halbach, "The Conceptual Evolution of 'Evangelization' and 'Catechesis,' from the *General Catechetical Directory* (1971) to the *General Directory for Catechesis* (1997): Tracing the Path towards the 'New Evangelization,'" (PhD diss., Catholic University of America, 2014), chap. 3.

98. Nebreda, *Kerygma in Crisis?* viii.

99. Hofinger, "Looking Backward and Forward," 351.

100. Hofinger, *Art of Teaching Christian Doctrine*, 187.

101. Hofinger, *Teaching All Nations*, 398. Cf. his *Art of Teaching Christian Doctrine*, 21, and his *Imparting the Christian Message* (Notre Dame, IN: University of Notre Dame Press, 1961), xx.

102. Hofinger, *The Good News and Its Proclamation*, 11.

103. Alfonso Nebreda, "East Asian Study Week on Mission Catechetics: 1962," in Warren, *Sourcebook for Modern Catechetics*, 1:43, 46; reprinted from *Lumen Vitae* 17 (1962): 717–730.

104. Nebreda, "East Asian Study Week," 52.

105. Erdozain, "The Evolution of Catechetics," 19.

106. Ibid., 20.

107. Ibid.

108. Still, the scholar Matthew Halbach points out that "by the time of the Second Vatican Council, kerygmatic catechesis began to wane in popularity among pastoral theologians and catechists" ("The Conceptual Evolution of 'Evangelization' and 'Catechesis,'" 87).

109. He would write that his "series of lectures on the kerygmatic renewal . . . [that he] gave during the summer 1955 at the University of Notre Dame seems to have been the first of this kind in the United States": Hofinger, "J. A. Jungmann (1889–1975)," 359.

110. Halbach, "The Conceptual Evolution of 'Evangelization' and 'Catechesis,'" 82 (italics in the original), citing and quoting Johannes Hofinger, *Evangelization and Catechesis: Are We Really Proclaiming the Good News?* (New York: Paulist Press, 1976), 10.

111. Dooley, "Evangelization and Catechesis," 148. She states, "The kerygmatic renewal called for a cohesive and unified presentation by an integration of the sources, or 'four signs' of revelation: liturgy, Scripture, Church teaching, and the witness of Christian living" (148).

112. Marthaler, "The Modern Catechetical Movement," S83.

113. Mongoven, *The Prophetic Spirit of Catechesis*, 48.

114. Marcel van Caster, "Signs of the Times and Christian Tasks," *Lumen Vitae* 21, no. 3 (September 1966): 324–366.

115. "General Conclusions of the Medellin International Study Week: 1968," in Warren, *Sourcebook for Modern Catechetics*, 1:3, 65–66. Reprinted in Warren from *The Medellin Papers*, ed. Johannes Hofinger and Terence J. Sheridan (Manila: East Asian Pastoral Institute, 1969), 213–219.

116. "General Conclusions of the Medellin International Study Week," 15, 69. See Mongoven's important review of Medellin, *The Prophetic Spirit of Catechesis*, 56–59. See *Evangelii Gaudium* on the importance of personal and spiritual accompaniment.

117. Carol Dorr Clement, "Catholic Foremothers in American Catechesis," *The Living Light* 37, no. 2 (Winter 2000): 60; entire article: 55–68.

118. Nolan, "Rosalia Walsh" citing Sr. Mary Rosalia Walsh, "The Lesson Plan in the Adaptive Way," *Journal of Religious Instruction* 13 (May 1943): 677ff., and "The Lesson Plan in the Adaptive Way (Concluded)," *Journal of Religious Instruction* 13 (June 1943): 775–785. Also see Walsh's *Teaching Religion the Adaptive Way* (Post Vatican II Edition) (St. Paul, MN: Catechetical Guild Educational Society, 1966), 321–325. She indicates in this book the successful applicability of *The Adaptive Way* method in parochial school classes in religion (3).

119. Mongoven, *The Prophetic Spirit of Catechesis*, 115ff.

120. Maria Harris, *Fashion Me a People: Curriculum in the Church* (Louisville, KY: Westminster/John Knox, 1989).

121. Clement, "Catholic Foremothers," 62.

122. Mary Perkins Ryan, "The Focus of Catechetics," *Worship* 38, no. 10 (November 1963): 235; entire article, 233–240.

123. The interested reader would benefit from Catherine Dooley, "Sister Maria de la Cruz, S.H., *Herald of Hope*," in Department of Religious Education, National Catholic Educational Association, *Proceedings of the 12th Annual National Association of Parish Catechetical Directors (NPCD) Convocation*, Boston, April 13–16, 2004 (Washington, DC: NCEA, 2005), 29–35.

124. Maria de la Cruz Aymes and Francis J. Buckley, *Jesus* (On Our Way Vatican II Edition), Grade 3, On Our Way (New York: William H. Sadlier, 1968), 3.

125. I was privileged to visit Fr. Buckley not long before his death. I remember him telling me that he first met Sr. Maria while she was participating in a retreat that he was directing. A longtime writing relationship would follow.

126. See, for example, LG, 17, and CCC, major heading above 781.

127. Citing Augustine, *De catechizandis rudibus*, c. 4, 8; *PL* 40, 316.

128. Daniel S. Mulhall, "A Brief Walk through the *National Directory for Catechesis*," *Catechetical Leader* 16, no. 2 (March 2005): 5.

129. See SLF, chapter VII, "Catechesis for Social Ministry."

130. For a (brief) 1970s discussion of the terms *catechesis* and *religious education,* see Berard L. Marthaler, *Catechetics in Context* (Huntington, IN: Our Sunday Visitor, 1973), 35, and Mary Charles Bryce, "Religious Education in the Pastoral Letters and National Meetings of the U.S. Hierarchy," *The Living Light* 11, no. 2 (Summer 1973): 249; entire article, 249–263.

131. The *General Directory for Catechesis,* in addressing briefly the reception of the Second Vatican Council, uses the phrase "deep ecclesial spirituality" in referring to the pursuit of "solid ecclesial cohesion" within the communion of the Church. GDC, 28.

132. For example, Pope Pius XII's encyclical, *Divino Afflante Spiritu* (September 30, 1943). See Bryce, "Evolution of Catechesis," 225.

133. Of benefit here is the outline of historical catechetical stages in Msgr. Francis D. Kelly's *The Mystery We Proclaim* (Huntington, IN: Our Sunday Visitor, 1993), appendix (129–134).

134. GCD, 20. This reference and term are cited in GDC, 59.

135. SLF, 40, referencing GCD, 20. See also *To Teach as Jesus Did* (Washington, DC: United States Catholic Conference, 1973), 43.

136. This reference and phrase are cited in the NDC, 48A.

137. United States Catholic Conference, *Our Hearts Were Burning within Us: A Pastoral Plan for Adult Faith Formation in the United States* (Washington, DC: USCC, 1999).

138. Contributors to this discourse were those who participated in what was known as the Catechetical Forum; they met periodically in the 1960s and early 1970s. See the section on the forum prepared by Joan Thiry in *Catechetical Leadership* 8, no. 4 (September/October 1996): 8–16. Separately, an excellent research source with detailed historical information about influential scholars is the website of the *Christian Educators of the 20th Century Project* (http://www.talbot.edu/ce20/). This impressive project is hosted by the Talbot School of Theology at Biola University, which houses the database. The list identifies many Protestant, Catholic, and Orthodox Christian educators and includes such prominent individuals as Sofia Cavalletti, Janaan Manternach and Carl Pfeifer, and Angela Ann Zukowski, M.H.S.H.

139. Sloyan, ed., *Shaping the Christian Message*. Gerard S. Sloyan, ed., *Modern Catechetics* (New York: Macmillan, 1960, 1963).

140. Gerard S. Sloyan, "Catechetical Crossroads," *Religious Education* 59 (March–April 1964): 145–149.

141. Gabriel Moran, *Catechesis of Revelation* (New York: Seabury, 1973), 69. See also his *Theology of Revelation* (New York: Herder and Herder, 1966).

142. Mongoven, *The Prophetic Spirit of Catechesis*, 61.

143. Moran, *Education toward Adulthood*.

144. Groome, *Sharing Faith*, 135ff.

145. Groome, *Christian Religious Education*, and Groome, *Sharing Faith*.

146. Groome, *Christian Religious Education*, xvii, n1.

147. Groome, *Sharing Faith,* 187.

148. For example, consider Maria Harris's *Fashion Me a People*; one chapter is titled "Curriculum: The Course of the Church's Life."

149. See the outline for this stage of catechetical development in Kelly, *The Mystery We Proclaim*, 133.

150 John XXIII, Address Delivered by His Holiness Pope John XXIII at the Solemn Opening of the Second Vatican Council, Vatican City, October 11, 1962 (Washington, DC: National Catholic Welfare Conference), 8.

151. Committee on Evangelization and Catechesis, *Disciples Called to Witness*, 11n35. Also see CT, 22.

152. Catechetical leaders in the United States benefit from the guidance of the *National Directory for Catechesis* in developing cohesive catechetical approaches: "Effective catechesis should feature no opposition or artificial separation between content and method. Similar to the dynamic present in the pedagogy of God, catechetical methodology serves to transmit both the content of the entire Christian message and the source of that message, the Triune God" (NDC, 29). Also, consult NDC, chap. 4, "Divine and Human Methodology," in its entirety and GDC, part three, "The Pedagogy of the Faith."

153. A partial list of documents and other sources that have helped to guide or impact catechesis since the council can be found in the appendix.

154. Berard L. Marthaler, "A New Meaning of Catechesis," *Catechetical Leadership* 14, no. 3 (Summer 2002): 5. A few years after the council, the book *Experiential Catechetics* would begin to influence the catechetical agenda. Jean Le Du and Marcel van Caster, *Experiential Catechetics* (Paramus, NJ: Newman Press, 1969).

155. The 1977 synod on catechesis, held between the appearance of *Evangelii Nuntiandi* and that of *Catechesi Tradendae*, helped to solidify and set the tone for reinvigorated, catechumenally driven catechetical foundations.

156. See also *Rite of Christian Initiation of Adults, Provisional Text* (Washington, DC: United States Catholic Conference, 1974).

157. Contributing to the discourse of the time were the participants in the International Catechetical Congress in Rome, conducted just a few months after publication of the *General Catechetical Directory*. In an address to the congress, Pope Paul VI said that catechesis "requires the living and direct work of the whole community of the Church." William J. Tobin, ed., "Importance of Catechetical Congress Address of Pope Paul VI" (unofficial translation), *The International Catechetical Congress* (Washington, DC: United States Catholic Conference, 1971), 4.

158. Synod of Bishops 1977, "Message to the People of God," *Origins* 7, no. 21 (November 10, 1977): 11. The convergence of clarifying documentation and educational advances continues to make for high expectations. It is fair to suggest that many catechists struggle not only with formulating appropriate means of addressing encounter, conversion, and experience of the Spirit but also with doing so within limited amounts of time. Effective time management is a necessity for maximizing exposure to catechetical themes. A corollary is that substantial catechist formation is a necessity that cannot be overlooked, especially when budgetary cutbacks are proposed.

159. The two national directories were preceded in time, respectively, by the two worldwide general directories, the first of which (GCD) has already been addressed here. Mulhall writes that the GDC and GCD "are substantially different in style, content, tone, and approach"; he states the

same of the relationship between the NDC and SLF. "A Brief Walk through the *National Directory for Catechesis*," 18.

160. The catechetical publishing world, in existence for many decades before the Second Vatican Council, has been an increasingly distinctive service to the Church in the United States since the council, especially with the publication of resources in various languages, adherence to the *Catechism of the Catholic Church*, and commitment to catechetical documentation. This part of the publishing industry has been a significant contributor to the catechetical enterprise through publications and catechetical consulting services to dioceses and parishes.

161. See GDC, 85–87, and NDC, 20, for fine treatments of the six tasks. GDC, 59, quotes the Synod of Bishops 1977, "Message to the People of God," which identifies the baptismal catechumenate as "the model for all catechesis" (8).

162. Mulhall, "A Brief Walk through the *National Directory for Catechesis*," 5. He also writes, "Where *SLF* was developed from the *General Catechetical Directory* (*GCD*), the *NDC* was developed from the *GDC*" (18).

163. See EN, 44: "The methods must be adapted to the age, culture and aptitude of the persons concerned; they must seek always to fix in the memory, intelligence and heart the essential truths that must impregnate all of life."

164. See *Go and Make Disciples: A National Plan and Strategy for Catholic Evangelization in the United States* (Washington, DC: United States Conference of Catholic Bishops, 2002).

165. Committee on Evangelization and Catechesis, *Disciples Called to Witness,* preface. Cf. "Message to the People of God of the XIII Ordinary General Assembly of the Synod of Bishops," October 7–28, 2012, 5, http://www.vatican.va/roman_curia/synod/documents/rc_synod_doc_20121026_message-synod_en.html.

166. Congregation for the Clergy, *Directory on the Ministry and Life of Priests* (Vatican City: Libreria Editrice Vaticana; Washington, DC: United States Catholic Conference, 1994), 47 (italics in the original). See also OT, especially 19–20.

167. United States Conference of Catholic Bishops, *National Directory for the Formation, Ministry, and Life of Permanent Deacons in the United States* (Washington, DC: USCCB, 2005), 31.

168. Committee on Evangelization and Catechesis, *Disciples Called to Witness*, 3.

169. Ibid., 10.

170. Hosffman Ospino, *Hispanic Ministry in Catholic Parishes: A Summary Report of Findings from the National Study of Catholic Parishes with Hispanic Ministry* (Boston: Trustees of Boston College, 2014), 38, https://www.bc.edu/content/dam/files/schools/stm/pdf/2014/Hispanic MinistryinCatholicParishes_2.pdf.

171. Ibid.

172. Ibid.

173. Cf. USCCB, *Co-Workers in the Vineyard of the Lord*, 33ff.

174. Committee on Evangelization and Catechesis, *Disciples Called to Witness*, 10.

175. Cf. USCCB, *Co-Workers in the Vineyard of the Lord*.

SUBJECT INDEX

SCRIPTURE INDEX

CHURCH
DOCUMENTS INDEX

Gerard F. Baumbach is professor emeritus in the McGrath Institute for Church Life at the University of Notre Dame and director emeritus of the Institute's Echo Program. He joined the faculty in 2003 after a distinguished career in publishing, writing, and parish catechetical leadership. He was the founding director of the Echo Faith Formation Leadership Program, which he led until July 2011. Baumbach was appointed senior catechetical advisor at the Institute, serving until 2013. He was a concurrent professor in Notre Dame's Department of Theology and served for many years on the department's Master of Divinity and Master of Arts in Theology committees.

Baumbach was the recipient, with the Institute's Center for Catechetical Initiatives, of the 2008 NCCL Catechetical Award, which recognized the Echo initiative. In 2003, he received the F. Sadlier Dinger Award for his leadership and service to catechesis nationally and internationally. He also was selected for inclusion in the "Christian Educators of the 20th Century Project," recognizing his contributions to religious education. Baumbach has served on task groups of the US Catholic Conference and the United States Conference of Catholic Bishops. He directed and/or participated in the publication preparation process for numerous catechetical publications during his almost twenty-five years at William H. Sadlier in New York City, where he ended his publishing career as executive vice president and publisher.

Baumbach earned a bachelor's degree from St. Michael's College in Vermont in 1968, a master's degree in education from the University of Maryland in 1975, and a doctorate in education from New York University in 1989, where he specialized in religious education. His service to catechesis began in 1967 and includes several years as a parish catechetical leader. Baumbach serves on the Ave Maria Press board of directors.

He and his wife, Elaine, have three married sons and six grandchildren. They live in Granger, Indiana.

AVE
Ave Maria Press

Founded in 1865, Ave Maria Press,
a ministry of the Congregation of
Holy Cross, is a Catholic publishing
company that serves the spiritual and
formative needs of the Church and its
schools, institutions, and ministers;
Christian individuals and families; and
others seeking spiritual nourishment.

For a complete listing of titles from

Ave Maria Press

Sorin Books

Forest of Peace

Christian Classics

visit www.avemariapress.com

AVE | AVE MARIA PRESS
| Notre Dame, IN
A Ministry of the United States Province of Holy Cross